PEOPLE AND POWER
IN BYZANTIUM
AN INTRODUCTION TO
MODERN BYZANTINE STUDIES

PEOPLE AND POWER
IN BYZANTIUM

AN INTRODUCTION TO
MODERN BYZANTINE STUDIES

ALEXANDER KAZHDAN

and

GILES CONSTABLE

Dumbarton Oaks
Center for Byzantine Studies
Trustees for Harvard University
Washington, District of Columbia
1982

Third Impression, 1996

Library of Congress Cataloging in Publication Data

Kazhdan, A. P. (Aleksandr Petrovich), 1922–
People and power in Byzantium.

Bibliographical references and index.
1. Byzantine Empire—Civilization.   I. Constable,
Giles.   II. Title.
DF521.K35   949.5   81-12640
ISBN 0-88402-103-3   AACR2

Once out of nature I shall never take
My bodily form from any natural thing,
But such a form as Grecian goldsmiths make
Of hammered gold and gold enamelling
To keep a drowsy Emperor awake;
Or set upon a golden bough to sing
To lords and ladies of Byzantium
Of what is past, or passing, or to come.

W. B. Yeats, "Sailing to Byzantium"

PREFACE

by

GILES CONSTABLE

IN spite of the two names on the title page, this book is in all essential respects the work of Alexander Kazhdan. It grew out of the lectures he gave late in 1978, soon after he left Russia, at the Collège de France in Paris, some of which he also gave in Vienna, Munich, Erlangen, Birmingham, Oxford, and London. It is based on the conviction, which he shares with Marc Bloch and the historians of the so-called *Annales* school, that history is concerned not so much with sources, monuments, events, or institutions as with the real lives, attitudes, and beliefs of people in the past, including not only the rich, wise, and powerful but also the poor, humble, and ignorant. With this he combines the belief that by using new research techniques, derived both from other areas of historical investigation and from anthropology, geography, and statistics, historians can force even limited source material to give new insights into the past and to answer questions that previously seemed unanswerable. He has a robust confidence in the relevance of historical studies to the main concerns of the contemporary world. Scholars, whether they like it or not, are part of the world in which they live and neither can nor should divorce it from their research. They must, on the contrary, respond to the needs of their society and approach the study of the past—and the work of other historians, both past and present—with an awareness of these concerns in addition to a desire to understand the reality of the past critically and impartially. "The proper task of historians," he says at the end of this book, "is to bring into consonance the two languages, the one of scholarship and the other of the age they are studying."

Seen from this point of view, the field of Byzantine studies today appears to Kazhdan—and to two other eminent Byzantinists, Paul Lemerle and Hans-Georg Beck, whose works are cited in the introduction—to be out of phase with other areas of historical study. I my-

PEOPLE AND POWER IN BYZANTIUM

self was present a few years ago at a half jocular, half serious dispute among a group of Byzantinists over whether their field had yet moved from the nineteenth century into the twentieth, and a young American scholar has recently stated with confidence, and some seeming satisfaction, that the main problems facing the field today, and blocking the way to the asking of new questions, are the same as they were before the First World War. This is to some extent true of all historical fields in which basic work still has to be done on the discovery, publication, and critical assessment of the sources, but this should not prevent scholars from asking new questions and seeking new answers. This concern for the state of the field explains the use of the term *modern* in the subtitle of this book.

The approach taken here is therefore in some respects critical of the work of other historians, but it is the criticism of a scholar who, like Lemerle and Beck, knows his field too well not to see its faults and who has contributed too much to it to be suspected of ignorant carping. Kazhdan brings to this work not only a lifetime of productive research into almost all aspects of Byzantine studies but also—and this is one of its most valuable features—a full knowledge of the contribution of Russian Byzantinists, many of whose works, inaccessible to western scholars, are cited in the notes. This background in Russian scholarship is another factor that enables Kazhdan to look at Byzantine studies in the West from outside as well as from inside. His approach is not that of one school or another, however, let alone that of one particular political or socioeconomic point of view, even if signs of his background and training—as is, by his own standards, inevitable—can be found in his work. He looks at the entire field as a modern scholar and is inspired by the belief, well put by H. M. Jones in his talk "What Is a University?" that "A wise and living scholarship is not content with research, it seeks also comprehension, and the freedom to seek comprehension untroubled by the clamors of those who insist that their own view is the only possible view."

Kazhdan is particularly concerned to grasp the distinctiveness of Byzantine life and culture and to understand the pressures, both old and new, that shaped Byzantine people, making them different from people who lived before or after or who lived at the same time in other parts of the world. He relies heavily on the concept of *homo byzantinus*, of which the Latin form is used not only to avoid the perceived, if etymologically incorrect, sexism of *man* but also, and more important, to convey some of the anthropological and even paleontological sense of a distinctive type of human being who flourished at one time in the past but no longer exists. Kazhdan is aware of the dangers of this concept and that there never was a type example of *homo byzantinus* as there is—or was—of the Neanderthal or Peking man. The term covers countless individuals, each differing from the others. "Beyond this diversity," however, he says, "looms a certain principle which determined the common traits of Byzantine social life and mentality and even the supreme and most sophisticated products of the individual brain." He therefore looks at *homo byzantinus* "from various points of view, including position in society, relation to power, attitudes toward material environment, self-image, and image of God," and he tries to show how "all these forms of Byzantine behavior converge on one point" and thus provide "a plausible definition of what was distinctive about the average Byzantine."

The approach of this work is therefore comparative, both in time and in space, though the material on which it is based is drawn primarily from Byzantine sources, and it is by its nature addressed not only to Byzantinists but also to non-Byzantinists, who will doubtless look critically to see whether or not the features described here as distinctively Byzantine can be found in other contemporary cultures. The concept of "individualism without freedom," for instance, will certainly be of interest both to Islamists and to western medievalists, or occidentalists, as Irfan Shahid prefers to call them in order to establish the parallelism between the major groups of medievalists. Kazhdan refers several times to "individualism without freedom" in order to distinguish the type of individualism he finds in Byzantium, where the *homo byzantinus* was isolated, fearful, and helpless before authority, from the concept of individualism that is current today, when it is closely associated with political and metaphysical freedom. "Individualism without freedom," even more than Christianity, according to Kazhdan, accounts for the distinctive nature of *homo byzantinus* and forms a central part of his concept of the ambiguity of Byzantium, which was marked by inner contradictions and where people were at the same time dependent upon themselves and yet subject to the higher powers of God and emperor.

All these and many others are among Alexander Kazhdan's distinctive contributions, to which I can lay no claim and which, therefore, I can freely describe here. My own contribution lies in two areas. Foremost, both in time and in importance, is the revision of the English text. The work is not a translation, since Kazhdan, knowing that he was coming to the United States, wrote and delivered the original lectures in English. While this may have created some problems, though in a good cause, for his distinguished audience at the Collège de France, it means that the present work is written largely in his own words, of which only a few had to be changed in order to express the meaning more clearly, and the grammar occasionally corrected, both by myself and the others, mentioned in the Acknowledgments, who looked it over in whole or in part.

This editorial work, which in itself would certainly not have entitled me to a place on the title-page, aroused my interest in the contents of the book, of which both the method and the substance call for comment by a western medievalist. Although I work in a very different field of historical studies from Kazhdan, an intellectual link exists between us that is based not only on our common background as medievalists but more specifically, as we discovered after we met, on the friendship and shared interests of our respective teachers Evgenij Kosminskij, whose pioneering *Studies of the Agrarian History of England in the Thirteenth Century* appeared in English in 1956, and Helen Cam, who also worked in local history. Our views of history are in many respects similar, and as director of an institution of which one of the principal concerns is the study of Byzantium, I understood his concern for the present condition of the field. We therefore decided to work together, though on a quite unequal basis, and the sole justification for my appearing as coauthor (besides the friendly insistence of Kazhdan) is the small contribution I made to the substance of the book. This consists principally, as the reader will soon perceive, in some—though by no means all—of the comparative material from the medieval West and in a few precisions and reformulations of such terms as *feudalism, the state,* and *freedom.* Some of my western medievalist friends and colleagues may feel that I have not gone far enough in this direction. If not, I hope it will provoke a serious discussion of the proper meaning and use of these terms in the context not only of Byzantine and western medieval studies but also of differing historiographical traditions. I should also take responsibility for some of the views on the progressive differentiation between the East and the West, since I am increasingly impressed, partly as a result of reading this book, by the continued parallelism, if not resemblance, in the early Middle Ages between the various parts of the Greco-Roman world that began to move along irrevocably distinct courses only after the turn of the millennium.

Finally, my small part in this work gives me the opportunity to express, in this preface, my admiration for Alexander Kazhdan both as a scholar and as a man and my deep satisfaction that he has become a member of the western scholarly community and, in particular, a Senior Research Associate at Dumbarton Oaks. Even if not all readers will agree with the judgments and point of view found in this book, and even if some are moved to dispute its conclusions, no one can question the learning, integrity, and seriousness of purpose of the author. Kazhdan is not one of those scholars, in the words cited above, "who insist that their own view is the only possible view." Both his purposes and mine will be well served if this book serves to stimulate interest and discussion, among both Byzantinists and non-Byzantinists, in the main problems of Byzantine studies and in their present and future direction.

Preface to Second Printing

The second printing of this work differs from the first only in this additional preface, which primarily concerns the reviews of the first printing. We are well aware that the indulgent opinion of one reviewer that the book "both in the facts and the interpretations it offers . . . is virtually free of errors" is too flattering, since works on general subjects are never entirely accurate in their facts or above criticism with regard to interpretations, but the errors that have come to our attention are not of a type to warrant a new edition at this time. The purpose and significance of our book, as we see it, lie not in the comprehensiveness of its facts or bibliography but in the effort to apply to Byzantium the methodology of western medieval studies.

The reactions of reviewers to this approach have varied substantially.[1] Some accepted both the methodology and the conclusions. Others accepted the methodology but questioned whether the conclusions could not be enriched and revised, as is undoubtedly true. The most interesting reviews, however, are those of P. Schreiner and W. Hörandner, who have serious doubts that western medieval methodology is, in general, applicable to Byzantium. These scholars express, we feel sure, not only their personal opinion but also the view of many Byzantinists, a very traditional view, against which we were arguing. If this book, and the development of Byzantine studies in the last two decades, have failed to convince them, we doubt whether a brief preface will change their minds. These critics have contributed greatly, however, to clarifying what is probably the most crucial problem facing modern Byzantine scholars: whether to follow the safe path of collecting individual sources and isolated facts or whether to aim, in spite of the risks of errors in facts and interpretations, at the goal of understanding both how Byzantine society worked and how this understanding can help in appreciating the modern world.

It is worth noting in this connection that no review of this book (so far as we know) has appeared in a journal published in the eastern bloc. We attribute this not to a lack of interest in the subject on the part of scholars in those countries but to the fact that one of the authors is an emigré from the Soviet Union and as such considered unworthy of scholarly attention. We sincerely hope that the policy of Glasnost will free Soviet scholarship from this prejudice against emigrés and open the way to a period of fruitful cooperation and exchange among scholars with common interests in the East as well as the West.

A.K. and G.C.

1. P. Charanis, *American Historical Review*, 88 (1983), 379 f.; J. Gouillard, *Revue historique*, 269/2 (1983), 489 f.; J. Gouillard, *Byzantinische Zeitschrift*, 76 (1983), 358 f.; J. Mossay, *Revue d'histoire ecclésiastique*, 78 (1983), 618 f.; M. Rentschler, *Historische Zeitschrift*, 237 (1983), 134 f.; L. Rydén, *Svenska Dagbladet*, 14 Jan. 1983; P. Schreiner, *Südost-Forschungen*, 42 (1983), 480–82; A. Failler, *Revue des études byzantines*, 42 (1984), 323 f.; W. Hörandner, *Jahrbuch der österreichischen Byzantinistik*, 34 (1984), 265–68; R. Morris, *Journal of Hellenic Studies*, 104 (1984), 270 f.; G. Weiss, *Deutsches Archiv für Erforschung des Mittelalters*, 40, 1 (1984), 357; M. Angold, *English Historical Review*, 100 (1985), 157 f.; A. J. van der Alst, *Het Christelijk Oosten*, 37 (1985), 139–41; T. Kiousopoulos, *Mnemon*, 11 (1987), 318–21.

ACKNOWLEDGMENTS

The critical advice and friendly discussions of many scholars, including Herbert Hunger, Hans-Georg Beck, Fairy von Lilienfeld, Paul Lemerle, Walter Kaegi, Anthony Bryer, Cyril Mango, and Robert Browning, helped to shape the general ideas of the lectures upon which this book is based. Our respective contributions are described in the preface. We worked together in the favorable atmosphere of Dumbarton Oaks, discussing it step by step with our colleagues. We are especially grateful for the contributions of Anthony Cutler, William Loerke, Alice-Mary Talbot, and Speros Vryonis. Angeliki Laiou read the entire work after it was completed and made many valuable suggestions.

A. K. and G. C.

CONTENTS

LIST OF TABLES

LIST OF ABBREVIATIONS

MichAk	Michael Choniates, *Ta sozomena*, ed. S. Lampros, 1–2 (Athens, 1879–80)
MM	*Acta et diplomata graeca medii aevi*, ed. F. Miklosich and J. Müller, 1–6 (Vienna, 1860–95)
NicCh	Nicetas Choniates, *Historia*, ed. J. L. van Dieten (Berlin and New York, 1975)
PG	*Patrologiae cursus completus, series graeca*, ed. J. P. Migne, 161 vol. (Paris, 1857–66)
PL	*Patrologiae cursus completus, series latina*, ed. J. P. Migne, 221 vol. (Paris, 1844–64)
Prodrom	D. C. Hesseling and H. Pernot, *Poèmes prodromiques en Langue vulgaire* (Amsterdam, 1910)
Sathas	K. Sathas, *Bibliotheca graeca medii aevi*, 1–7 (Venice and Paris, 1872–94)
Sym *Cat*	Symeon the New Theologian, *Catéchèses*, ed. B. Krivochéine, 1–3 (Paris, 1963–65)
Sym *Hymnes*	Symeon the New Theologian, *Hymnes*, ed. J. Koder, 1–3 (Paris, 1969–73)
Theoph	Theophanes, *Chronographia*, ed. C. de Boor, 1–2 (Leipzig, 1883–85)

SECONDARY LITERATURE

Angold, *Exile*	M. Angold, *A Byzantine Government in Exile* (Oxford, 1975)
Averincev, *Poetika*	S. S. Averincev, *Poetika rannevizantijskoj literatury* (Moscow, 1977)
Beck, *Byzantinistik*	H. G. Beck, *Byzantinistik heute* (Berlin and New York, 1977)
Beck, *Jahrtausend*	H. G. Beck, *Das byzantinische Jahrtausend* (Munich, 1978)
CMH	*The Cambridge Medieval History*, IV. *The Byzantine Empire*, 1–2 (2nd ed., Cambridge, 1966–67)
Guillou, *Civilisation*	A. Guillou, *La Civilisation byzantine* (Paris, 1974)
Hunger, *Prooimion*	H. Hunger, *Prooimion. Elemente der byzantinischen Kaiseridee in den Arengen der Urkunden* (Vienna, 1964)
Kazhdan, *Sostav*	A. P. Kazhdan, *Social'nyj sostav gospodstvujuščego klassa Vizantii XI–XII vv.* (Moscow, 1974)
Koukoules	Ph. Koukoules, *Vie et Civilisation byzantines*, 1–6 (Athens, 1948–57)
Laiou, *Peasant*	A.E. Laiou-Thomadakis, *Peasant Society in the Late Byzantine Empire* (Princeton, 1977)

Lemerle, *Cinq*   P. Lemerle, *Cinq Etudes sur le XIe Siècle byzantin*
Etudes   (Paris, 1977)

Litavrin, *Obščestvo*   G. G. Litavrin, *Vizantijskoe obščestvo i gosudarstvo v X–XI vv.* (Moscow, 1977)

Ljubarskij, *Psell*   Ja. N. Ljubarskij, *Michail Psell. Ličnost' i tvorčestvo* (Moscow, 1978)

Ostrogorsky,   G. Ostrogorsky, *Pour l'Histoire de la Féodalité byzantine* (Brussels, 1954)
Féodalité

Patlagean, *Pauvreté*   E. Patlagean, *Pauvreté économique et Pauvreté sociale à Byzance. 4e–7e Siècles* (Paris and The Hague, 1977)

Sjuzjumov,   M. Ja. Sjuzjumov, "Problemy ikonoborčestva v Vizantii," *Učenye zapiski Sverdlovskogo pedagogičeskogo instituta*, 4 (1948)
"Ikonoborčestvo"

Toynbee,   A. Toynbee, *Constantine Porphyrogenitus and His World* (London, New York, and Toronto, 1973)
Constantine

Weiss, "Antike"   G. Weiss, "Antike und Byzanz. Die Kontinuität der Gesellschaftstruktur," *HistZ* 224 (1977)

Weiss,   G. Weiss, *Joannes Kantakuzenos—Aristokrat, Staatsmann, Kaiser und Mönch—in der Gesellschaftsentwicklung von Byzanz im 14. Jahrhundert* (Wiesbaden, 1969)
Kantakuzenos

Introduction

BYZANTINE studies seem to be flourishing at present, to judge from the number of periodicals and monographs, congresses and conferences devoted to them. Until 1892 there was no special review dedicated to Byzantine research; now there are dozens. The meager bibliographies in nineteenth-century dissertations rarely exceeded a page or two, whereas the bibliographies in modern works often include thousands of items. Who among Byzantinists has never regretted the steady expansion of the third, bibliographical section of the *Byzantinische Zeitschrift*, where the constant growth in Byzantinological production is reflected in ever increasing listings, which seem to leave almost no room for a summary of the book or article in question? While Franz Dölger was editor many notes were developed into little reviews, but authors are now forced to restrict their notes to purely bibliographical notices.

Byzantine studies were founded in the seventeenth century, but until the end of the nineteenth they were commonly regarded as part—usually the concluding part—of the history of the Roman empire or of the Hellenistic world. Byzantine literature was seen as a direct continuation of the late Greek literature, both pagan and patristic, and Byzantine law was unhesitatingly placed within the framework of late Roman legal history. Byzantine art, which could less easily be tied to its Greco-Roman predecessors, was by and large neglected until the last decades of the nineteenth century. This approach has now changed. Byzantine history and culture have to a great extent been separated from their ancient past, both in space and in time, and form a distinct body of research. Scholars are beginning to understand that the Byzantines had their own ethical and aesthetic values. This does not mean that modern Byzantine studies have the aim of severing Byzantium from its roots in Antiquity or from its common elements with its neighbors to the East, West, and North. The task ahead is rather to show the distinctiveness of Byzantium in the common traditions and ways of thought that collectively made up the Middle Ages.[1] What matters is the tendency to single out Byzantine studies as a special scholarly discipline.

Under the surface of this thriving discipline, however, an attentive observer can detect the characteristics of a curious and unexpected development that can be described as a crisis of confidence. The dean of living Byzantine historians, Paul Lemerle, recently emphasized that Byzantine studies had failed to participate sufficiently in the renewal of historical studies in other fields and were, in their methodology and tools, half a century behind classical and western medieval studies. In order to close that gap, Byzantinists should now abandon the traditional type of narrative and descriptive history and acquire new scholarly techniques, perspectives, and disciplines. Byzantine studies should cease to be an autonomous and self-contained science, he said, and should no longer be divided by centuries but by major questions, which would be open to study by comparative techniques.[2]

The need for new methods and perspectives was also emphasized by Hans-Georg Beck in a paper delivered at the Byzantine congress in Athens and published as a booklet that marks a break with tradition in both form and content. The core of this work consists neither of a dissection or an explanation of the sources nor of an enlargement of the mass of so-called facts. Indeed, Beck, heretically, expresses severe doubts whether the application of renewed energy—if we understand correctly the German term *Fleiss*, criticized by Beck at the beginning of his work—in these directions can promote our understanding of Byzantine history and civilization.[3] There is in Beck's attempt a kind of responsibility for the fate of our discipline and an effort to give an account of the real nature and purpose of Byzantinology, which is not tantamount to gathering new facts and adding new texts to old ones. Is the main task, in other words, to enrich our minds with new facts or to approach, with the support of the facts already known, a new insight into Byzantine society and culture? In order to reach new shores, is our primary need new sources or new perspectives?[4]

We pose this question as a contrast in order to make it as clear as possible, although in reality the two sides of the investigation are not and should not be in opposition to one another. Since a scholar of Beck's standing has felt it necessary to raise this question, however, we can assume that the normal balance between the two is missing in Byzantinology today and that the traditional type of source analysis and commentary now has the upper hand. Beck proposes to stop for a while, to restrain our *Fleiss*, and to think about the basic issues of Byzantine studies.

Beck's questioning is a starting point for the considerations that follow. They are, to some extent, an answer to his challenge, an answer that will, in many cases, differ from the perspectives and solutions proposed by Beck himself. First and foremost, we have to examine his interpretation of one of the most important questions, which he formulated as follows: Why do we study Byzantium?[5] This question can be reformulated more precisely so as to bring out its hidden meaning: Why is Byzantium, a state that has been dead for more than 500 years, interesting, significant, and worthy of the attention of our contemporaries? Beck's answer is that in contrast to Antiquity, which remains an unattainable model and exemplary ideal, Byzantium displayed modest patterns that are closer and more comprehensible to modern people. Beck calls the Byzantine world "unassuming" because "it always knew how to be humble in the end, even if its final aims were set very high, even if it boasted about this to the barbarians." According to Beck, Byzantium was decadent in certain respects. "Decadence, however, is workaday, hard bread and little leisure."[6] Seemingly so clear and nonheroic, this explanation needs to be carefully examined.

First of all, we should ask whether Antiquity as a whole can really be evaluated as an unattainable, heroic model and as lacking the concept of humility. Even the confrontation between Achilles and Hector in the Homeric epics appears to some extent as a contrast between a lofty hero capable of despising, for the sake of glory and pride, his own destiny, and a man who displayed another kind of human behavior and who knew gentleness and sorrow.[7] Though Aeschylus constructed one type of heroic model, personages of quite another type are portrayed in the dramas of Euripides. And it would perhaps not be untrue to regard Plutarch as a poet of humility. The traits of humility and decadence were not therefore alien to Antiquity.

Byzantium, on the other hand, had not only a humility but also a heroism of its own kind, and the martyrs who defended Christianity against their relentless enemies were no less heroic than Aeschylus's defenders of Hellenic liberty. The difference between Byzantium and Antiquity is one not of humility and heroism, commonplace and classic, but of two different kinds of heroism and humility. Later we shall consider the particular features of Byzantine heroism; for the time being it is enough to assume that while earlier generations of scholars understood and accepted only the ancient kind of heroism, later ones could sympathize with other forms of heroism and other ethical norms.

The same problem can be approached from another point of view. Beck's distinction was based on the idea that the concept of the unattainable model is unchangeable, depends on absolute criteria, and is ethical rather than historical. Antiquity is treated by him as a classical model and eternal ideal, and Byzantium as an eternal symbol of humility. But are human evaluations of past values really unchangeable? When the attitude toward Antiquity that dominated the Middle Ages is compared with the new attitude born in the epoch of the Renaissance, it becomes clear how radical these changes could be. During the last century, on the other hand, a basic shift in the appreciation of Gothic art can be seen, and subsequently appreciation of the Russian icon was substantially altered. This is not the place to explain these changes; the point here is only that cultural values change and that the exemplary ideals created by men undergo birth, death, and rebirth.

Unlike Beck, we are going to seek the reasons for the growing interest in Byzantium and its culture not in an eternal and moral approach, but in historically conditioned factors. If the decline of the ancient model in the eyes of modern man and the simultaneous rise of what may be called the Byzantine ideal can really be assumed, the underlying reason lies hidden in the modern world conception. Byzantium is important today not because it was humble and human in contrast to a heroic and "divine" Antiquity but because the ideals and values of mankind are shifting, and modern society and culture seem to be drawing closer to the world of Byzantium. The process of this shift is still not complete, it should be noted, and it has affected different fields of Byzantine studies in varying degrees.

In comparison with Byzantine art, for example, Byzantine literature remains underappreciated, since present-day evaluation of the Byzantine literary inheritance still depends on the criteria of Antiquity and the Renaissance that force the modern student to see in Byzantine literature either the degradation of Antiquity or the awkward and undernourished harbinger of the Renaissance. That the sphere of Byzantine art is better appreciated than that of literature may be attributable to the fact that art is an open field of aesthetics, speaking directly to its observers without the mediation of a dead language, whereas Byzantine literature is separated from the modern reader by the high wall of the Greek language. The directness of art may account for the greater effect that this branch of Byzantine studies has had on the public at large, thereby accelerating its reassessment. As is often the case the historian has followed in the wake of common opinion. Whereas we believe that the lofty symbolism of Byzantine art can be found behind its clichés and distortions, or we are enchanted by the decorative beauty of great and minor Byzantine creations, the hidden meaning of literary stereotypes continues to escape us and therefore leaves us cold and weary. But this is not the only possible explanation, and it need not be emphasized to the exclusion of others. What matters is that the attitude of the present generation toward Byzantium and its culture has changed and that this change apparently cannot be attributed to the influence of any eternal or moral tenet. How, then, can these changes be accounted for?

Before trying to answer this question in a different way from Beck, we should mention some general trends in modern historical research, of which our discipline is and must be a part. The main topics that attracted the attention of scholars and the public in the nineteenth century were the Greek polis, the Roman republic, the medieval town, and the so-called feudal hierarchy of personal dependencies, in which each person had his or her place. The common element of these institutions was understood to be freedom, in the sense of clear individual rights, whereas the oriental monarchy was identified with slavery. Ancient and feudal free communities of different kinds were treated as normal sociopolitical forms, and nineteenth-century historians were interested above all in the problem of why these forms alleged to be normal gave way to the successive autocratic regimes of the Hellenistic kingdoms, the Roman empire, or the absolutist monarchies. In other words, the autocratic forms of the past were regarded by the nineteenth-century historian as deviations from the normal social and political structure. From a philosophical point of view, this concept displayed an optimistic and rational attitude: Mankind, led by enlightened philosophers, by the spirit of history, by mystical national sentiment, or by class interest, was thought to have proceeded in a direct line from slavery to freedom. In this way any regeneration of the autocratic forms seemed to be a deviation from the general tendency and therefore in need of explanation.

After the close of the nineteenth century historical research underwent radical changes. Scholarly work was concentrated more and more around new centers of gravity, including the ancient oriental monarchies, the Hellenistic kingdoms, and the late Roman empire. The growing interest in Byzantine studies, to which we referred at the beginning of this introduction, should be seen in the context of this increasing interest in the autocratic states of the past. From this point of view, the advance of Byzantine studies ceases to be a fortuitous or isolated event in modern historiography, since we are concerned with not only the interest in Byzantium but also the general interest in the destinies of the ancient and medieval empires. The traditional evaluations have been turned upside down, and today the autocratic states of the past are once again regarded as normal forms of social and political structure, while the so-called free structures have come to be seen by many scholars, especially in the East, as an exception, as a cul-de-sac of historical development, and as a phenomenon without a future. The Hellenic *poleis* seem to have embraced an insignificant part of human population and cultivated territory in comparison with such oriental monarchies as Egypt, Assyria, and Persia and to have been chronologically restricted by the rise of the Hellenic kingdoms and the Roman empire, which repeated or even imitated the autocratic features of the oriental monarchies. The free world of feudal dependencies and independent towns is likewise now seen as limited in space and time, as surrounded by the vast autocratic states of the Muslims, Russians, and Mongolians, and as lasting for only a short time before the reinstallment of the autocratic powers of the sixteenth century. In the light of this reassessment of the past, the new question for scholars is, How did such exceptional forms of freedom emerge from the sea of darkness and natural autocracy?

The recent change in the historiographical attitude toward the past can be seen in the new view of the origins of feudalism, a term that was used by historians and philosophers of the nineteenth century in several senses, including: as a phenomenon that appeared at various times and in various regions—that is, a specific period in the development of various regions, including Egypt, Homeric Greece, and ancient China as well as Europe in the Middle Ages; as an expression of a national spirit, such as of the Germanic people; and as a particular historical age that could be conceived as a stage in the development of the spirit of history, or as a socioeconomic formation inevitably following the preceding age of slavery. A common feature of these theories was to view feudalism as a phenomenon of general significance and as a necessity brought into existence by the activity of hidden forces of either an idealistic or a materialistic nature. Recent historiography, on the contrary, has introduced a new concept, recognizing that feudalism was neither a result of an esoteric quality of a time, space, or people nor a child of historical inevitability, but that it was produced by a specific historical situation, the concrete encounter of forces in western Europe after the downfall of the Roman empire.

The concept of feudalism, moreover, has been restricted to the particular form of mentality born "in the narrow world of fighters who little by little became nobles."[8] Some scholars have gone further and questioned the value of using the term *feudalism* at all, arguing that it is better to describe the precise social or economic relationships in question rather than to conceal them under a vague and ambiguous generalization.[9] Whether or not the term is used, the mentality and institutions to which it refers are seen by many historians not as a normal historical condition or stage but as a more or less random deviation from the continuity of the autocratic late Roman empire, which embodied, in its turn, the tradition of the oriental monarchies.

The reasons for this shift in historical viewpoint must be connected with modern political and social experience. By making such a shift, however, we come to the point that will appear particularly debatable to most Byzantinists—that is, the problem of the objectivity of our discipline.

There are two radically different images of the historian created or accepted by the general public and also, mutatis mutandis by the learned world. The first depicts the ideal historian as a scholar working in an ivory tower of so-called scholarly independence and gathering facts about the past purely for the sake of the truth. This image, which has been cultivated by positivistic historians, ultimately derives from poetry and possesses the power of poetic seduction. The opposite image is by comparison immoral and monstrous, since it shows the historian as distorting the truth for the sake of political, ethnic, social, or religious aims. It is no less popular than the image of the searcher for truth, but it tends rather to disparage than to praise historians. This tendency was incorporated in the formula attributed to an official leader of Soviet historians in the twenties and thirties, Michael Pokrovskij—but not found in his works, which is in itself a nice example of a legend—"History is a policy projected into the past."

The inclination to condemn this crude formula is as great as the inclination to praise the pure researcher of facts. Even those who consciously and clumsily used history for political aims struggled to avoid the stigma of the dictum attributed to Pokrovskij. But—and this may sound heretical—we cannot so easily dispel the idea that is the central element of this formula. We cannot reject the connection of historians with their sociopolitical environment and return to the concept of the ivory tower. The truth lies between the two extremes. For while it is a truism that historians should collect facts, they have never been able to do so without premises. The very choice of facts or sources is determined by influences of various kinds. Historians cannot turn deaf ears to the voices of their times and cannot decide that they will or will not be objective. Their only choice is whether to recognize openly and consciously the influence of the contemporary situation in their constructions of the past. Unconscious influences can be as dangerous and distorting as the open uses of history for political aims. There is thus a constant—and in our view fruitful—tension between the desire of historians to be objective, in accordance with the first image, and their inevitable involvement in the attitudes and interests of their own day, in accordance with the second.[10]

Mankind has passed through different stages in its attitude toward the past and has known periods of increasing and of diminishing interest. Sometimes it has assumed ancient garb—biblical, Greek, or Roman; at other times it has arrogantly rejected its own past, announcing the arrival of an absolutely new era. But even the rejection of the past is a way of dealing with it. Each new generation has tended to measure the past from one of two opposing points of view, looking either for differences that are alien to its way of life or for similarities that seem to be analogous to contemporary events. By using both kinds of juxtaposition the new generation has tried to understand and come to terms with itself in the light of its past.

The investigation of the past thus has two sides that are dialectically bound together. On the one hand, we study the facts of the past in order to understand the contemporary situation; on the other, we try to comprehend the facts of the past for their own sake but in accordance with contemporary experience. Scholars doubtless distort to some extent the actual reality of the past, as did their forerunners, but if they are sincere they are not doing so for the sake of fitting the facts of the past to their own presumptions. If they distort reality, it is because they are seeking an understanding of their own destiny.

Sociopolitical inquiry is certainly not the only force in the development of historiography. Other causes must be taken into account, including the trends of contemporary science. It was no accident that the discovery of relativity and the crisis of Newtonian physics coincided with the growth of historical criticism. The effects of new sources and new methods should be borne in mind, but the fact that new sources tend to appear just at the moment when scholars are searching for historical material of a particular kind should not be forgotten. The rich sources of the history of the ancient and Hellenistic empires of the Fertile Crescent and its environment were put into the hands of historians at the same time as interest in autocratic structures increased!

We can now return to the problem posed by Beck and consider the possibility that Byzantium is important and significant for our contemporaries, not simply because of the humility of its culture, as Beck suggests, but primarily because it can serve as a tool for consideration of the destiny of the modern world. Mankind is unable to experiment with its fate. It cannot turn back and begin anew. But it can afford a cheaper kind of experiment by rereading its past with new eyes. There is no investigation of the past, except perhaps some very narrow research, that is not in some degree influenced by contemporary tasks and problems. There is no ivory tower of pure objectivity.[11] Even before the mighty autocratic states of our time became political realities, scholars began to look for analogous empires in premodern history. The interest in Byzantium, in our view, was connected with the general interest of our epoch in autocratic and bureaucratic regimes.

Byzantium was the only autocratic state of long duration in medieval Europe. The medieval West knew autocratic rulers and even, for brief periods, autocratic regimes, but the decentralization of authority and the hierarchy of personal dependencies, or freedoms, hindered the development of permanent autocratic structures or concepts. Byzantium, furthermore, occupies a special place in the series of ancient empires, since it can claim a direct link with some of the political bodies of the modern world, especially in eastern Europe. In contrast to the Assyrian or Roman autocracies, of which traces remain only in the historical sources or popular legends, Byzantium can be regarded as having living heirs in present surroundings. The nature and reality of this link are open to debate,[12] but even imaginary links are an added stimulus to Byzantine research for the present generation. It is no accident that the foundations of the study of Byzantium were laid in the Age of Absolutism or that the great *Corpus byzantinae historiae*, published between 1645 and 1711 and later used for various standard nineteenth-century editions of many Byzantine historians, was compiled under the patronage of Louis XIV and is still known as the Louvre Corpus. Both Catholic and Protestant scholars sought the roots of their own religious preferences in the works of the Greek fathers that were edited at that time. Scholars such as Du Cange, Combefis, Le Quien, Labbe, and Montfaucon can truly be said to have laid the basis for the serious study of the Middle Ages in the East, and their works are still of value today. The reaction against absolutist government and orthodox Christianity in the second half of the eighteenth century, however, tended to bring the entire Middle Ages, and Byzantium especially, into neglect and disrepute. It is from this time that the pejorative use of the term *Byzantine* to mean devious and intricate, not without a suggestion of corruption and intrigue, appears to date.[13]

Upon consideration of the main currents of Byzantine historiography it can be seen that they were called to life, at least in part, by some important preconceptions, which could be called exoteric or "extrahistorical," because their roots should be sought above all in the social and political conditions of the time and in the dominant ideological tendencies.

For many scholars of the late eighteenth century and the first half of the nineteenth century Byzantium was either practically unknown or, if known, was considered, as the young Karl Marx said, "the worst state." The reasons for such negative perceptions varied, but they are in all cases clear-cut and associated with the political and social developments of the time. Charles Le Beau's attack against the bad qualities of the Byzantine emperors in his *Histoire du Bas-Empire*, which was published just before the French Revolution, was in fact directed against French absolutism.[14] For Le Beau the real problem was whether a good king could save an ailing state and prevent its decay. Edward Gibbon, in his *History of the Decline and Fall of the Roman Empire* (London, 1776–88), followed the same line, adding an enlightened animosity toward Christianity to French enmity toward absolutism. According to Gibbon, Byzantium was the worst of all states not only because it was ruled by bad absolutist emperors but also because it was thoroughly Christianized. The decline and fall of the Roman empire depended to a great extent upon the influence of the Christian religion.[15]

The ideological and political sources of Le Beau's and Gibbon's views are beyond doubt, as are those of the opposite view found in the now forgotten book of Louis-Philippe de Ségur, one of Napoleon's generals, who wrote at the time of the restored monarchy after the French Revolution and who glorified the noble Byzantine rulers, such as Alexius Comnenus, who had to lead "a ruined and corrupted people."[16] The emphasis here is different: the emperor was declared talented and modest, and base qualities were ascribed to the crowd. But even for Ségur Byzantium remained bad, a state with bad people. A pejorative view of Byzantium was also taken by Jacob Fallmerayer, but in his case the causes must be sought in culture and demography as well as in politics. The problems of absolutism were less important for

Fallmerayer than for the French writers of the preceding generations, and he could afford to praise Andronicus I, who was a symbol of tyranny for the French Byzantinists and who was condemned even by Ségur. For Fallmerayer Byzantium was bad because it was Slavic. The ancient Greek element had disappeared and had been replaced by new, entirely alien, ethnic elements.[17] Even authors who reacted against this negative view of Byzantium were influenced by similar considerations. The seven-volume *History of Greece* down to modern times by George Finlay (London, 1844–61), which is still one of the most comprehensive accounts in English of the eastern empire, was a product of the Pan-Hellenic enthusiasm associated with the establishment of Greek independence. Later national movements have stimulated interest in the history of the Byzantine empire on the part of almost every ethnic group that lived within its historic borders. It is not our intention at present either to confirm or to refute these theories. We wish only to stress that none of these writers were scholars in an ivory tower. On the contrary, they were deeply interested in contemporary foreign and domestic affairs, and they hoped to draw some instruction from the Byzantine experience.

As time went on, the political background of historiographical conceptions became less obvious and the language of investigation became more sophisticated. Historical views were not simply proclaimed but increasingly supported by references to sources. Increasing attention was given to Byzantium by classicists and philologists, who laid the basis for the proper interpretation of Byzantine texts by examining the variety and changes in the meaning of words. Not the political idea but the historical fact came into prominence. In spite of these scientific investigative techniques, however, the theories concerning Byzantine history and civilization continued to be influenced by sociopolitical considerations.[18] Two principal theories to explain the peculiarities of Byzantine society emerged but neither retained the negative attitude toward Byzantium of earlier scholars. On the contrary, beginning with the nationalistic historians of the mid-nineteenth century and especially with the so-called scientific scholars of the end of the nineteenth century, Byzantium began to receive a progressively more positive appreciation. Among scholars who contributed to this shift of attitude were Karl Krumbacher, John Bagnell Bury, Charles Diehl, and Vasilij Vasil'evskij. We shall not describe their activities in detail, since it is enough for our purposes to understand the connection between the scholarly basis of both theories and their political and social background.

The first of these theories presented Byzantium as an immovable stronghold of the view of ancient civilization as an ideal. Byzantium was the only medieval state that retained Greek science and literature, Roman law and administration, and Christian faith—the greatest achievements of Antiquity. This view was in part the result of the worship of classicism and of the Greek ideal in the nineteenth century, but its origins go back to the self-image of the Byzantines, who saw themselves as genuine Romans [*Rhomaioi*], as the heirs of Greek civilization, and as the followers of the apostles. We shall argue later that although instability was one of the cardinal features of the society ruled by the emperors of Constantinople, stability and tradition were the mainstays of the Byzantine mentality. Scholars from the end of the nineteenth century onward promoted the revival of old Byzantine views of the political and cultural stability of the kingdom of *Rhomaioi*. The very titles of John Bagnell Bury's volumes on the later Roman empire (to 800) and the eastern Roman empire (to 867) show his stress on continuity and perhaps also a desire to avoid the pejorative term *Byzantine*. This trend was not caused, however, by the discovery of sources that were unknown to earlier writers. Neither Psellos, the Farmer's Law, nor other texts that were first published just before or during this reappraisal of Byzantium could by themselves have led to such a shift of opinion, which can only be explained by causes drawn more from contemporary events and attitudes than from history.

The supporters of the theory of Byzantine continuity tended to defend the Byzantine administrative machinery that had been criticized and disdained by scholars of the Enlightenment. The activities of Byzantine tax collectors and judges were rehabilitated and even admired by many twentieth-century Byzantinists. The continuity of the Byzantine social and cultural structure and the merits of the Byzantine political and administrative system have been emphasized by two gifted contemporary scholars, one Russian, the other German, whose contributions deserve to be examined here in order to illustrate the point we are making.

Michael Sjuzjumov, the senior Soviet Byzantinist, stressed that the late Roman empire suffered heavy blows from the barbarians, which forced Roman society in the West to revert to more primitive conditions. The eastern Roman empire was faced at that time, according to Sjuzjumov, with the alternatives of following the path of the West, which led to the reorganization of society—with an implied decline in urban life, jurisprudence, and spiritual culture—or of taking another direction, aimed at conserving Roman traditions. Each possibility was supported by different social strata, and the decision was made after an acute struggle, in which the victory was finally won by the followers of the old traditions. Byzantium conserved the urban life and significant elements of ancient civilization, including the old state machinery, experienced bureaucracy, and military science. Sjuzjumov's conception is more complicated than earlier theories of Byzantine continuity, which were closely connected with the Byzantine self-image. In Sjuzjumov's view, the continuity was not a simple and mechanical inheritance from Antiquity. It was established in a social struggle, and Byzantium stood for a while in danger of what he calls the "Merovingian development."[19] Byzantium actively rescued its political and cultural heritage rather than passively receiving it from distant ancestors, and by so doing, it retained its position as the first state of early medieval Europe. Byzantine institutions were more just and more rational than those of the West, which suffered a setback from the invasions of the barbarians. In this context it is natural that for Sjuzjumov the struggle against the barbarians always appeared as a just and holy war. The triumph of tradition and of the urban forces was realized in the tenth century by the victory of the Macedonian emperors over the centrifugal tendencies of the landlord class. The balance of power changed from the eleventh century on, however, and in spite of the stubborn resistance of the bureaucracy and of the merchant class, the landlords won the day and the urban elements were beaten. The last attempts at resistance were, according to Sjuzjumov, the revolt of the Zealots (1342–49) and the antiaristocratic policy of Alexius Apokaukos. The destruction of the antique principles of the Byzantine empire were for Sjuzjumov the main cause of its final downfall.

A somewhat different view of the theory of Byzantine continuity is found in a recent article by the German historian Günter Weiss, who disregards the problem of the struggle around the heritage of Antiquity, which forms the core of Sjuzjumov's views, and concentrates on an effort to prove the existence of Byzantine continuity, which was taken for granted by Bury and his contemporaries, for whom it went without saying that Byzantium was the eastern Roman empire of the Middle Ages. Weiss attempted to work out principles for comparing Byzantine and Greco-Roman society and to analyze the changes—or better, the lack of changes, the immobility—in various branches of economic, social, and political life. Although there are many differences in tasks and methodology between the works of Sjuzjumov and Weiss, both of them represent a tendency to rehabilitate the Byzantine administration, particularly the Byzantine judicial system.[20] Is there any connection between this desire to justify the Byzantine autocracy and bureaucracy and the lamentable experiences of the German and Soviet peoples in the middle of the present century? Sjuzjumov was silent on this subject, but Weiss, in the introduction to his important book on Psellos, admitted that his interest in Byzantine administrative organization was closely connected with the destiny of modern bureaucracy, in the ranks of which his father had been active.[21]

The other modern theory of Byzantine history seems at first sight quite different from the theory of continuity, since it begins with the recognition that Byzantium was not an ancient but a medieval state, created after the downfall of the late Roman empire and based on the Slavic village community, absolute monarchy, and Orthodox creed. This view originated with the great Russian Byzantinist Vasil'evskij and his contemporaries, such as Fedor Uspenskij and Nikolaj Skabalanovič, and it clearly reflected Russian problems of the end of the last century, when the idealization of the village community as the main support of the Orthodox monarchy was transplanted from contemporary Russian social and political discussions into the field of Byzantine studies. The evaluation of imperial agrarian policy by Russian historians was especially striking in this connection. Not only were the Macedonian emperors highly praised for their concern to defend the village community, but Andronicus I was even proclaimed to be a peasant tsar and a head of the national movement against the rule of foreigners.[22]

It would be easy to neglect this theory created by authors whose first works were published a century ago, closer to the lifetime of Ségur or Fallmerayer than to our own, were it not that significant remnants of this view are still found, particularly in one of the most popular modern outlines of Byzantine development, the work of the late George Ostrogorsky.[23] Certainly, Ostrogorsky's construction differs from the Russian conception of the end of the previous century in many respects. Vasil'evskij, for instance, dated the radical change in eastern Roman society to the eighth century and connected it principally with the Slavic invasions, which had brought new forces and regenerated the half-ruined empire. Ostrogorsky, on the contrary, suggested that this upheaval took place earlier, in the seventh century, and was the result of the reforming activity of the Heraclian dynasty. The Slavic background of this change was thus brought out less explicitly by Ostrogorsky than by his predecessors. Aside from these minor deviations, however, the main lines of the theory remain the same. According to both views, the rebirth of the empire or the birth of Byzantium (whether it is dated to the seventh or eighth century) is associated with the introduction of the themes, the system of peasant and soldier holdings, and a well-organized tax system. Contrary to the views of Sjuzjumov, the ideal Byzantine state was, according to Vasil'evskij and Ostrogorsky, based not upon the old urban organization but on the new agrarian and military conditions.

According to both theories the Golden Age of Byzantium lasted until the beginning of the eleventh century. Both Ostrogorsky and Sjuzjumov connected the breakdown of the ideal Byzantine state machinery with the growth in the eleventh and twelfth centuries of the landed aristocracy, whether or not it is called feudal. In the period before 1000 however, the real Byzantium was for Sjuzjumov a Roman empire, based on and supported by the town with its officials, merchants, and craftsmen, whereas for Vasil'evskij and Ostrogorsky it was a medieval and primarily peasant state. The great struggle of the tenth century was seen by Sjuzjumov as a controversy between the town and the "Merovingian" landlords, while for Ostrogorsky it was a conflict between landlords and the government. Ostrogorsky did not deny the existence of Byzantine cities—on the contrary, he insisted that urban life continued in Byzantium, at least in its Anatolian regions—but the town was irrelevant for him, because the entire destiny of Byzantium was decided in the area of agrarian conditions.[24]

Finally, it can be said that the sum of Byzantine research in the past shows how hard it is to escape from the influence of present-day problems on the understanding of the past. It is better, therefore, to understand than to ignore the link connecting our view of the past with our interest in modern issues. The development of modern Byzantinology is connected with the understandable interest of present-day society in totalitarian regimes, in the autocratic experience of the past, and in the concepts of organism, society, and people that are of great importance in many modern political developments.[25] Until recently most historians have seen the centralization of authority as good and decentralization as bad. It is not necessary to enter here into the differences in definition between totalitarianism, autocracy, and absolutism in the Middle Ages and in the contemporary world, because they were not taken into account by scholars who have been influenced more by the parallels than by the differences. The process works in both directions, since modern experience is an aid to understanding of the Byzantine reality and, on the other hand, the Byzantine reality sheds some light upon modern issues.[26]

What aspects of the autocratic experience of the past are of especial importance for present-day society? Is it the Byzantine political experience, the diplomacy, the military organization, or the system of taxation? An answer to this question can be found in the parallel scholarly discipline of modern western medieval studies. The French medievalists of the so-called New History school have emphasized that the proper subject of historical research is the history not of events but of society and of the men and women who made up this society.[27] As its founder, Marc Bloch, said in his *Apology for History*, "History is a vast experience of human variety, a long encounter with people."[28] The subject of modern Byzantine studies must therefore be the *homo byzantinus* in the sense of Byzantine people and their place in society, and all traditional topics—politics, diplomacy, and the like—must be reconsidered in the light of the interests, intentions, and hopes of these people. The attention of previous generations of historians was concentrated above all on the activity of the Byzantine state, and it was hardly by chance that the best survey of Byzantine history—Ostrogorsky's classic work—was entitled *The History of the Byzantine State.*[29] Earlier generations believed in the rational background of state organization and saw in it the real instigator of historical development. The accent has now shifted from the state to the individual, and man's reaction to the machinery of the state now seems more important than the activity of the machinery itself. The material conditions of human existence, the social organization of people, their collective psyche or mentality, their hopes, fears, and beliefs, their highest personal achievements—these are the topics that are attracting the attention of Byzantine researchers today. This New History school has recently been criticized by Lawrence Stone, among others, who attacked many of its principles and called for a return to narrative history and the organization of material in chronological order.[30] Calling "scientific history" a myth, he contrasts narrative history and individual biography, the New Old History, to "the decaying corpse of analytical, structural, quantitative history" and argues the need for a shift from the analytical to the descriptive mode. He rejects cliometrics, what he calls "statistical junkies," and the concept of history as the study of impersonal forces. This attack is on the methods rather than the objectives of the New History, since like its practitioners he insists that descriptive narrative and individual biography are aimed at discovering the mental attitudes, the history of people.

At this point some hesitations and objections must be faced. There are two main difficulties in the search for *homo byzantinus*. First, did a particular kind of Byzantine man ever exist? Were the desires and passions of the Byzantines not like those of people throughout the history of mankind? Second, may not the idea of *homo byzantinus* be without real content, embracing not one but various kinds of human beings, since the Byzantine population was divided into many social and regional groups? A peasant from Cappadocia did not have the same social position as a merchant from Constantinople. In other words, we are faced with the double danger of diluting Byzantine man in a broad notion of man in general and of splitting him into multiple and unconnected diversities.

The present work is a response to this challenge. We shall try to overcome these difficulties and to understand something about Byzantine people, remembering that they formed a link in the general chain of human development and are therefore somehow bound to us and that we have inherited some of their cultural achievements and some of their social and political problems. The theories discussed above, both of continuity and of change, emphasized the distinctiveness, not to say uniqueness, of Byzantium in the world of the Middle Ages. Scholars today are more interested in common features that link societies in the past; comparative studies are in fashion. Without denying these links, or that Byzantium inherited a great deal from the past and resembled in many respects the societies and cultures on its border, we shall try to show that Byzantine people differed not only from us but also from their antique predecessors and medieval contemporaries. They were in certain respects creators of a specific civilization. Though unique, they were certainly not uniform, differing as have all peoples at all times, and they changed in the course of time. Nonetheless, we believe that beyond this diversity looms a certain principle which determined the common traits of Byzantine social life and mentality and even the supreme and most sophisticated products of the individual brain. We will approach the *homo byzantinus* from various points of view, including position in society, relation to power, attitudes toward material environment, self-image, and image of God. We will try to show that to some extent all these forms of Byzantine behavior converge on one point, come into focus, and by doing so offer a plausible definition of what was distinctive about the average Byzantine.

The aim of this approach is to investigate the past in all its complexity and contradictions, including both the differences and the similarities between the past and the present. We shall try to show that Byzantine society and mentality were far from being simple and one-sided and can be understood and evaluated only in the light of their internal ambivalence. These tasks, while not absolutely new, are in a real sense modern. The answers depend to some extent on new methods and new research organizations, which are still being born, and at present it is possible only to summarize the scattered attempts and to understand the direction of this important movement.

CHAPTER ONE

Homo byzantinus in Society

IN the introduction we declared that the study of Byzantine people in society is a relatively new task, which until now has been almost totally ignored by our discipline. This statement may well provoke doubt and bewilderment. If this is so, the question may be asked, about whom are all the Byzantine histories or histories of Byzantine civilization written? Are not Byzantine people constantly present in any average book on any Byzantine topic? Are they not always there—acting, fighting, pursuing their goals, succeeding or failing—on every page of every history of the Byzantine empire? All this is correct, but not without some reservations. Some restrictions must be introduced, and their implications considered.

The selection of the characters who appear in the pages of histories of Byzantium is to some extent one-sided and does not correspond to the real stratification of Byzantine society. This can be seen clearly in a table showing the social standing of the people mentioned in—to take a noteworthy example—George Ostrogorsky's work on Byzantine history cited earlier (see Table I).[1] Some preliminary observations are necessary. First, this is not intended as criticism, since the result would be the same if the calculations were based on any other history of the Byzantine empire. The point is to illustrate, not a personal error of Ostrogorsky but a common tendency of Byzantine research. Second, the figures in the table may not all be exact, since the calculations present some difficulties, and it is not always clear to which category any specific person belongs. What is needed in this case is not absolute accuracy but general tendencies, which are shown even by approximate figures. The following table naturally includes only Byzantines, but not all Byzantines, because we have rejected those who appear in Ostrogorsky's book not as persons acting in their own right or as the subject of narration but only as sources of evidence, above all as historians.

Table 1
Persons Mentioned in Ostrogorsky's *History*

Social Position	Number
Emperors, empresses, princes, and so on	218
Usurpers	14
Generals	50
Great officials	35
Patriarchs, bishops, abbots	70
Theologians	23
Scholars	7

No representative of the common people—merchants, craftsmen, peasants—is mentioned in this book, and even scholars appear but rarely among those who were said to have made history. Women, likewise, except for crowned persons, figure very rarely, and then only those of exalted rank. A defender of the traditional point of view might insist that emperors, bishops, and generals have played a greater part in Byzantine history than simple merchants or peasants and that their activity is of greater significance for an understanding of Byzantium. But would this statement be correct and would it correspond to modern views of historical development?

Byzantine sources, in spite of their paucity, reveal many kinds of activity of the average Byzantine, of which a few may be cited at random. About 1285, a certain *nomikos* named Keramares, an official with judicial functions, seized some property belonging to a *paroikos* named Koutoules. Koutoules fled to the Polovcy, who lived then in the region of Smyrna. With their help he took revenge on Keramares and stole his ploughing oxen. Keramares was able to recover his yoke of oxen only by making a gift of wine, which cost, as the author of the document describing this story stresses, two hyperpyra.[2] The characters in this little drama were humble villagers and the neighboring Polovcy, and the objects of the controversy were also modest: a small piece of land and a pair of oxen. Nevertheless, this simple story provides more information about Byzantine social relations than, for instance, the descriptions that are found in almost every history of the Byzantine empire, and even of Byzantine civilization, during the short reign of the Emperor Alexander (912–13).

Among the many people portrayed by the great Byzantine historian Nicetas Choniates in his *Chronika diegesis* there is a rich and greedy merchant named Kalomodios whose wealth was unexpectedly and unlawfully confiscated by the exchequer and who was put in jail. A riot immediately broke out in Constantinople. The angry mob threatened to throw the patriarch out the window unless he forced the Emperor Alexius III Angelus (1195–1203) to release the arrested merchant.[3] Every detail in this picturesque story is precious for a historian of Byzantine life.

It is not necessary to cite further examples. The common people have a right to be represented within the framework of Byzantine history. The result of their exclusion from history is inevitably a distortion of historical perspective. Seen from the point of view purely of the palace and the battlefield, the eleventh century has been unequivocally condemned by earlier generations of Byzantinists as a period of disintegration and political collapse. Recently, there has been a significant shift toward a reappraisal of this supposedly lamentable epoch. We shall return to it later, but it is essential to emphasize at this point that this shift became possible and necessary because the bourgeois were introduced into Byzantine history,[4] and the commercial activities of the urban population were depicted in a new light.[5] The eleventh century was also a turning point in the history of the intellectual life of Byzantium, and the small scholarly groups in Constantinople, with their harmless discussions of ancient authors, may have had a greater effect on the future of mankind than the intrigues of palace eunuchs and military upheavals. Psellos was attacked by a contemporary for concocting iambs and anapests and being stupidly concerned about eloquence at a critical moment in the history of the empire,[6] but the eloquence of Psellos was among the most important creations of eleventh-century Europe. Both the average person and the intellectual deserve a place in descriptions of Byzantine history as important as that which they had in real life.

A second source of concern is less obvious. In most histories of the Byzantine empire, even recent ones, the actors are presented not as the real people of a specific region and period but as the personifications, if not allegories, of eternal passions, such as greed, lust for power, frivolity, courage, and statesmanship. The better the book, the more consistently this tendency appears. Charles Diehl, who was one of the best writers among Byzantinists, considered his heroes worthy of attention precisely because they could be easily transplanted from the Byzantine into any other field. Let us look, for instance, at his description of Justinian II (685–95, 705–11), who, according to Diehl, "was not a very solid head. Having almost since infancy been invested with the most absolute authority that ever existed, he went on to govern imprudently and foolishly both externally and internally." He had "a vindictive, violent, and blood-thirsty character." His cruelty, Diehl concluded, "precipitated anarchy and the demoralization of the monarchy."[7] Whether or not this image of Justinian II is true need not be discussed here, since for our purposes it is enough to note that the virtues or defects of the Byzantine emperor as enumerated by Diehl tend to obscure rather than bring out the particular social and psychological features of the man in his specific time and place. Although Diehl said that Justinian was "fairly representative of the age in which he lived," he showed him not as a man of his own age and country but as an abstract symbol of a senseless tyranny that can be compared with the government of cruel rulers of any time. Precisely in order to include Justinian in a series of cruel adventurers without any specifics of time or place, Diehl introduces him with the following words: "Few adventure stories are more animated and vivid than the life of this sovereign."[8] He presents a fully shaped personality, but one that is only externally bound up with Byzantine reality, although it is placed in a network of Byzantine names, toponyms, and dates. Diehl's aim seems almost to be ahistorical, since his works are less inquiries into the Byzantine experience than efforts to find eternal human qualities in the framework of Byzantine history, and eternal qualities usually turn out to be modern qualities.

No one will deny that *homo byzantinus*, like people of all times, had two legs, needed food, married, and raised children. But does this mean that people at all times have been the same? Certainly the similarities between human beings in different epochs can be stressed, but was not this similarity accompanied by marked diversity? People always needed food, but there were different means of providing it at different times and different attitudes toward it; they concluded their marriages differently, and their children were brought up differently, in order to conform to specific social standards and values. In studying the Byzantine model not only the traits common to mankind in general must be dealt with but also the particular features of the Byzantine way of life. The only means of reaching a solution is to keep in mind the complex duality of the problem and to study both the common and the particular features in the social structure of the time and in the human psyche.

Even if the existence of the specific quality of Byzantine people is accepted, however, how can it be grasped? If different historical eras and different geographical areas are assumed not to be identical, a further step must be taken to the assumption that they had different languages and that a different style of life was accompanied by a different style of expression. Cannot the past, including the Byzantine past, now be seen on its own terms or are we separated from Byzantium by a hazy border, an iron curtain, or an unbridgeable gulf? Can sense be made of the incomprehensible information in the scanty sources of this remote age? Or can only historical similarity be understood, while historical diversity or historical specifics are veiled in terms whose meaning and significance has been already obliterated? Although absolute knowledge of the past is unattainable, the attempt to approach it is justified by the fact that history deals with human beings who can be compared with one another. In the introduction we stressed that the starting point for the study of Byzantine history was a silent comparison of the Byzantine past with the modern age and an attempt to interpret Byzantine material in terms of modern issues. This concealed comparison is inevitable. We now turn to another kind of comparison, the comparative study of sources.

In order to compare the Byzantines with their western, Slavic, and Muslim contemporaries, any comments from medieval sources, whether Byzantine or non-Byzantine, both by Byzantine authors about the surrounding peoples and by neighbors concerning the empire, must be collected. Various pitfalls await the scholar on this course, especially the tendency of medieval authors to see their neighbors in the social relations or psychological characteristics typical of themselves.

Western observers who mention the upper strata of Byzantine society in the eleventh and twelfth centuries, for instance, usually treated them as barons and *nobiles*—that is, in accordance with the concepts and terms common to western society—while in the eyes of contemporary easterners the merchants formed the principal social grouping of the Byzantine empire.[9] Opinions of this kind reveal more about the self-awareness of the authors than about the relationship they describe. There are nevertheless a few medieval writers whose treatment of foreign people remains relatively free from a presupposed model. Thus, William of Tyre, a Latin author of the crusading period, described the representatives of the Byzantine ruling class in terms and concepts that correspond to those found in the contemporary Greek sources.

For such purposes especially not so much simple descriptions of foreign countries are needed as direct comparisons drawn by medieval writers between the Byzantines and other peoples, in particular those comparisons that bring out any points that obviously surprised the author and therefore show the differences between the two worlds, social structures, and psychological systems. An examination of some comparisons of this kind will make clear the potentialities of this method and define some special features of Byzantine social organization.

In his account of the arrival of the crusading army at Constantinople in 1147, Kinnamos, the Byzantine historian of the twelfth century, noted with apparent surprise the hierarchy among the leading group of the crusaders: "Their offices [or dignities—ἀρχαί] are peculiar and resemble distinctions descending from the height of the empire, since it is something most noble and surpasses all others. A duke outranks a count; a king, a duke; and the emperor, a king. The inferior naturally [φύσει] yields to the superior, supports him in war, and obeys in such matters."[10] Translated into the terminology of modern scholarship, it is clear that Kinnamos's surprise was caused by the fact that every Latin warrior had his own lord. This fact, taken by itself, is of little value, since the existence of a hierarchy of personal dependencies in the West is well known, and Kinnamos's reference to it adds nothing significant to our knowledge of western social structure. The importance of this evidence is not in its content but in the author's surprise. The hierarchical ladder of the crusading army was alien to Kinnamos, since he had not previously encountered this form of social structure. Thus we touch on a radical difference between two societies: the hierarchical structure of the western world on the one hand and the lack of hierarchy in twelfth-century Byzantine society on the other.

The contrast between the two societies in Kinnamos is so general that it takes no account of any regional or social units. It can certainly be assumed that within the frontiers of the empire were some ethnic groups with a relatively well developed hierarchical organization, but Kinnamos's surprise makes plausible the suggestion that hierarchy was not typical of the Byzantine system.

Kinnamos's note is not the only evidence of this cardinal difference between the two societies. A striking parallel from the western side is found in a story narrated by his contemporary Nicetas Choniates.[11] In the autumn of 1189 a Byzantine embassy was sent by Isaac II to Frederick Barbarossa, who, says Choniates, ordered the ambassadors to be seated in his presence and had chairs placed in the hall even for their servants. By so doing, comments Choniates, the German ruler made fun of the Byzantines, who failed to take into consideration the virtue or nobility of different people and who appraised the whole population by the same measure, like a herdsman who drove all the hogs into the same pigsty. In this case, if Choniates' tale is true, the contrast between Byzantium and the West is formulated by a western onlooker. But although they approached the problem from different points of view, both observers shared the same difference. Kinnamos was surprised by the hierarchical organization of the western army, and by implication western society, and Frederick was scornful of Byzantine social uniformity. Barbarossa's words need not be taken literally, and it does not matter for our purposes whether he in fact thought so or whether this opinion was ascribed to him by Choniates. Byzantine society in the twelfth century was not uniform; it had its own gradations. But there is every reason to believe that it did not have hierarchical links of the western kind.

Another example of direct comparison between Byzantium and the West is the statement by Theodore Balsamon, the patriarch of Antioch at the end of the twelfth century, that religious communities (*koinobia*) of the type described in the law known as Novel CXXIII of Justinian I (527–565) did not exist in his day, in sharp contrast to the practice in the West where the monks ate and slept together.[12] Balsamon thus drew attention to a fact of prime importance. On the basis of his information the relative weakness, in comparison with those in the West, of social ties in the Byzantine monasteries can be surmised, possibly a reflection of the weakness of the ties between people in Byzantine society as a whole. This individualism, stressed by Balsamon, is the counterpart of the lack of hierarchical relations noted by Kinnamos and Frederick Barbarossa.

Byzantine polemics against pagans, Muslims, and Jews can also be studied from this point of view. Primarily religious in essence, the Byzantine polemic contains some valuable confrontations with alien modes of life and social thinking. John Chrysostom's treatise "On vainglory and the right way for parents to bring up their children" is a polemic against pagan institutions and pagan morality. He addresses his criticism not against slavery or wealth, however, but above all against the social system of Antiquity, especially the social functions of citizens, including the organization of public games, for which Chrysostom expresses scorn at the beginning of the treatise, the *nomen gentile,* and the tendency to consider wealth as a sign of social prestige.[13] John's sharp criticism of circus games was not simply an expression of the competition between the church and the hippodrome for the attention of the public. He berates horse races and theatrical performances as traditional forms of social gatherings and contrasts them with the most private social unity, the nuclear family. The same point is made by later Byzantine theologians in their writings against the Muslims, whom they accused not only of believing in a false and impotent God but also of immorality, attacking what they regarded as the unrestrained hedonism of Muslim life and the strange concept of polygamy by which wives were easily and frequently divorced.[14] This criticism of Muslim ethics is based on the same veneration for the nuclear family as Chrysostom's polemic against pagan customs. Comparison with both the pagan and Muslim worlds, as with the western, therefore leads to the same conclusion; the special character of Byzantine society begins to emerge, and it appears to be weakness of social ties above the level of the family.

Another means of approaching this question is through self-portrayal. There are comparatively few Byzantine literary works in which the author shows an awareness of himself. Autobiographies are rare, and their evaluations of human characters are as a rule trivial. Most of the Byzantine moralists were dependent on biblical and ancient Greek sources, and most of the letter writers deal not with their own feelings and impressions but with clichés and *topoi*. Among the few works that give an idea of the writer's character one that has recently attracted particular attention is the so-called *Strategicon* or *Precepts and Anecdotes* by the eleventh-century author Kekaumenos.[15] It is a collection of tales and counsels addressed to various members of the ruling class, from the emperor and patriarch to the military commander or landlord living in seclusion far from the capital. Although the sections differ in nature and subject, the work is united by the main theme of the author's conception of human behavior, which can be summarized as his belief that life is fraught with danger. First, Kekaumenos was obsessed by fear of natural dangers, such as poisonous mushrooms or rocks that might fall and destroy his house. Second, he was frightened of political forces and of any kind of authority—the emperor, the department head, and even lower officials—including the mob ready to riot. Finally, he was afraid of social life, and this fear is interwoven in his mind with his fear of authority. Kekaumenos advised his readers to avoid evening parties so as not to be accused of plotting against the emperor. His negative attitude toward friendship is especially striking. "I know many people who have perished because of friends," he proclaimed, and he advised against letting a friend stay in one's house lest he seduce one's wife and discover the secrets of the family. This fear of friendship and avoidance of social life are surely related to the trait shown by the two contrasts already mentioned between Byzantium and the West and between Byzantium and the pagan world. Analogous conclusions have emerged from several directions.

Valuable observations on Byzantine social psychology are scattered through various literary works, some of which reflect the general

Christian attitude toward the universe and God. The sixth-century poet Romanos the Melodist stressed in his hymn "On Earthquakes and Fires" that catastrophes were sent by God to make people obey Him and seek eternal life.[16] Although this point of view was questioned by several contemporaries, who explained the origin of earthquakes in terms of exhalations and smoky vapors, as the famous engineer and architect Anthemius of Tralles tried to prove by sophisticated experiments,[17] and although this "naturalistic" explanation is often found in later authors, the concept of the edifying role of catastrophes prevailed in Byzantium as it did throughout the medieval world. Some observations, however, are of more specific significance. The early fourteenth-century Byzantine historian Pachymeres says that it is strange—and this strangeness immediately commands our attention—that although the Patriarch Joseph I Galesiotes (1266–75, 1282–83) lived in simplicity and righteousness and followed the monastic style of life with regard to vigils, fasts, and the like, he nevertheless did not disdain "human virtue" [ἡ κατ᾽ ἄνθρωπον ἀρετή], and liked to meet people, converse, laugh, and arrange revels.[18] That an eminent churchman should thus combine traditional ascetic values with a more worldly social attitude and stress on *humanitas* seemed strange to the Byzantine author, and from this we can see both that a new ideal of behavior was beginning to emerge at the end of the thirteenth century and that it struck contemporaries as alien and contrary to traditional Byzantine norms.

Another important source for understanding the social position and social psychology of *homo byzantinus* is the internal antagonisms within Byzantine society. These socioethical controversies could be direct or indirect (implied). The difference between Kekaumenos and his learned contemporary Psellos is one of the most revealing indirect controversies, since they may never have heard of each other, whereas the opposition between the Patriarch Michael Cerularius (1043–58) and Psellos was direct and open. Both controversies, however, were rooted in the same socioethical antagonism.

The clash between Cerularius and Psellos was noticed and studied long ago, and it has been interpreted in the light of the traditionally hostile view of Psellos's personality. In the book on Psellos by Pavel Bezobrazov, for example, Psellos was rebuked as an unscrupulous schemer who was ready to serve all rulers and Cerularius was seen as a haughty patriarch conscious of the dignity of his office and filled with self-confidence and the desire for power.[19] The whole conflict, and especially Psellos's accusations against the disgraced patriarch, were seen in Bezobrazov's description as the result of a court intrigue, not of an intrinsic social and ethical antagonism. But it is now time to reconsider the essence of this conflict and also the personality of Psellos. Jakov Ljubarskij has already taken the first steps in this direction by showing that the Cerularius-Psellos conflict reflected a confrontation between two different ethical positions of rigorism and tolerance.[20] This confrontation can be seen, according to Ljubarskij, not only in the accusatory speech by Psellos delivered at the time of the patriarch's disgrace but already in the panegyric addressed by Psellos to the still powerful church leader and in a letter to the patriarch. This is a case not of court servility or incidental and superficial accusations against a banished and defeated patriarch but of an attack by Psellos on the central tradition of Byzantine ethics.

The conflict between Psellos and Kekaumenos is reflected only indirectly in their works, but it throws further light on the heart of the controversy between the patriarch and the scholar. The salient features of the social behavior of Kekaumenos were his avoidance of social life and his fear of friendship. In contrast to Kekaumenos, Psellos praised friendship, φιλία [philia], as the best form of human relationship. His letters not only contain lofty definitions of friendship[21] but are full of sober, matter-of-fact concern for his friends. In contrast both to the Patriarch Photius, who instructed and rebuked his correspondents, and to Psellos's younger contemporary Theophylact, archbishop of Ochrid, who was above all concerned with the privileges and possessions of his church, Psellos thought and wrote a great deal about his friends and showed concern both for their troubles and interests and for their leisure and careers.

The notion of *philia* was rather complicated in eleventh- and twelfth-century Byzantium; it involved elements from both the classical literary ideal of friendship and the harsh world of political reality, where "friends" were allies and supporters as much as kindred spirits. For Nicetas Choniates *philia* meant a form of relationship or alliance between states,[22] semifeudal allegiance,[23] political support,[24] respect,[25] and—on the whole rarely—"pure friendship."[26] Psellos, on the contrary, emphasized the last meaning of the term: the tight personal bonds buttressed by common interests, especially in scholarship. In this view Psellos differed from the traditional ethical concept of the Byzantines, as expressed in the works not only of Kekaumenos but also of Symeon the Theologian, the famous Constantinopolitan monk and preacher of the turn of the eleventh century. Symeon's hostility to *philia* was connected with his rigoristic individual asceticism, which linked him to Cerularius. Symeon declared his break with the secular world, abstained from all social ties, and labeled friendship as a desire to feast and chatter. Man's main concern must be, according to Symeon, his individual salvation, realized as the vision of divine light. He even stressed that helping another person may be dangerous, since one's own house may be destroyed if one becomes involved in other people's affairs.[27]

The existence of a significant current of rigoristic ethics can thus be assumed. Its exponents in the eleventh century were Symeon the Theologian, Cerularius, and Kekaumenos; its main opponent was Psellos. It may be that this ethical contrast lies behind the well-known difference between the eleventh-century mural decorations in Hosios Loukas in Phocis and those at Daphni near Athens. The mosaicists of Hosios Loukas, the contemporaries of Symeon the Theologian, worked in the Byzantine tradition, presenting heavy isolated figures against an abstract gold background, while toward the end of the century at Daphni the manner is more supple, mild, and human, and the figures, presented in grouped compositions, seem more closely linked. The mosaics at Daphni are unanimously accepted by art historians as having been inspired by classical models, and this trait should also be connected with the scholarly and antiquarian tendencies of Psellos. What seemed to be a political intrigue, therefore, emerges as a serious controversy, which sheds some light on the contradictory Byzantine attitudes on social, ethical, and, perhaps, aesthetic issues in the eleventh century.

Homo byzantinus was at the same time both a unity and a conglomeration. Although Byzantine people appear as more or less a unity in opposition to the West, they show important antagonisms in their internal relations. It is still uncertain whether the conflict between Cerularius and Psellos was influenced by any regional differences and whether it originated in social contradictions or reflected the struggle of new trends against old traditions. Be this as it may, this conflict displayed two kinds of socioethical attitudes. Beside the characteristic Byzantine individualism and avoidance of social ties, there was a search to inaugurate a system of social relationships. The problem of *philia* appeared to be a crucial element in the Byzantine system of human behavior.[28]

We have tried to trace the principal ways of approaching and understanding the special character of Byzantine social life, which was closely connected with the social self-consciousness of the Byzantine people. These observations can now be summarized in order to propose a brief overview of Byzantine social structure and social ethics.

In comparison with the municipal society of Antiquity and the hierarchical society of the West, Byzantium appears to have had weak social ties. The Byzantines lost the social ties that originated in kinship and the polis and did not acquire new links, analogous to those established in the West, where society was arranged and bound together by links that can be variously described as vertical and horizontal. The vertical links are represented by the hierarchy of dependencies, as between lord and vassal, the horizontal links by the family, the village community, trade guilds, city organizations, and other types of association. Although these forms can also be found in Byzantine society, the two basic forms of western medieval social ties were slight, loose, and undeveloped in Byzantium, as was noticed even by medieval observers.

Some vertical ties existed in Byzantium, from at least the eleventh century onward. The question to be asked, however, is whether the Byzantine quasi-seigneurial retainers had the same origins as their western counterparts. Hélène Ahrweiler surmised that the Byzantine institution originated in the self-defense of inhabitants faced with the disorganization of state and had no feudal character.[29] But on this point there is no radical difference from the West, where the retinues of vassals were also formed during the period of disorganization in order to establish a system of self-defense. Paul Lemerle looked for another solution to the problem and assumed the existence of retainer relationships in Pakurianos's *Typikon*, but he denied its Byzantine origin and connected it with Caucasian influence.[30] This must be to some extent correct since the intermediate, or frontier, zone was a place of important social development in Byzantium, and the Caucasian effect on Byzantine aristocratization was potentially immense. Nevertheless, these retinues existed on Byzantine soil and not only "in Georgian micro-society," as postulated by Lemerle. As in the West, the Byzantine retinues served to sustain and prop up the private power of Byzantine nobility. So the difference may have been only quantitative in nature, but it did exist, and even in the fourteenth century the Byzantine *hetaireia* remained an embryonic, loose, undeveloped form of organization.[31]

It should be emphasized in this connection that the idea of faithfulness or fealty [*fides*], which was of central importance in Western society, remained practically alien to Byzantine political ideology. Nicetas Choniates emphasized the lack of fidelity [πίστις] in Byzantine society and complained that all tribes called the Byzantines *echidnae* and mother killers because of their treacherous attitude toward the emperors.[32] Choniates was astonished when a certain Pupakes preferred to be loyal to his benefactor rather than to receive a reward

from the emperor and was punished for such behavior, which in Byzantine eyes was incredible.[33]

Horizontal social ties were also not especially well developed in
Byzantium. The Byzantine village community has long been the object of study, and differing opinions have been expounded and defended by various schools of Byzantinists. According to Vasilij Vasi-
l'evskij, the village community dominated Byzantine agrarian history,
whereas Boris Pančenko affirmed that the Byzantine village community did not exist.[34] This historiographical disagreement can be explained by the complicated, ambiguous nature of the Byzantine village community. Village solidarity did exist, but it did not consist, as
Vasil'evskij suggested, in collective sovereign rights to the soil. The
salient feature of Byzantine agrarian relations was the individual
peasant's perpetual possession of his allotment, of which the economic independence was marked by a surrounding brick wall. The
common rights of the villagers consisted primarily of neighbors'
rights *in re aliena*, such as making hay and collecting chestnuts on the
neighboring lands. They had the right of pre-emption, if neighboring
land was sold, and were liable for the taxes of their impoverished or
absconding neighbors by virtue of the law of "common responsibility." In other words, the solidarity of a Byzantine village appeared as a
sum of distinct individual links connecting independent owners.[35]
This does not signify the absence of any form of village community,
since the villagers celebrated together [κοινὸν τοῦ χωρίου] their common feasts,[36] and references to common pastures are found in various
sources. In general, however, the individualistic marks of the Byzantine village community seem to have predominated. The Byzantine
system of guilds and crafts, *somateia* or *systemata*, is known from the
so-called *Book of the Eparch*, which was issued in the tenth century in
order to regulate the economic activity in the capital. Its regulations
were designed primarily to protect the guilds from the competition
both of unorganized craftsmen or peddlers and of noble owners of
workshops, and to this extent they had the same function as the later
craft rules in the West. The internal links of Constantinopolitan trade
guilds were weaker than those in the West, however, and the individual atelier more nearly independent from the community. The control
over production was exercised not by the guild authorities but by the
state machinery. The hierarchy of masters, journeymen, and apprentices normally found in western guilds did not develop in Byzantium,
where the masters employed in their workshops members of their
own families, slaves, and laborers who were hired, according to the

law, for a brief term. The difference between apprentices and hired laborers was insignificant.[37] We do not know whether the Byzantine guild system extended to the provinces, and there are reasons to believe that even in Constantinople the guild organization declined from the twelfth century onward.[38]

Nobody doubts that urban self-administration was weak in Byzantium. According to most scholars, indeed, Leo VI (886–912) abolished what remained of the autonomy of the provincial towns by depriving the *curiae* of the last vestiges of their authority.[39] This statement needs to be corrected, since there are several references to an urban population functioning as a group in the eleventh and twelfth centuries. Kekaumenos provides evidence that the crowd could act as a political power influencing the sentences of a judge,[40] and Psellos tells of a provincial *notarios* [secretary of a judge] who publicly praised his patron in Constantinople, delivering his speeches not in the exchequer or in other restricted meetings but in the crowded squares.[41] More important is the description by Eustathius of Thessalonica in the twelfth century of a man plunged into public activity, who was always in the square or in the city council, and who was visited by myriads of people for advice concerning marriage, trade, or various contracts.[42] And Michael Choniates, the metropolitan of Athens at the turn of the thirteenth century, complained that the Greeks forgot their ancient order and transformed their proper and quiet meetings into mad, noisy gatherings.[43] Be that as it may, these loose Byzantine city organizations cannot properly be compared with either the ancient *curiae* or the administrative, financial, or judicial authorities of western medieval towns after the eleventh century.

In the absence of public social life, the one form of association that flourished in Byzantium was the family. Herbert Hunger has drawn attention to the fact that the decline of the ancient order and the establishment of the Christian relationship brought with them a strengthening of marriage and family life.[44] In this connection the words of the Pope Nicholas I (858–67) in his *Responsa* addressed to the Bulgarian ruler Boris (852–89) are particularly significant.[45] The pope tried to persuade Boris to submit to Rome rather than to Constantinople and therefore praised the advantages of medieval Roman institutions in comparison with those of Byzantium. By stressing, among other points, that the possibility of divorce *solo consensu* still existed in ninth-century Rome, the pope showed that family connections were stronger, and perhaps more restrictive, in Byzantium.[46]

The *nomen gentile* that was so fervently attacked by John Chrysostom disappeared throughout the empire from the fourth century on, as can be seen from many epitaphs of the later period.[47] In the West the notion of clan was revived, partially under the impact of the barbarians, and in many areas the clan rather than nuclear family became the basic unit of medieval society.[48] The allotment was then regarded as the indivisible property of the extended family, whereas in Byzantium the clan connections remained embryonic at least until the eleventh century. The reappearance of the patronymic system took place at the same time as a regeneration of nobility but remained inconsistent, since the *nomen gentile* could be inherited in Byzantium from either father or mother, or even mother's mother.

The predominance in Byzantium of the nuclear family is brought out by the contrast between the systems of inheritance found in the Peloponnese after the conquest of the Latin crusaders, who brought with them from northern Europe the concept of preserving the unity of the estate held from a lord, while the native Greeks adhered to the Mediterranean practice of dividing their lands among all their children.[49] The demographic study by Angeliki Laiou-Thomadakis further shows the difference in family structure between the predominantly Greek theme of Thessalonica and the region of Strymon, which was populated mostly by Slavs.[50] The Greek family was as a rule nuclear and individual, whereas the Slavic family was often an extended, many-layered structure similar to the lineage.

The nuclear family was the real unit of civil society in Byzantium, and heavenly society was depicted by Symeon the Theologian as forming "one house," where all people will be brothers.[51] But the family was not a final ideal of Byzantine ethics, since it was treated as a transitional stage on the way to celibacy and as a means of subduing and restraining human lust. The final aim of *homo byzantinus* was, in principle, a solitary, eremitical life, free from any form of social relationship.

The loose structure of Byzantine social ties was particularly apparent in monastic life.[52] We have already shown how Balsamon distinguished between monastic regulations and organization in the East and West. Byzantine monasteries were as a rule small and weak, with an apparent prevalence of eremitic and semifamilial ways of life which allowed the individuals to dispense with the set discipline of a community. Byzantine monks, like some hermits but unlike most monks in the West, could dispose of their own property and even make wills, of which some examples survive. To this degree of individualism in the style of life within the monastic community corresponded the individualism of monastic communities themselves.[53] Not only were no monastic orders established in Byzantium, but even the so-called monastic republics consisted of independent units. The unity of the Athonite monasteries remained superficial. As with the Byzantine village community, this was only a territorial conjunction, a neighborly proximity, without any real submission and supervision. The external sign of Athonite administrative looseness was the acquisition of greater rights and privileges by the abbots of certain monasteries than by the *protos*, who acted as a nominal head of the whole Holy Mountain. The constant rivalry among monastic communities led to many lawsuits and completely disrupted the theoretical unity of Athos.

An absence or looseness of social relationships—in other words, individualism—was the most prominent feature determining the position of *homo byzantinus* in society. The term *individualism*, however, needs to be defined, since Byzantine individualism differed radically from the Renaissance or modern type of individualistic behavior and will be called here, in order to distinguish it from its more recent analogies, individualism without freedom. The average Byzantine, deprived of any substantial form of social relationship, consciously kept within the narrow circle of the nuclear family and, lacking the means of collective defense and help, felt alone and solitary in a dangerous world, naked before an incomprehensible, metaphysical authority.

The earthly embodiment of this authority was the emperor. The Byzantine concept of imperial authority was essentially different from the theory of kingship in the West, where the king was treated to some extent as first among equals, as the best among the nobility, and, later, as the uppermost link in the hierarchical chain. The Byzantine emperor, in addition to his supernatural and supertemporal— that is, biblical—epithets such as the Brilliant Sun and the Image of Christ or New Moses, was characterized by two important definitions drawn from the social sphere: the Lord and the Father. The application of the father epithet[54] is significant for a society that strictly emphasized family connections. As the lord of his slaves, the emperor was the only authority, placed beyond any hierarchy, high above his subjects. An unbridgeable gulf separated the holy person of the emperor from his humble children and slaves. The subtle ceremonial of palace life and sophisticated imperial ideology, which German scholars call the *Kaiseridee*, elevated him to the level of a semidivine being.

The gap between authority and subject dominated the Byzantine political imagination and made it impossible for any Byzantine to consider participating in administering the state. The delegation of power to the people seemed absurd to a Byzantine. If our city, wrote

Symeon the Theologian, were to call you and promise to appoint you a *praepositus* or imperial *protovestiarius* and send you to the palace in order to talk with the emperor about the needs of the people, you would never do it and, moreover, you would consider the people who proposed it mad.[55] More than three centuries later, Nicephorus Gregoras wrote that the republican polity established by the Zealots in Thessalonica of 1342–47 was a strange kind of state created by the mob, a state that had never existed either in Greece or in Rome.[56] Byzantine historians severely criticized their celestial rulers, whom in other types of works they compared to Moses, David, or even Christ himself, but they regarded their sins and shortcomings as deviations from the ideal image of the emperor. The rulers could be better or worse, but the political system itself, in the Byzantine imagination, was perfect and needed no correction. The Byzantines understood the empire as a just state, and therefore created only a very small literature of eschatological dreams.[57] Even the fifth-century pagan historian Zosimus, despite his criticism of Constantine and Christianity, admitted that the pagan oracle had predicted the greatness and prosperity of Constantinople.[58] In these conditions man's highest fate was to serve the emperor, and the servants who surrounded him and who really participated in the administration were proud to describe themselves as imperial serfs, δοῦλοι τῆς βασιλείας, and were aware that their privileges had been delegated for a restricted term and might be taken away at any time.

The difference between the Byzantine and western administrative systems is clear, since the Byzantine administration was strictly centralized and in theory directed from a single point, the imperial palace. Every subject of the empire had a nominal right to appeal to the emperor for justice. Administration in western Europe, on the contrary, became increasingly hierarchical, and justice in particular was exercised by different lords in varying degrees. Not only towns but even village communities exercised jurisdiction and obtained certain limited legal and administrative privileges. To belong to a social body signified possession of certain rights and participation in administrative, fiscal, and judicial activity. Freedom in the West thus came to be defined as personal privilege, as when someone today is said to be free to do something, and in some areas "freedom" and "nobility" were equated.[59] Whereas power in Byzantium was ideal, unattainable, and alien, in the West there was an illusion of participation in the administrative activity.

This gap between authority and subject, combined with the lack of social relationships, resulted in the constant instability of the Byzantine way of life. The subjects of Byzantine emperors were defenseless in the face of corporal punishment, confiscation of property, or banishment. The only restriction on governmental executions was the morality of the ruler. In all Byzantine political instructions, the emperors were called upon to imitate the best examples of the past and not to coordinate their aims with any constituted political body. There were no means, however, of enforcing this good advice.

The threat of ruin, whether or not it was realized, hung over society, and its existence forced Byzantine men and women into a pattern of political and cultural conformity, engendered by an almost Kekaumenian universal fear.[60] The alienation both from social ties outside the nuclear family and from power primarily accounted for this social fear, but it was also strengthened by other reasons ranging from human defenselessness before disease and starvation to frequent and dangerous invasions.

The yearning for security and stability that arose in this precarious society lasted longer in Byzantium than it did in the West, where it was associated particularly with the decline of Rome and the barbarian migrations and with the fragmentation of political power in the early Middle Ages.[61] In Byzantium the sense of insecurity was rooted in the nature of society and found its reflection, as will be seen in the following chapters, in various branches of Byzantine ideology.

CHAPTER TWO

The Material Environment
of *Homo byzantinus*

THE material aspects of Byzantine life have until recently been on the whole disregarded by scholars. The only works on this subject are in essence collections of raw data, such as the material scattered through the voluminous work by Phaidon Koukoules on everyday life in Byzantium. In spite of its value, however, this book shows the shortcomings of today's historiography, since Koukoules describes the various aspects of Byzantine material life as if they were unrelated to each other, the period, or the social conditions. In reality the various forms of external human existence were interconnected and interwoven because they were the product of the activity of the same people or groups of people; they bore the stamp of their epoch and developed in time; and they influenced and were influenced in their turn by the social structure and ethical values of the Byzantine world. It is not enough simply to collect the facts concerning Byzantine agriculture, housing, or food, however, since scholars today want to know whether there was a specifically Byzantine relationship to the material environment that was reflected both in human productivity and in the way people saw this productivity.

Among the most important aspects of the material environment that need further study are the geographical space and the historical geography of the Byzantine world.[1] The *Tabula Imperii Byzantini* will be an indispensable tool for research, but at present it is simply an alphabetical list of place names accompanied by a few introductory remarks concerning—quite naturally in view of the limited goals of the series—a single region without any connection with the general geographic patterns of the empire.[2] André Guillou's book on Byzantine civilization was the first work to treat geographical space as an important element of the civilization, but even there pure description of isolated areas prevails.³ His approach emphasizes regional variety and the territorial reduction of the empire, which was transformed from a Mediterranean power into a state on the Bosphorus. The first of these problems is purely geographical while the second is political and military, but until now neither has led to a serious study of the place of *homo byzantinus* in the geographical environment of the eastern Mediterranean. Two important issues, both closely connected with this problem and still practically untouched by scholars, are, first, the social aspect of Byzantine geography, which in turn can be subdivided into several questions, and, second, the Byzantine attitude toward the natural environment.

Asia Minor and Greece, geographically a series of small isolated valleys surrounded by mountains and badly linked with one another, were the geographical heart of Byzantium. Ravines, streams, and mountain rivers hindered traffic, and snow on the passes often made the roads impassable in winter. There were no broad plains or navigable rivers to promote political centralization. Modern historians of ancient Greece affirm consistently and convincingly that the territorial dissection of the country into small valleys led to the political disintegration of Greece. In Antiquity Asia Minor was likewise covered by a network of independent political bodies. This consideration forces us to ask why such a geographical milieu, which fostered political disintegration, served in the Middle Ages as a basis for a centralized autocratic state? Centralization in the Nile valley may be regarded as an organic result of natural conditions. In Byzantium, on the contrary, centralization seems to be in sharp contradiction to the geographical environment, and the establishment of Byzantine autocracy therefore needs to be explained.

Another special feature of the Byzantine geographical pattern was the lack of connection between the coastal cities and the interior. Most Greek and Anatolian rivers were narrow streams that dried up during the summer and flooded broadly in the rainy seasons. Their swampy estuaries sometimes caused serious obstacles to the establishment of settlements on the lower banks. The big rivers, such as the Danube and the Euphrates, were not used for internal traffic but were the frontiers of the Byzantine empire. Theophanes mentions the Danube—or Istros, as it was called—only as a frontier between Byzantium and the neighboring Slavs, Avars, and Bulgarians. It had been crossed by the invaders, its banks served as battlefields, and the Byzantine fleet entered its estuary. In Skylitzes there are twenty-one references to the Danube, most of them to crossings of the river. It is connected seven times with the verb περαιόω [to carry over or across], three times with διαπεράω [to cross over], once with παρα-πλέω [to sail along] and once with διαβαίνω [to cross over]. The chronicler also speaks four times of the castles on the Danube, once of the cities, twice of the plains close to the river, and once of the swamps. Finally he mentions the Danube in connection with the baptism of the Pečenegs. Choniates likewise saw the Danube primarily as the border between the empire and its northern neighbors, the Pečenegs, Polovcy, and Hungarians. The Byzantine fleet, in Choniates, entered the river only to fight against the Hungarians.

The main trade routes in the North Balkans were not along the Danube but over the mountain passes, with all their disadvantages. The regions of Asia Minor were also connected, or rather divided, by mountain passes rather than, as in the West and North, by rivers such as the Rhine or the Dnieper.[4] This geographical feature accounts for the fact that Byzantine cities turned their backs on the interior and faced outward across the sea. Even Constantinople, with her tiny rivulet, the Lykos, about six kilometers long, had no natural hinterland and was primarily a coastal city, linked both in reality and in the popular imagination with the Golden Horn.

To judge from its geographical situation, Byzantium, with its long coastline and many convenient bays, should have been a maritime state. Medieval reality, however, offers a sharp contrast to such geographical presuppositions. D. A. Zakythinos has already drawn attention to the strange wanderings of late Roman cities in the seventh century and later and to the tendency of towns to change locations, especially to move from the seashore to the summit of a hill. Corinth and Ephesus, as well as many smaller cities, left their original sites, and part of their populations moved away from the coast.[5] Martin Harrison has drawn attention to the tendency, only recently reversed, of people to move into upland valleys, away from the coast, in Lycia in late Antiquity.[6] One of the causes of urban migration may have been the change in the maritime situation. The sea grew dangerous because of Arab attacks, and the constant threat drove people away from the coast. This attractive hypothesis needs to be examined carefully, however. Byzantium was not seriously threatened from the sea before the second half of the seventh century, when Muawiya, the able Arab general and statesmen, began to ravage the Greek islands and the Lycian coast, but by this time the process of urban migration had already started and the new city of Ephesus had already been founded on the neighboring hill farther inland. Both internal and external explanations must therefore be sought for this striking contrast between geographical requirements and economic trends.

The problem of the Byzantine frontier has several aspects, including the administrative, which have long attracted the attention of researchers. There are a classic survey of the eastern boundaries by Ernest Honigmann,[7] various works on the Byzantine administrative network in southern Italy,[8] and an accurate study by Gennadij Litavrin of the complex—and politically involved—problem of the Danubian frontier.[9] The social significance of the frontier needs further study, since in Byzantium, as in Spain, Germany, and other parts of Europe in the Middle Ages, the frontier regions were marked by a ferment of new social developments.[10] It is probably not accidental that most of the aristocratic families of the eleventh and twelfth centuries originated in the frontier zones, either in Asia Minor or in the North Balkans. In these areas, which were relatively far from the unifying forces of the capital and where sudden attacks from enemies required quick decisions, there spread a new mode of life and new types of social relationships, which are reflected particularly in the Byzantine epic *Digenes Akritas*.[11] The social peculiarity of the Byzantine frontier was connected with an ethnic peculiarity. On the eastern borders of the empire the Armenians prevailed, as did Slavs in the Balkans, where the Vlach population was also considerable after the eleventh century.

The particular social and ethnic situation in the frontier zone raises two questions. The first, and simplest, is the possibility of establishing what can be called a collective ethnic portrait of the various border tribes or peoples. References to such tribes are to be found in Byzantine sources, including depictions of them in book illustration, and from these the Byzantine image or perception of the tribes can be reconstructed.[12] We can also try to understand the reality—that is, whether a particular tribe or people, such as the Armenians, Slavs, or Vlachs, in fact played a special part in the social, political, and cultural life of Byzantium.[13] It is not enough to answer simply that they played a "great part," since the way they differed from the Byzantines in such matters as administrative activity, landholding, or participation in rebellions must be examined, and the ethnic and topographic diversity that lay beneath Byzantine social attitudes must be uncovered.

The second question is that of regional tendencies, since the frontier was a constant source of centrifugal movement. We have inherited from the long tradition of panegyrics of national unity and in particular from the antifeudal historiography of the nineteenth century the identification of regional forces with the centrifugal tendencies that were held responsible for the military defeats of the empire.[14] This view, although widely held, is one-sided. In reality it was the centralizing forces that tended to suffocate new elements in the provincial towns and frontier villages and were responsible for the fact that the new urban forces and social structures of the frontier zones found no place in the framework of the Byzantine system and were therefore forced to strive for complete independence.

A second significant issue of our geographical investigation is to understand the Byzantine attitude toward the natural environment. Medieval attitudes toward space were always tinged with emotion or ethics. Space was seen as either good or evil. For the inhabitants of western Europe, the contrast between good and evil space was realized as the opposition of field and forest, for the inhabitants of the Fertile Crescent as that of oasis and desert. The Byzantines had their own opposition of the town and the mountain, or, more generally, of the inhabited and uninhabited worlds. Beyond the world of the *oikoumene* lay the *eremos*, which conveyed the idea of "uncivilized" as well as "uninhabited." [15] If the definitions of the city scattered in the Byzantine sources are collected, it can be seen how far they are from the modern idea of urban life. For them the indispensable features of an ideal city were mild climate, abundance of drinking water, and civilized, arable soil and orchards. [16] Another aspect of the Byzantine concept of urban life was brought out by Michael Choniates, when he openly opposed the ancient idea of the town and asserted that towns consisted not of strong walls, high houses, markets, and shrines, but of men with high morals, piety, courage, and justice. [17] The town was thus appreciated not as a center of commercial activity or as a community with self-government but rather as a place for rest and pleasure or as a cornerstone of Byzantine morality. Even if trade is mentioned, its function is as a vehicle of supply rather than of production for export. Merchants are praised for bringing silk, precious stones, or vases into the city, in the same way that the nearby lakes are praised for being rich in fish. For the Byzantines, therefore, the city was the pious center of what would today be called a consumer society.

In contrast to the city stood the mountain, which was understood as a wilderness infested with beasts and robbers. But the Byzantines also had an opposite image of the mountain. It was a place of escape as well as of danger, the home of those who either were forced or wished to cut themselves off from human society. [18] The holy existed side by side with the evil, and the mountain, since it was a terrifying wilderness, served as a holy place, where hermits dwelled. Some Byzantine monks lived in real mountains, or at least in hills or rocks, but sometimes the pious image of the mountain appeared imposed on the relatively flat reality. The most famous monastic congregation in Byzantium, Mount Athos, was understood as the mountain par excellence, the Holy Mountain, although the most important monasteries there were located as a rule by the sea. Depictions of hermit saints almost always show them in mountainous surroundings. The Byzantines were thus at the same time frightened by and attracted to mountains, but the attraction was of a negative sort, aimed at withdrawal from the world.

The Byzantines were afraid not only of mountains and wilderness but also of the sea.[19] Byzantine literature is filled with images of storms or shipwrecks. Human life itself was depicted as a sea voyage, on which the individual was in constant danger of shipwreck. Dread of the sea was a fact of real life, however, as well as of literature. The Byzantines were not courageous mariners; they preferred to navigate, in the words of Theophylact of Ochrid, touching the shore with the oar.[20] Ships moved slowly. Nicholas Muzalon, the future patriarch of Constantinople (1147–51), described his voyage from the capital to Cyprus, sailing, as he said, under the special patronage of the Trinity and with the Holy Spirit Himself filling the sails. Even with such patrons the voyage lasted ten days.[21] The Byzantines commonly used the so-called *strongyla*, or round vessels, which were broad and stable but rather slow.[22] They therefore easily fell prey to the pirates, both Christian and Muslim, who were endemic in the Mediterranean world and presented a constant threat not only to sailors but also to established coastal settlements. This dread of the sea helps us to understand that the downfall of the Byzantine navy and the defeat of the Byzantines in their struggle with the Italian maritime republics were the result not only of the mistaken policies of some Byzantine emperors but also of Byzantine social psychology. Byzantine merchants were not normally adventurers, ready to sail across the foreign seas; they preferred to stay at home, protected by the emperor and exploiting their privileges. The nomadic life was for the Byzantines bestial or barbaric and found its natural pendant both in the sumptuous stability of the imperial ceremonies[23] and in the principle of stability, which dominated monastic life. In reality many Byzantines traveled for administrative or commercial purposes, but in the Byzantine imagination the disturbance that required constant changes of place was regarded as evil, and the never-ending movements of Andronicus I were seen by Nicetas Choniates as as bad as his lewdness. Though monks sometimes moved in order to avoid crowds of admirers, in doing so they were not regarded as having broken the obligation of stability.[24] The continual rhetorical appeals addressed to the emperors not to leave the capital and not to be involved in military

expeditions also originated in the traditional idea of serenity and re-
pose as the most honorable type of behavior.

It would be interesting to know when the sociopsychological
shift took place by which the geographical curiosity of someone like
Cosmas Indicopleustes, who lived in the sixth century, was replaced
by the more passive attitude and when his acute perception of the
surrounding world gave way to pseudoscientific lists of ancient place-
names. The world grew narrow and its outskirts took on, in Christian
legend, curious features. The *Life* of St. Macarius of Rome may have
been written by a contemporary of Cosmas. It begins with a sober description of a journey to Jerusalem by three monks from a Mesopota-
mian monastery. The trip took eighteen days. In Palestine they visited
various holy places and then, after fifty-five days away, crossed the
Tigris. The road led them through Ctesiphon to India, where they encountered many strange beings and saw many fantastic sights, including the *kynokephaloi* [dog-headed people], whose lairs were under
rocks, and the highest mountain, where the sun did not shine, no
trees or grass grew, and venomous snakes, buffalos, leopards, bas-
ilisks, and unicorns abounded. They saw a man twenty feet tall,
chained between two hills with fire all around him, who wept and
mourned and whose cry could be heard thirty miles away. After
drinking from the river, they were able to stay there for a hundred
days without any food save the marvelous water, and they saw the
strange winds, of which one was green, another the color of acorns,
the third pure gold, and the fourth white as snow.[25] In this account
only the apparently precise figures that measured the distance between miraculous sights remain from the external form of the travel
descriptions written in Antiquity, a form that reappeared only in the
twelfth century, when a certain John Phocas wrote a modest and fac-
tual account of his voyage to the Holy Land.[26] By the time the Byzantines again showed an active curiosity toward the world around
them, they had lost the struggle for control of the seas, and the Italians soon gained maritime control even over the Bosphorus. This development paralleled that on land, where the towns from the seventh
century onward gradually moved away from the sea and yet were not
transformed into commercial or cultural centers in the interior.

It was not enough simply to observe the surrounding environment, however. In order to survive, the Byzantines had also to appropriate it, since the existing environment could not supply their needs.
The modes of appropriation and distribution of material goods form
in their totality what is called economic life. In the introduction the
desire of all peoples, particularly of historians writing about the past,

to find themselves in history was mentioned. This can be seen in many works on the Byzantine economy, where there is a tendency to modernize economic life. We are told about a pure money economy in Byzantium, about the struggle for markets, and about industrial competition. One of the most striking examples of this type of judgment is the identification of Byzantine gold coins with modern currency, as when the solidus is referred to as the dollar of the Middle Ages.[27] The Byzantine economy was in reality more complicated and contradictory than these comparisons imply, since it combined a natural economy based on barter with a monetary system. Coins were struck throughout Byzantine history, but the intensity of minting varied from century to century. Even Philip Grierson, a cautious scholar, has admitted, ". . . a strong case can be made for the view that Byzantine rural society from the late seventh century was less differently organized from that of the Germanic states in western Europe than we are accustomed to think."[28] Gold and silver coins were produced primarily for the needs of the state, such as the taxation of subjects and payment of mercenaries, rather than for more purely economic purposes, and Byzantine currency served not only as a medium of exchange but also as a special tool of administrative activity and government propaganda.[29] Every usurper, after acceding to the throne, immediately ordered new gold coins to be issued. Coins were used as a means of accumulation, not only in their natural form as treasure but also as a means of adornment and even for magical purposes.[30] On the other hand, wages were paid partially in kind, even in the twelfth century, as can be seen in the *Typikon* of the monastery of the Pantokrator,[31] not to mention peasants' corvées and taxes in kind.

The medieval foundations of the Byzantine economy left their mark on social psychology and consequently on imperial economic policies. The notion of just price and just profit penetrated Byzantine economic and juridical thought. John Tzetzes relates a typical anecdote. He saw that his contemporaries in twelfth-century Constantinople blamed the dealers in fish and fruit for selling their wares in the city market for more than they had paid for them on the shore. Mass psychology could not accept the source of profit in this case. Since he disapproved of the complaints lodged by the crowd, Tzetzes offered an explanation of this profit, but still within the realm of the idea of a just price, saying that the dealers were entitled to more than they paid because they had carried the produce on their shoulders and were compelled to share their income with the state officials.[32] Even Tzetzes could not understand the nature of commercial profit.

The prevalence of the idea of a just price explains various measures undertaken by the Byzantine government, including the attempts to prohibit interest. The history of usury in Byzantium, in spite of its importance, has not yet been written, but we know that it was at most tolerated and sometimes restricted. Kekaumenos felt a superstitious fear about lending or borrowing money, and some emperors, such as Nicephorus I (802–11) and Basil I (867–86), promulgated—without success—decrees prohibiting interest. Money lending did not therefore serve the function of promoting agrarian or industrial development in Byzantium. In most texts the usurer appears together with the tax collector as the supporter—later as the destroyer—of insolvent taxpayers who were awaiting the whip or imprisonment. Since the agrarian policies of the Macedonian dynasty have been studied in detail by various scholars from Vasilij Vasil'evskij to George Ostrogorsky and Paul Lemerle,[33] it is necessary here only to recall that they were based on the principle of a just price and designed in accordance with the traditional sociopsychological ideas of the Byzantine world.

The idea of noneconomic exchange is characteristic of preindustrial societies. Evelyne Patlagean showed its existence in the early centuries of Byzantine history and argued that the downfall of the late antique economy created an imbalance between the services rendered and the return.[34] From then on, the procedure of exchange was not limited to the simple movement of goods but included the establishment of various personal obligations between the contracting parties. The idea of noneconomic exchange can be studied further on the basis of documents from the thirteenth and fourteenth centuries. This raises the important question of whether there was a direct and comprehensive relation between the size of a piece of land and the tax or rent that was paid and the price for which it was sold.

Under Diocletian the basis of taxation consisted of a piece of land of definite value and extent and the individual who cultivated it. All possessions were strictly measured, and tax collectors assessed payment according to the quantity of land and its quality in terms of implements, cattle, and manpower. Although some old terms, such as "land of the first quality," survived from Diocletian's system into the later period, the principle of the strict relationship between landholding, including manpower, and so on, and tax payment seems to have disappeared, and Ostrogorsky stated as a general rule that the poorer the peasant, the higher the tax liability. Even in the same village peasants who owned quite different properties might pay equal sums to tax collectors, and greater taxes were sometimes levied on smaller properties.[35] Recently, the application of mathematical methods, including the use of computers, has shown that the factors determining the rate of taxation in a Byzantine village at the beginning of the fourteenth century were not purely economic. Different economic items were taxed differently in different villages. Ksenia Chvostova showed on the basis of seventeen late Byzantine *praktika* [inventories] that the tax was based primarily on the number of yokes of oxen (seven inventories), the size of family (eight cases), or number of cattle (again eight cases). In some villages the correlation was so low that it confirmed the absence of any connection between those items and the amount of tax paid. Chvostova further concluded that in one of the villages even the extent of arable land did not influence the amount of the tax.[36]

It should be added that Chvostova's results, though eloquent, are nevertheless incomplete and, to some extent, misleading. The fact that she dealt with villages as a whole inevitably led her to neglect the individual disparities within a village. When each peasant household is taken into account a yet more varied picture of the interdependence between the elements of household and taxes emerges. To sum up, it can be said that the late Byzantine peasant tax, the so-called *telos*, was not based upon a precise calculation of various liabilities, as presupposed in Diocletian's system, but was a sort of a hearth tax. The rate of the *telos* was doubtless to some degree dependent on those elements, but the connection was not direct; it varied from village to village, and the *telos* was influenced by various noneconomic factors, including the relations between the lord or the government and the peasant, tradition and *consuetudo loci*, and the real structure of power in the village. Precisely the poorer and weaker farmers were therefore compelled to pay relatively more than the well-to-do.

Even more striking is the lack of direct correlation between the price of a holding and its real size, value, or rate of rent. Although the incongruity of prices and land size has been already acknowledged,[37] scholars have tried to explain it by changing economic situations or by the influence of factors not mentioned in the documents, such as the quality of the land or of the fruit trees. The preference of scholars for calculating the average prices of land has distorted the multiplicity of noneconomic origins typical of medieval relationships. Table 2 shows the lack of connection, not only between the price of a holding and its real size, which could be explained by the changing economic situation or the variation in the quality of land, but also between the *epiteleia*, the rent imposed on the holding, and its size or price. All the

Table 2
Connection between Price, *Epiteleia* (both in Hyperpyra),
and Real Size of Property[38]

Epiteleia	Price	Object of Purchase
2	4	arable land
1½	70	arable land
1½	70	27 olive trees
1⅓	43	44 olive trees
1	8	arable land
1	7	24 olive trees
1	6	7 olive trees
1	5	18 olive trees
1	5	7 olive trees
1	4	arable land
½	20	arable land
½	13	14 olive trees
½	10	arable land, 14 olive trees, other trees
⅓	donation	46 olive trees
⅙	11	2 *modii* of vineyard

data come from the cartulary of the Lembiotissa monastery, in the region of Smyrna and refer to the brief period from 1246 to 1283.

An important witness to the fact that the Byzantines understood that the mutual relationship between the parties in a land transaction did not cease after the purchase is found in an act of 1433, by which the monks of the small monastery named Alypiou on Mount Athos conceded to the monastery of Saint Panteleimon a piece of land for the construction of a harbor. They included in the text of the act not only the price but also a pledge of the purchaser to support them. "You are obliged," according to the document, "as you are faithful and virtuous people, to love and sponsor us, in accordance with Christ's commandment, since we are feeble and weak."[39] Another case is described in a purchase deed of 1271 by which Michael Archontitzes, a peasant from the region of Dryanubaine, sold his holding to his lord Nicholas Maliasenos for twelve hyperpyra, even though—as was plainly put in the document—Maliasenos, being the lord of all Dryanubaine, could have taken it [κατακρατῆσαι] without payment.[40] These examples show that both land rents and land prices in Byzantium were determined not only by purely economic factors but also by personal and social relations, which accounts for the other-wise inexplicable vacillation in prices and rents.

The free play of economic forces was restricted in Byzantium, not only by medieval social psychology, but also by the Byzantine government, which served as a regulating power. In the period after the dark ages of the late seventh and eighth centuries, the regeneration of Byzantine trade, monetary system, and urban life as a whole—early in comparison with the West—may have been attributable in part to imperial protection, especially to the regular need of the imperial court and the bureaucracy for supplies. This protection gradually turned into a system of restrictions, owing to changes, not of the regulations but of circumstances, above all to the competition of the Italians. Until the middle of the eleventh century Constantinople enjoyed a trading monopoly in the eastern Mediterranean, but from the second half of the eleventh century the Byzantine merchants, who had been accustomed to anticipating profits at home under the powerful protection of the emperor, were compelled to contend with more flexible and mobile Italian competitors.

It has become traditional to blame Alexius I Comnenus (1081–1118) for his treaty of about 1082 with Venice, which is alleged to have led to the economic and political collapse of the empire. This opinion rests on the wisdom of hindsight, since scholars are looking at the Byzantine situation of the late eleventh century from the viewpoint of the contemporaries of the Fourth Crusade, who actually saw the installation of Venetian power on the Bosphorus. It is necessary to reconsider the problem and to compare the content of the Venetian treaty with that of the tenth-century agreements between Byzantium and the Russians, who in 911 were granted full exemption from customs, a special residence in a suburban quarter of Constantinople, and free board for six months. In 1082 the Venetians were allowed unrestricted trade, with exemption from all customs, and were given several warehouses and quays on the shore. Alexius thus introduced nothing radically different from what had been granted in the agreements of the tenth century. The content of the privileges was practically the same, and it was specified that Venice should continue to recognize the sovereign rights of the emperor. In the changed conditions after Alexius I, however, the Venetian privileges grew dangerous. What was appropriate to the tenth century, with its low level of commercial activity, became disastrous in the twelfth century, when the Byzantines were forced to compete with the new type of Italian merchant. It is necessary to emphasize again that the economic defeat of Byzantium in competition with the Italians was caused

not, or not only, by the mistaken policies of a single emperor or a si
gle dynasty—the Comnenian—but by the body of traditions, experience, geographical situation, and social psychology of the Byzantine
people.

In the preceding chapter the individualistic traits of Byzantine social organization, which were parallel to the individualistic organization of labor in Byzantium, were brought out. Individualistic labor
was typical of all preindustrial modes of production, but in Byzantium it seems to have lacked some of the communal features that are
found in both oriental and western countries. In Byzantium, for example, the light plow of the so-called ard type was used rather than
the English eight-oxen yoke, which presupposed collaboration among
the users; much peasant work was done by spade and hoe; the wind-
mill did not appear before the thirteenth century; and as a rule use
was made of a mill worked by hand or by a donkey, which did not
exceed the power available in a single household.[41] Small parcels of
land were enclosed by a brick fence and were not transformed into
common pastures after the harvest. There were no large-scale irriga-
tion works or mechanical devices of the type found in the Muslim
world, which were so costly as to be beyond the means of small landowners,[42] and there are only occasional references in the sources to
the draining of swamps and clearing of forests. The history of Byzantine land clearing has yet to be written, and we do not know whether
the tendency was to expand by assarting or to reduce by abandoning
arable land. The few extant sources concerning the opening of new
lands, such as the will of Eustathius Boilas of 1059, suggest that they
were cleared by individuals rather than by the government or by any
community.

Most Byzantine craftsmen worked separately, in small ateliers,
using the help of their families and one or two apprentices. The remains of a glass factory excavated at Corinth that dates from the eleventh or twelfth century show the nature of an average handicraft establishment of the middle Byzantine period. It had only one furnace
and about eleven square meters of work space.[43] The evidence concerning Byzantine manufacturing is sparse and difficult to interpret.
Construction was by cooperative labor, not only in the case of large-
scale works. According to hagiographic sources, the stonemasons
formed actual communities, working and living together, and took
care of coworkers who had lost their eyesight or their health in this
difficult job.[44] State workshops are mentioned in various sources, but
there is no evidence that they were any more than simple agglomera-
tions of individual artisans, and governmental needs were to a great

extent filled by levies assessed on craftsmen. Even arrows for the army and sailcloth for the navy were provided, at least in part, by private workshops. The Byzantine state occasionally tried to organize agrarian and handicraft production, but as a rule it functioned primarily as a supreme power to check and restrain commercial activity.

The everyday life of the Byzantines was as individualistic as their social system. They were a southern people, and traditionally they spent a considerable part of their day in the streets and market. But to share one's house with a stranger seemed a tragedy to a Byzantine. Tzetzes complained in a letter that he had been compelled to live in a house with an alien family, and this encounter became in his imagination a catastrophe. The strangers who occupied the upper story had almost as many children as Priamus or Danaos, and certainly more than Niobe or Amphion. They brought up pigs with the children; and the pigs and children, unlike Xerxes' horses, who dried up rivers by drinking the water, made navigable rivers of urine from which Tzetzes suffered as much as from the rain.[45] This description may have been in order to get a new apartment from the high official, the mystikos Nicephorus Serblias, to whom the letter was addressed; but Tzetzes' suspicion of his neighbors, even if exaggerated, is typical of the cult of the closed nuclear family in Byzantine society.

The establishment of Byzantium coincided with a change in the ancient principles of private building, at least among the classes who could afford to build their houses in accordance with their social tastes. The ancient upper-class house, the villa, which predominated in late Roman architecture until the sixth century, was a one-story building, of which the openness to nature was stressed both by the *impluvium* over the inner garden and by the decorative scheme, especially the floor mosaics, which suggested a direct continuation of nature. The medieval Byzantine house, on the other hand, was a two-story or three-story building covered by a roof and with restricted contacts with outside society and nature. As a rule, the courtyard was enclosed by walls, and the main economic activity was concentrated inside the walls. The ground floor was used for storage and animals, often including a mill run by a donkey, as on the Constantinopolitan estate of Michael Attaleiates.[46]

The plans of cities also changed. Public buildings, except for churches, and public places disappeared. Private houses, separated by curved and narrow streets, were built over old squares or gymnasia. Commercial activity, which in the ancient polis was concentrated in the central square, had already begun to move into the streets in the late Roman period.[47] Such streets were at first wide, with broad sidewalks and arcades, but as such remnants of Hellenic public life vanished, the town assumed a medieval aspect.

The individualistic means of production and forms of everyday life were counterbalanced by the centralized means of distribution. The main part of Byzantium's wealth was produced from agriculture, and the greatest part of the surplus produced by the peasant was taken not by individual landlords but by the state, which spent part of it on the needs of the court, army, and bureaucracy and distributed other parts among the members of the ruling class. Litavrin has shown that at the end of the eleventh century the Byzantine aristocracy possessed vast movable property, although the relatively small size of its landed estates shows that this movable wealth was not acquired from the income of these estates.[48] The same economic situation apparently still prevailed in the twelfth century, when according to William of Tyre the niece of Emperor Manuel I Comnenus (1143–80), Theodora, received as her dowry on marrying Baldwin III of Jerusalem (1143–62), 100,000 hyperpyra, plus 10,000 for wedding expenses, and various gifts of clothing, jewelry, carpets, silk tissues, and vases. The absence of any reference to new holdings of land is especially remarkable, since she was to receive in return, as her marriage portion, Acre and its territory.[49] In this connection it is worth remarking that when in the fourteenth century Kantakuzenos calculated his losses during the civil war, he did not mention either arable land or vineyards but listed the exact numbers of his oxen, horses, camels, mules, donkeys, pigs, and sheep.[50] Even in the eyes of a fourteenth-century nobleman land was not the most important source of wealth.

Rents from land, salaries, and imperial donations were not the only means of support for the Byzantine ruling class. Some groups were involved in commerce, though trade was regarded as being unworthy of a nobleman. The story about the Emperor Theophilus (829–42), who was so enraged when he learned that his wife owned a ship and its cargo that he ordered the ship to be burned, is typical of the Byzantine aristocratic attitude towards mercantile profit.[51] Other kinds of surplus income, however, were regarded as normal and legitimate. When the law school in Constantinople was created, in about 1047, the imperial directive emphasized that it was important for students to give gifts to their teachers before leaving the school benches. Byzantine judges were paid officially by both parties to a trial, and it was well known in Byzantium that a fiscal office could bring in a great deal of money. Bribery and fiscal extortions were a normal element of Byzantine state machinery and found their corollary in the practice of selling titles and offices. The fact that the price of a title was incomparably higher than the salary even for several years shows that the social prestige and additional income of an official were in excess of his direct material reward.

It can safely be said that the system of taxation was more important in Byzantium than in any country of medieval Europe and that in no other area was the ruling class so dependent on the centralized distribution of surplus production. Here we find on another level the contradiction already mentioned of individualism without freedom. Though the Byzantine ruling class was in many respects individualistic, it was highly organized in its appropriation of the labor of peasants and craftsmen, except when it resorted to semilegal robbery on an individual scale.

The recently developed discipline of demography has contributed significantly to the investigation of our problem. Byzantine demography in the past was concerned primarily with ethnic movements and was on the whole restricted to qualitative results. Scholars discussed whether the Slavs invaded Byzantine territory but not which part of the Byzantine population became Slavic. Demography now deals with a wide range of questions and tries to approach a quantitative expression of the data, although it still faces severe obstacles. Any calculations concerning the fate of the Byzantine population remain uncertain owing to the lack of exact numbers.[52] The only exception appears to be southern Macedonia in the fourteenth century, for which scholars have several detailed monastic inventories. In spite of the scarcity of information, however, some demographic questions can be asked that may contribute to a better understanding of the place of Byzantine people in their material environment. One of these questions is that of life expectancy. Angeliki Laiou-Thomadakis, in her book on the southern Macedonian peasantry, assumed that sixty years was the normal life span of the Byzantine rural population.[53] Since there are no exact data about the age of peasants in the *praktika*, she deduced this from indirect testimony, arguing that no family of more than three generations was described. This information can be compared with the references to life spans found in various narrative and rhetorical sources. Constantine X Ducas (1059–67), who died at sixty, had exhausted his lot, according to Psellos, who apparently regarded sixty as the normal life span.[54] The Patriarch Nicholas Mysticus at the beginning of the tenth century gave a somewhat longer term and assumed that the Byzantines seldom reached seventy.[55] Basil Pediadites, on the contrary, wrote that in Corfu at the end of the twelfth century a man of fifty was considered to be old and one of sixty senile and decrepit.[56] By putting it as he does he suggests that life expectancy elsewhere in the empire was longer. These figures agree approximately with those found in the eleventh and twelfth centuries in the West, where anyone over fifty was regarded as *gravis* or *senex*, and old age was said by different authors to begin sometime between fifty and sixty.[57]

It is possible to go a step further and try to find some figures that will permit a comparison of the life expectancies in different periods. The following analysis is based on a particular professional group, writers, for whom the dates of birth and death are indicated with some frequency in the sources, though not always exactly, or can be calculated on the basis of indirect information. Table 3 shows the average life spans of the authors whose biographies are included in the *Tusculum Lexikon*.[58]

These tentative calculations, though of limited validity, open the way to further research, and if they reflect demographic reality to any extent, they indicate that the Byzantines of the eleventh and twelfth centuries lived somewhat longer than their late Roman predecessors and western contemporaries. This conclusion, if valid, makes it necessary to reconsider the traditional view of the economic situation of Byzantium in the Comnenian period.

Another demographic question is that of the size of the family and the birth rate. It is often said that the celibacy of monks in Byzantium artificially restricted the birth rate, but it is less often emphasized that marriage of the clergy was recognized in the East throughout the Middle Ages. There is abundant information concerning the size of families in the southern Macedonian *praktika*, and Laiou-

Table 3
Average Age of Writers

Period	Size of Sample	Average Age
Late antique authors, fourth century	27	67
Greek and Roman writers, sixth century	13	62
Western authors from the end of the eleventh to the twelfth century	more than 100	68
Byzantine writers of the end of the eleventh to the twelfth century	15	71

Thomadakis estimates, by using these inventories, that the crude birth rate for the years 1317–21 was approximately 44 per thousand a year. She also proposes that there was a dramatic decline from 3.5 to 2.15 in the number of children born and surviving per couple during the first 40 years of the fourteenth century.[59] For the preceding period there are only scattered data in narrative and rhetorical sources, most, if not all, of which refer to aristocratic families. The task of collecting them would be worth while, though difficult, and might yield valuable results.

It would also be useful to study the appearance of similarities in family patterns and attitudes among the Byzantine nobles of the Comnenian period, particularly because of the part they played during which they seem gradually to have grown to resemble noble families in the West. The successors of the Emperor Heraclius (610–41) like the members of the Merovingian dynasty and, later, the Ottoman rulers of Constantinople, regarded their close relatives as dangerous enemies, and the brothers of emperors were almost always either put in prison, mutilated, or killed. At the end of the eleventh century the Caesar John Ducas still advised the Emperor Nicephorus III Botaneiates to marry the Georgian princess Maria precisely because she had no relatives.[60] The fact that the Comneni, on the other hand, saw in their relatives a firm support for their power may be associated with their origins as a noble family of which the members looked to each other for help in the troubled times of the eleventh century. A parallel development can be found at about the same time in western Europe, where the position of the corporate or consortial family was firmly established by the tenth and eleventh centuries and where natural communities of kin came together to defend their position and property.[61]

An important aspect of demographic research is the calculation of the population of cities, for which archaeology provides a comparatively firm basis. Anatolij Jakobson calculated the population of Cherson in the tenth and eleventh centuries, when it was the most prominent center on the northern coast of the Black Sea, at about 5,000 inhabitants.[62] David Jacoby determined the population of Constantinople at about 400,000 in the sixth century.[63] If this figure is correct, there was an amazing demographic expansion in Constantinople, which remained the same size even when the empire of which it was the capital had been radically reduced in size. Here is another typical Byzantine contradiction. The coexistence of an oversized capital and relatively small provincial towns is no less contradictory than the existence of social and economic individualism under the sway of the imperial power.

Among the most important economic and demographic issues is that of poverty or wealth in society. Can the question be answered whether Byzantium was rich or poor? If the test of wealth, in medieval communities, as Bernard Berenson said, was the quantity of gold used in works of art, Byzantium was certainly rich.[64] And it continued to give the appearance of wealth until at least the fourteenth century. It is unnecessary to enumerate the many Byzantine articles of gold, precious stones, silk, and enamel, from all periods, preserved in various museums. No less eloquent are the words of Latin authors of the period of the Crusades, who were amazed at the wealth of Constantinople and Cyprus. The same awe is recorded by the twelfth-century Jewish traveler Benjamin of Tudela. But was Byzantium really rich under its glittering surface?

One of the aspects of wealth is diet. The traditional view is that food was cheap and plentiful, and this seems to be confirmed by the large list of foods drawn up by Koukoules.[65] John Teall was among the first to question this traditional opinion,[66] and his idea was recently supported and developed by Patlagean,[67] who showed that the death rate increased during the spring and early summer months and that the life expectancy of women was less than that of men, both phenomena typical of an undernourished society. Patlagean dealt with the late Roman period, and Teall went, with a few exceptions, to the first quarter of the eleventh century. For the later period there is in the monastic rules or *typika*, an eloquent source in which the diet of a particular element in the Byzantine population, the monks, is described in detail, the evidence agreeing exactly with the conclusions of Teall and Patlagean. The normal Byzantine menu consisted of bread, vegetables, and wine; meat and even fish were seldom served. Recent research on the diet of monks in the West in the early Middle Ages shows that the food was plentiful but unwholesome and not nourishing.[68] Food was hard to store and often spoiled, and both the fear and the reality of famine were very real at that time. People took meals once or at most twice a day. This sparse diet was further reduced both by fasts and by various disasters, such as bad harvests, enemy raids, floods, and hail.

There is, however, one fact that needs special explanation. According to Patlagean the average consumption of grain from the fourth century to the sixth oscillated between three and six pounds a day, diminishing in the areas where the supply of meat was relatively rich. In sharp contrast to these figures, the Byzantines ate about a pound of meat daily: the *typikon* of the monastery of Saint John the Baptist, *tou Phoberou*, calculated the ordinary diet as between a half and two pounds.[69] Attaleiates conveys the figure 26.7 pounds a month,[70] and in Prodromus the similar figure 12 *medimnoi* a month for 13 people.[71] If the figures are correct, it must be asked why the consumption of grain was so sharply reduced. Does it signify that the products of cattle-breeding were more prominent in Byzantine alimentation than in that of the late Roman empire? Tentatively the hypothesis sounds correct, but it is difficult to prove. The problem can be approached from another direction by trying to calculate the productivity of arable land. While the evidence is scanty, except for the later period, that which is available has not been gathered. The boast of Eustathius of Thessalonica[72]—that is that he had reaped twenty times as much as he had sown—is hardly credible. The figures reported in the late fourteenth-century documents vary between 5:1 and 1.6:1,[73] which is comparable to those from other Mediterranean districts in the Middle Ages.

It is difficult to look at the Byzantine economy as it changed in the course of time. The traditional view is that Byzantium preserved a high economic level from late Antiquity until the eleventh century, when economic and demographic decay set in, primarily on account of the invasion of the Turks; but this assumption is based upon general considerations, primarily of political character, and needs to be re-examined. Some archeological evidence provided by excavations in Bulgaria suggests that in the eleventh and twelfth centuries the importance of cattle in relation to that of sheep and goats increased in the Balkan economy.[74] This idea is to some extent supported by the foreign witnesses who testified to the high level of Byzantine cattle-breeding in the twelfth century, such as the Russian traveler Daniel, who was surprised by the herds he saw on the islands of Patmos, Rhodes, and Cyprus.[75] From the twelfth century onward, moreover, Byzantium began to supply Italy with agricultural produce. Particularly important in this connection is the evidence in an unpublished eulogy by Eustathius of Thessalonica in MS Escorial Y-II-10 (fol. 35) that the metropolitan of Athens, Nicholas Hagiotheodorites, provided grain to the inhabitants along the shores of the Adriatic and off "famous Sicily." The calculations of the deserted villages made by Hélène Antoniadis-Bibicou[76] show that, after a temporary demographic decline at the end of the eleventh century, the process of agrarian desertion was interrupted until at least the second half of the thirteenth century. No great distress is mentioned in the twelfth-century sources, in spite of abundant evidence for bad harvests and other disasters throughout the eleventh century.

These indications may all be fortuitous, but they must be taken into account. Only numismatic material gives abundant numerical evidence, and this again does not support the traditional opinion. Both numismatic and archeological evidence indicate a shortage of coinage and a decay of city life in the seventh century. The recent works by Clive Foss[77] are convincing in this regard, though some questions may be asked concerning the causes—the Persian invasion—and his exact dating—about 618—of the end of urban life in Asia Minor. Even in Constantinople economic life decayed for a time, as can be seen in the decline in quality of Constantinopolitan ceramics[78] and in the reduced number of monastic foundations. Only two new monasteries are known to have been founded in the seventh and eighth centuries. The first is mentioned about 695, and the second is said to have been founded by the wife of Leo III (717–41).[79] It is uncertain why so few new monasteries were founded at this time, but it was not the result of Iconoclasm, because the building of monasteries stopped long before the beginning of the Iconoclast struggles. The economic revival started in and around Constantinople in the ninth century, spread to the provinces in the tenth century, and reached its acme in the eleventh and twelfth centuries.[80] It may even have survived the defeat in 1204 and have continued through the thirteenth century. Both Michael Hendy and Michael Angold regard this century with good reason as a direct continuation of the Comnenian period and consequently deny that the Fourth Crusade interrupted Byzantine monetary and economic development.[81]

The economic history of the eleventh century, which was long characterized as a period of deep economic collapse, has recently been reconsidered. Cécile Morrisson has shown that the monetary crisis of the eleventh century did not reflect a general economic crisis, and Lemerle has brought out several progressive traits in the economic, social, political, and cultural life of the eleventh century that account for the growth of the urban middle classes.[82]

In summary, it can be said that Byzantine social and economic life, especially the relationship of people to their environment and the relationships among people in using natural resources is now seen as more complicated and contradictory than it was some twenty years ago. The old simplistic views are being reconsidered, and Byzantium is understood in the complexity of its many apparent contradictions, of which the most significant was the contrast between the individualistic mode of production and the centralized form of appropriation.

This contradiction, reinforced by the particular geographical framework of the country, aggravated the difficult position of Byzantine cities within the framework of the medieval world. The contradiction was not limited to social and economic spheres and can also be found in the various branches of Byzantine spiritual life, to which we shall return in chapter seven.

CHAPTER THREE

Byzantine Life and Behavior

THE history of social behavior is a fresh field, and except for the role of the emperor in the state ceremonial, Byzantine social behavior has hardly been touched by scholars. Social behavior can be seen as a system of traditional, inherent, and partly unconscious responses, reactions, or adjustments of human beings to situations that occur repeatedly in society. Here social behavior will be considered as a stable and at the same time changing phenomenon, differing both from regular responses and reactions of the human organism and from political decisions designed to meet the challenge of concrete situations in domestic or foreign affairs. When on a cold January day of 532 Justinian I appeared before the rebellious crowd in the imperial box at the Hippodrome in solemn dress and with the Gospel in his hands, he played the role of the basileus; but his order to suppress the riot was the result of a political decision rather than social custom, since it was taken deliberately on the basis of the danger that he saw in the situation. Many political decisions were influenced, even determined, by traditional behavior, however, and it is not always possible to distinguish political reason and will from a standard of social behavior.

The ancient Greeks created, according to Werner Jaeger, a "new awareness of the position of the individual in the community," and "a new conception of the value of the individual." They accepted as the main goal of human beings the tendency to develop as fully as possible both their physical and their spiritual qualities. "The variety, spontaneity, versatility, and freedom of individual character" were taken for granted, and the ideal of behavior included the human body in free motion, a noble and proud attitude toward the trials of life, and *paideia*, or education, as the conscious mastering of a sophisticated and contradictory cultural heritage.[1]

Early Christianity accepted many images and renderings of classical authors but rejected and denied the essence of Greek ideal behavior.[2] The relationship between the *zoon politikon* and the community was replaced by a relationship between people and God, between human beings and a superior being. Men and women were responsible not to their fellow citizens but to God, and their attitude became therefore in its essence not one of nobility and pride but of prostration, the *proskynesis*. Educated urbanity and merry enjoyment of creature comforts also gave way to strict confinement far from city life and to an utter indifference to clothes, food, and secular knowledge. The classical ideal of harmony and beauty was replaced by the new perception of human appearance that was embodied in the image of the holy man, who was admired by contemporaries but would have seemed to the theorists of the Greco-Roman world a denial of their most cherished values, since it represented the discovery—or rediscovery—of the beauty of disharmony and distortion. The emphasis in early Christian behavior on the dignity of obedience, rather than the dignity of boundless freedom, was likewise the antithesis of the classical ideal of behavior. Although Christian rhetoric, which was to a great extent addressed to urban audiences, retained some broken elements of Greek *paideia*, hagiography created the ideal of a cultural dissenter whose behavior could only shock the urbanized inhabitant of a classical polis. Symeon the Fool, the hero of a Life written by Leontios of Neapolis in the first half of the seventh century, ran through the streets of the city of Emesa dragging a dead dog by a rope; in church he threw nuts to put out candles; he overturned the tables of pastry cooks; even more, he defecated openly in the square in the view of the crowd, or entered the women's baths without compunction.[3] The early Christian hagiographers rejected the principles of classical behavior in the same way that modern social critics have reacted against many aspects of middle-class behavior.

The negative and dissenting aspects of Christian behavior were gradually pushed back and replaced by a new, positive ideal which gave no place for the exaggerated license of Symeon the Fool. Already in the legend of Philaretos the Merciful, written about 822, the activity of the hero, though resembling the scheme of the story of a holy fool, is presented as silly only from the viewpoint of household economy.[4] Philaretos did not transgress the bounds of acceptable behavior as he lavishly distributed his animals and other belongings among those whom he considered to be in need.

The central aspect of Byzantine behavior was *taxis* or order,[5] which contrasted sharply with the disorder introduced into social life by "the holy man." Earthly institutions, both ecclesiastical and temporal, were considered to mirror the order of the universe, the cosmic array created by God. The church building was seen as a microcosm mysteriously embracing within its walls all of space and time, and, according to Constantine VII Porphyrogenitus (913–59), the imperial power, being exercised with measure and order, reflected the harmony and motion arranged by the creator for the universe. The imperial ceremony was a visible expression of the heavenly harmony and order and made the power of the emperor more solemn, agreeable, and admirable to his subjects.[6] Solemnity was the very essence of the imperial attitude, with its slow processions, well-thought-out gestures, frequent halts, and repeated acclamations. But solemnity was not restricted to the emperor and his surroundings.

Psellos, while lamenting the death of his daughter Styliane at the age of nine, stressed the majesty [$εὐπρεπές$] and solemnity [$σεμνυνο-μένη$] of the child; her "solemn smile," he says, opened snow-white teeth.[7] On the other hand, an anonymous priest, scoffed at by Psellos, is described as completely without calmness. He twisted his lips unnecessarily, shifted his eyes violently, breathed hate and lewdness out of his nostrils, shook his head, twitched his shoulders, moved his hands, touched his back, scratched his belly, stroked his thighs, or did, Psellos concluded, "even more disgusting things."[8]

The classical concept of the image in visual art as an imitation of man or woman was retained by the Byzantines, and Byzantine authors of *ekphraseis*, descriptions of the monuments of art, copied ancient models by evaluating paintings and sculptures according to their adherence to nature.[9] But the opposite idea of human imitation of the statue arose in about the fourth century and gradually gained a foothold. Ammianus Marcellinus in his portrayal of Constantius (337–61) affirms that the emperor looked *tamquam figmentum hominis*, as a statue, and depicts the solemnity of his behavior: "No one ever saw him wipe his mouth or nose in public, nor spit, nor turn his face to this side or that."[10] The ideal of behaving like a statue evolved in the works of such Byzantine authors as Michael Psellos.[11] Solemnity was a precious and desirable quality. It was quite natural for Symeon the Theologian to urge monks to stay calm during the service[12] and for Byzantine artists to try to present their heroes as calm as possible, in frontal view and poised. To an observer of our time they seem motionless, though the Byzantines saw them as moving and could smell Lazarus after his resurrection.[13] The motion of heroes was solemn and full of dignity, whereas restless movement was a mark of a barbarian or a rebel,[14] and even the incessant mobility of an Odysseus seemed suspicious to the Byzantines.

Byzantine solemnity of behavior was closely associated, almost permeated, with humility. In other words, it was deprived of inner pride. The ceremonial act of *proskynesis* was the symbol of servility and self-abasement and signified a complete rejection of self-respect and nobility. When Andronicus Comnenus, the rebellious cousin of Manuel I, made peace with his imperial lord and master and returned to the capital, he staged a scene of utter self-abasement. Winding around his neck an immense chain that he concealed under his cloak, he entered the reception hall, instantly threw off the robe, prostrated himself at the feet of the emperor, and asked his imperial cousin to drag him by the chain. Modesty and humility were considered virtuous and became part of the system of behavior. Another physical expression of self-abasement was the tendency to tears. Medieval people in general wept more easily than we do, both at the prospect of misfortune and in happiness. Symeon the Theologian called tears the *energeia* of the Holy Spirit and said that they were necessary to the soul as food and drink are necessary to the body. Those who did not weep every day, he said, ruined their souls by famine, though he stressed that neither tears nor vigils would spontaneously provide salvation.[15] An example of the practice of weeping is found in the *Life* of the Patriarch Euthymios. After Leo VI (886–912) was excommunicated by the Patriarch Nicholas Mysticus, he came on Christmas day to the church of Saint Sophia, accompanied by the Senate, in the hope of being received there. The patriarch prohibited his entrance, and the humiliated emperor retired, without a word, "with tears springing to his eyes, and watering with his tears that sacred ground." After the feast of the Epiphany the emperor again presented himself at the church and was again repulsed by the patriarch. Though the members of the Senate protested, Leo stood a moment speechless and then he cast himself on the ground and after weeping a long time rose up and bade farewell to the patriarch.[16]

While tears were habitual and honorable, smiles and laughter were rejected by the church fathers and were regarded by the Byzantines as signs of lewdness and obscenity. The gods of Antiquity laughed frequently and noisily, but Christ can only be imagined weeping. The words of the Gospel, "Woe unto you that laugh now! for you shall mourn and weep" (Luke 6.25) give a clue to understanding the Byzantine attitude toward laughter.

Byzantine behavior was ritualized in the sense of being governed by habits and customs that acquired the force of law and created established patterns for bringing individual members of society into relation with each other and with the higher powers, both seen and unseen.[17] The ceremonial of the palace and the church was institutionalized, and a breach of ritual was considered tantamount to breaking one of the essential principles of the economic and social system. The questions of priestly vestments or of the use of leaven for the sacred bread became problems of primary importance. Private life was also pervaded by ritual. Three important points in human life especially surrounded by ritual acts were birth, marriage, and death. Associated with birth was primarily the ritual of aid to the woman in childbirth, who lay on a couch, or sat on a stool, or even stayed upright, supported by three other women, relatives, or friends.[18] If the delivery was abnormal, special actions had to be performed, as when Anna, mother of the future Empress Theophano, was in labor, suffering greatly from pain, and an old man helped her by bringing a girdle from the monastery of the Virgin and ordering her to fasten it around her loins.[19] Special formulas, both written and oral, were also supposed to help.[20] If a baby was born surrounded with the *derma*, or inner membrane, this piece of skin was retained as an amulet.[21]

Childbirth was regarded as soiling not only the mother but also the midwife, the women who attended and assisted, and even the house itself, which afterward needed to be anointed.[22] The object of this ritual cleansing was to exorcise the evil spirits who could inflict harm, particularly fever. According to Pseudo-Psellos, an old Armenian drew out a sword and by using Armenian spells drove away demons after the accouchement.[23] Attention gradually shifted from the mother to the newborn child. The relatives and friends prayed that the baby would not cry, would have enough milk to suck, and would love his or her mother not out of habit but out of sincere affection.[24] The presents and birthday feast arranged a few days after the birth fulfilled the ritual of the first stage in human existence, not to mention the religious ceremony of baptism.

We know nothing specific about age classes in Byzantium or about special initiation rites to mark the attainment of maturity, but it can be presumed that the generation existed as a cultural and demographic group in Byzantium as it did in the medieval West, where the widening gaps between the ages of bride and groom contributed to the varying attitudes of children toward their mothers and fathers.[25] In Byzantium it was marriage that marked the end of youth. The wedding ceremony was customarily performed at dusk. The crowd of relatives and friends approached the house of the bride with musicians and torches; the groom entered the house bringing the wedding robe, and as the bride appeared the relatives threw apples and roses, the symbols of love and fecundity. Death, the final step on earth, was also accompanied by ritual actions, including ablutions with special sponges, investiture, and ceremonial carriage. The hands of the dead were crossed on the breast and the icon set upon them, and the relatives followed the corpse, wailing and sometimes even tearing hair from their heads.[26]

Ritual acts and gestures were also associated with judicial practice. After the resolution of a case concerning a borderline between two estates a ceremonial procession carrying wooden crosses went around in order to sanctify the boundaries. A suspected thief was forced to look at a "magic eye" painted on the wall, since the Byzantines believed that a real criminal would be unable to bear looking at the magic eye and would be forced to divert his eyes. The ordeal by hot iron, borrowed from the West, appeared in Byzantine territory only in the thirteenth century, at the same time that it came to be regarded with disapproval by the Roman church.[27] Those who were required to prove their innocence spent three days in fasting and prayer before the ordeal. Their hands were bound to prevent their using ointments in order to lessen the effect of the ordeal. They then had to take a hot iron and walk three paces with it. George Pachymeres, who claims to be an eyewitness of these trials, records that those who came through the ordeal unharmed were acquitted of evil intentions.[28]

Verbal ritual was widespread. Legal acts, purchase deeds, private letters, and official speeches were all subject to strict formulas, and special reference books containing various models were compiled. An average letter included expressions of friendship, complaints at a correspondent's silence, a description of a writer's loneliness far from the capital, and so forth.[29] A standard set of metaphors, comparing a letter to a gift, festival, or the coming of the spring, was suited to each topic. The object of speeches was to praise, and the Byzantines regularly and deliberately contrasted the genre of speeches with that of history, the aim of which was to reveal the truth. Like the standard letter, an average speech or laudatory poem was permeated with standard metaphors, similes, biblical quotations, and images. Though restricted in the display of emotion by the ritual of words and gestures, the Byzantines could freely indulge in laughter and crude obscenity. They liked practical jokes and earthy buffoonery at their feasts; they used sharp irony in their political arguments. When at a feast Isaac II Angelus (1185–95) asked for the salt, ἅλας, an actor, *mimos*, who was present interpreted the word as ἄλλας, meaning other [girls], and re-torted: "First we must lie with these, and later we shall order others to be brought." Nicetas Choniates boldly described a jovial game in which the participants kicked each other in the buttocks, Andronicus Comnenus pretending to have diarrhea and squatting behind a bush, and the princess Anna Comnena, while blaming her husband for cowardice, wishing him to have a hollow vagina instead of a male organ.[30] A carnival license of tongue prevailed alongside the solemn order of speech.

In Byzantine ritual it is often difficult to distinguish ceremonial solemnity from an attempt to dispel, by religious or magical means, the evil forces surrounding mankind. The universe seemed to be populated by demons, witches, and wizards, who attacked people with temptations or sent them suffering. Byzantine historians tell of various sorcerers who attained their goals with the help of witchcraft. One of them, Skleros Seth in the twelfth century, was said to have desired a girl who had only just reached puberty and who had repelled him when he had tried to seduce her. He managed to send her a bewitched peach, however, and after eating the fruit she fell in love with him and allowed him to lie with her.[31] Rituals, especially processions, were used against evil forces as well as against rains or drought, invasions of locusts, or floods. An even more effective means against evil forces was the miracle, an instant action performed by a holy person who could read the future, expel evil ghosts, and wield power over nature. The miracles described in Byzantine histories and lives of saints are either edifying or pragmatic. They open a crack into the future, urging sinners to repent and live in accordance with God's will, or they consist of healing, overcoming natural disasters, saving from enemies, and the like. There is no evidence in the Byzantine sources of purely emotional phenomena or imitations of the passions of Christ, such as the stigmata that occasionally appeared on the bodies of Christians in the West in the twelfth and thirteenth centuries.[32]

The games stood in psychological contrast to ritual. The heart of each ritual action is certainty. From beginning to end all the steps are known to the participants. However long and complicated a liturgy, an imperial triumphal procession, a wedding, or a birthday feast may be, its order is stable and its accomplishment visible and predictable. The games, conversely, always involved an element of chance and a touch of the unknown. Ritual presupposed a physical effort, and an emperor in his heavy and precious garments was sometimes close to dizziness and fainting during a ceremony, but psychologically it brought calm, relaxation, and appeasement. The games also involved ritual, and their outcome may not always in fact have been entirely a matter of skill and endurance. But in essence they involved tension and uncertainty. They strained the nerves and excited the emotions, often violently and crudely.

Various types of games, most of which died out with the late Roman empire, were created in Antiquity. Gladiatorial combats were abolished by Constantine the Great in 325, but they survived for almost a century after the prohibition. An eastern monk, Telemachos, was murdered in Rome during the reign of Honorius (395–423) when he rushed into an amphitheater in order to part the gladiators and stop "this dirty spectacle."[33] The Olympic games were prohibited by Theodosius I in 393, though there are some vague references to their survival in the first half of the fifth century. The chariot racing in the circus seems to have had greater vitality, and the Hippodrome at Constantinople flourished during the sixth century. The circus, an enclosure with parallel sides and semicircular ends, divided down the middle into two runs by the spina, a low fence marked at each end by turning posts, was understood as a microcosm. The arena symbolized the earth, the spina, with its water tanks, the sea, and the obelisk pointed up to the sky. At the open end were the vaulted stables for the horses, who competed under various colors. Green and Blue were particularly popular in Constantinople,[34] and the fans there cheered their heroes. Thirty-two surviving epigrams are dedicated to just one successful charioteer, Porphyrius, who was evidently tough and did not give up easily. His first monument was dated c.500 by Alan Cameron and his last c.545. He drove alternately for the Greens and Blues and was rewarded with many statues. The victorious charioteers were popular idols. They made fortunes and exerted influence. At the same time, many of them were believed not only to consult magicians but to be sorcerers themselves. Three charioteers were prosecuted for the practice of magic in Rome between 364 and 372. One was acquitted, but another was beheaded and the third burnt.[35]

The charioteers customarily asked for the blessing of the church before races, but the Greek church fathers were always hostile to the Hippodrome. John Chrysostom named it the Satanodrome, calling the games a devilish procession and satanic spectacle. In his works, however, John repeatedly conjured up images from the Hippodrome. The prophets were for him the charioteers of the truth; the apostles, God's chariot-horses; and the church, a spiritual horse race.[36]

It seems probable that by about 600 the traditional rivalry of the Hippodrome had given way to the ceremonial function of circus organizations that was gradually included in the imperial *taxis*. John

Moschus in the *Pratum spirituale* compared circus activity with the ecclesiastical services. The chanting of the emperor's praises reminded him of the continual reading of the psalms. Tension was soothed, and the supporters of the Greens and the Blues no longer took offense and resorted to insults.[37] As described by Constantine Porphyrogenitus, the so-called circus parties had developed by the tenth century into semiofficial groups whose principal function was to praise the emperor by standard acclamations. They were absorbed into the imperial ritual.

Although the games did not vanish completely, they took on a more restricted and aristocratic character. The chariot races are still mentioned in twelfth-century sources, but they do not seem to have been a significant part of the life of the capital, and there are no references to them in the sources after 1204.[38] In the twelfth century Byzantine noblemen and even emperors readily participated in tourneys, vying in the lists with crusaders and sometimes receiving severe wounds. The aristocratic *polo*, a kind of competitive ball game on horseback, which required adroitness and skill, became popular at this time. Hunting was also popular among noblemen of the twelfth century. Not only were various descriptions of the chase composed by various writers, hunting motifs were included in imperial symbolism. Prodromus regarded the emperor not only as an ideal warrior but also as an ideal hunter.[39]

The Hippodrome became the scene of various innocuous spectacles, such as tame bears or acrobats dancing on the rope,[40] and the tendency toward carnival feasts spread side by side with aristocratic competitions. Christopher of Mytilene described a procession of disguised students in notarial schools on the day of Sts. Markianos and Martyrius.[41] Theodore Balsamon records similar masquerades, blaming both the actors who during the January festival represented monks and clerics and the clergy who put on masks in the likeness of soldiers and even of animals.[42] We also find in Balsamon a description of a festival that was banned by the Patriarch Michael III (1170–78) and that was traditionally celebrated on June 23, when people gathered in their homes privately with friends and put bridal clothing on the eldest daughter of the family. After a carousal and dancing they poured sea water into a brass mug, threw in all sorts of objects, and then asked the "bride" various questions, each of which she answered by taking from the mug an item that alluded to coming misfortune or success. On the next day, the participants in the fortune-telling went with tambourines to the seashore, scooped up water, spilled it over their houses, burned heaps of hay, jumped over the

fires, and adorned their houses.[43] It is difficult to interpret this festival, to which Balsamon was opposed, but it was clearly familial in
nature and combined foretelling the future with ceremonies aimed at
ensuring the welfare of the family house.

Was the Byzantine way of life in general more restricted by the
limits of the household than it had been in Antiquity? A comparison
of the Lives of two saints is revealing on this subject. In the first, the
seventh-century *Life* of the Holy Fool Symeon, mentioned earlier, the
scenes presented by the hagiographer occur in the streets and squares
of late antique Emesa, where poor citizens are to be found washing
their linen in the river, girls are playing in the street, and there are
workshops in which passers-by gathered round the fire during the
winter days, schools, and theaters. In the tenth-century *Life* of Basil
the Younger by Gregory, on the contrary, all the activities of the saint
are connected with the interior aspects of Byzantine everyday life.[44]
Basil found his abode with Constantine the Barbarian, who gave him
a couch, a chair, a lamp, and a table; he ate with the family of a man
whom he had healed of a fever; he visited the *patrikia* Irene and found
in her house a company of women; he predicted the death in three
days of a sick woman, addressing her relatives and friends who had
gathered in her house; he sent a vicious woman from his apartment
by raising a glass of wine and sweeping crumbs off his table. Even
heaven was seen by Gregory in a dream as a large atrium filled with
vases of white stone containing sacred oil. In the neighboring hall,
vaulted and dark, he saw St. Basil killing an enormous serpent, the
cause of all evil. Is this difference between the Lives of the two saints
fortuitous, or does it reflect a real social change and the growth of private familial elements? An investigation of these changes might be
rewarding.[45]

Worship of the body, courage, and physical strength was as typical of Antiquity as worship of reason and noble behavior. The Byzantines, on the contrary, seem to have been a bit ashamed of having
bodies, and they tried in art and literature to make the body subject to
the spirit and in everyday life to conceal it beneath a heavy dress. The
history of Byzantine costume has not yet been written, largely because the evidence is sparse. Byzantine artists tended to reproduce
antique fashions and to pay no attention to what was actually worn.
Only from written sources is it known that trousers were introduced
and became the most prominent feature of masculine costume. Indeed, the western writer Rupert of Deutz, in the twelfth century, divided Europe into regions where trousers were and were not worn.
He classified among those who wore no trousers the inhabitants of

Ireland, England, and Italy, "where the vestiges of this disreputable custom are still found, as we ourselves have seen when we have sat while visiting in these places among men stretched out in front of a fire."[46] The exact date when trousers and the sleeved shirt began to be worn in Byzantium is not known, but they marked the victory of the restrictive type of medieval clothing over the ancient type, which—except for the sumptuous garment of the toga—left both legs and arms free.[47]

This is not to say that the Byzantines rejected the flesh completely. A complete rejection of the body was typical of dualism, while the Byzantine church officially praised the flesh as one of the wonderful creations of God. A good example of this attitude is found in a hymn by Symeon the Theologian, who exclaimed that every limb of our body is Christ, Who made all our shameful parts graceful and decent by His divine beauty and glory and said that people must not be ashamed of their limbs or of their nakedness.[48] Symeon knew, however, that this bold statement was far removed from normal Byzantine judgments, and he asked especially that this hymn should not be made the basis of a charge of heresy. Although the flesh was made by God, it was considered to be of a second, lower level.

Thence, in theory, all activities that concentrated on the body, including hygiene, make-up, gluttony, and revelry, were disdained by Byzantine moralists. They could not be eradicated and were found in every stratum of society, but they stood in apparent contradiction to the Byzantine ideal of solemn behavior. The decline of bathing in Byzantium was a result both of this new attitude toward the body and of a reaction against the social role of public baths in Antiquity. Some of the public baths continued to function, but the ancient sanitary norms were probably not retained by most of the population. Nicholas Mysticus, at the beginning of the tenth century, defended an unassuming notion of hygiene, saying that it was shameful to have a dirty face, but he was not bothered by filth on other parts of the body, whether it was visible or not.[49] Symeon the Theologian exaggerated when he recommended washing the face, feet, and hands only with tears and never with water,[50] as did Prodromus when he derided a monk who had not bathed between two Easters.[51] Monastic *typika* of the eleventh and twelfth centuries varied between washing twice a month to three times a year, but the most usual frequency was once a month. Bathing ceased to be a normal element of everyday life and was regarded as a remedy for ailments. Doctors recommended that sick people wash twice a week. Balsamon's reference in the twelfth century to the rebuilding of the old baths into a Christian temple is symbolic in its own way. Kekaumenos testified that in the Bulgarian town of Servia at the beginning of the eleventh century there was only one bath, on a sheer rock, that functioned outside the city walls.[52] This fact did not seem to surprise him, even though Servia was a foreign town. Michael Choniates was struck by the shabby appearance of a bath in the country, which was heated by an open hearth in a hut of which the door could not be closed, so that the bathers suffered from smoke and heat and at the same time shivered in the chilly draft. The local bishop, according to Choniates, wore a hat while bathing lest he catch cold in the bath.[53]

The Byzantines nevertheless in fact kept adorning their attire and putting on make-up. They loved carousing and drank so much that Nicetas Choniates saw in drunkenness a national disaster. The all-powerful eunuch John Orphanotrophus in the eleventh century, who was the favorite of several emperors and was the effective ruler of the country, was renowned for his skill in drinking. However much wine he drank, he remained sober and alert, attentively watching his political rivals. A century later, John Ducas, an influential official and courtier, was considered to be a glutton capable of swimming across a river simply in order to have a feast of sweet beans. In Byzantine literature of the twelfth century, moreover, the earlier simple and ascetic attitude toward food was abandoned, and Eustathius of Thessalonica described with delight the dinners served after hard winter trips and the fat, white fowl that had been washed with red wine and stuffed with pastry balls.[54] Nicetas Choniates compared the delicious Byzantine cuisine with the food cooked by the crusaders in captured Constantinople, which seemed to him too fat, pungent, and crude, consisting mostly of big slices of meat with beans, garlic, and sour juices.[55] These are almost exactly the criticisms of Byzantine food made two and a half centuries earlier by Liutprand of Cremona, who was sent as an emissary to Constantinople by Otto I and complained repeatedly at the oil, garlic, and fish sauces he was served at the table of Nicephorus Phocas.[56]

The same contradiction existed in the Byzantine attitude toward sexuality. Marriage was an honorable social institution in an individualistic society, but virginity and celibacy were the highest ideals of behavior. Whereas Islamic polemicists against Christianity criticized these two points of Christian morals,[57] the hagiographers regularly praised sexual abstinence or temperance. Theophanes Confessor, saint and chronographer, told his young wife immediately after his wedding that they should preserve their chastity and renounce conjugal duties,[58] and Cyril Phileotes, an eleventh-century saint, proposed to his wife, after their first child was born, to restrict their sexual intercourse to several times a year.[59]

On the other hand, piety was interwoven with sexual imagery in the East as in the West, where the symbolism of the Song of Songs and that of Ovid were fully exploited in the twelfth century. The church in Byzantium was seen as the bride of Christ, and the Greek erotic romances were interpreted as pious books in which the longing of lovers appears as an allegory of the soul's yearning for salvation. The authors of several ancient erotic romances, such as Achilleus Tatios and Heliodoros, were proclaimed Christians, even bishops, and Heliodoros was said to have endorsed celibacy in his diocese.[60] The attitude of Symeon the Theologian toward God is described in one of his hymns by the term *eros*,[61] which normally signified love as a sexual passion. In another hymn Symeon dwells on this topic in even more detail, calling Christ a groom and the soul His bride with whom He unites and commingles in a real marriage, so that it receives His seed.[62] The borderline between celibacy and sexuality was vague and uncertain, a fact that helps account for the occasional appearance of a former harlot as the heroine in the *Life* of a saint.

In practice neither Christian morality nor canon or civil law presented insurmountable obstacles to adultery. Leo VI tried to keep decorum. After the death of Theophano, his pious wife who was proclaimed a saint by the Byzantine church, he married his old mistress Zoe, the daughter of his minister Zautzes. When she died soon after without issue, although a third marriage was prohibited by canon law Leo married a beautiful girl named Eudocia Baiane, who died in labor, as did her baby soon afterward. Since a fourth marriage would inevitably have created a scandal, Leo preferred to live with his new mistress Zoe Carbunopsina, without the blessing of the church, but after she gave birth to a boy, the future Emperor Constantine VII Porphyrogenitus, Leo's decision to legitimize his son and only heir led to a long dispute over the fourth marriage, which was settled only fourteen years later, after Leo's death.

Emperor Constantine IX Monomachus (1042–55), a jaunty character, was very fond of his elderly wife, whose death he mourned. His mistress Sklerena lived openly in the palace, however, and was even sponsored by the Empress Zoe. Adultery flourished at the court in the twelfth century. Since power was wielded by the Comnenian clan and the upper layer consisted of relatives, this adultery was often tinged by incest. Manuel I set an example by living with his niece Theodora, while his wife Bertha of Sulzbach was completely disregarded. Theodora later married the *sebastos* Nicephorus Chaluphas, but her son by Manuel was openly accepted as the emperor's child and given the highest title, *sebastokrator*, usually bestowed on the sons of an emperor. Manuel's cousin Andronicus was equally free in his liaisons and took as his mistress Theodora's sister, the widow Eudocia. The adultery caused a scandal, and Eudocia's relatives formed a plot to murder Andronicus. When they surrounded the lovers in Eudocia's tent, she tried to persuade Andronicus to escape in woman's dress, but he rejected the idea lest he appear ridiculous, took his sword, came out, and with incredible agility jumped over the fence and ran off. Subsequently Andronicus fell in love with Philippa, the sister of the Emperor Manuel's second wife, then with another niece of Manuel, also named Theodora, who was the queen of Jerusalem, and finally he forced Agnes, the young widow of Manuel's heir Alexius II, who was strangled at Andronicus's order, to live with him. The adulteries of Manuel and Andronicus were not simple conjugal infidelity. In contrast to legal conjugal relations based on considerations of politics, property, or genealogy, these love affairs were regularly imbued with passion and self-sacrifice. Though ephemeral, they were based on sentiment and not on calculation, and the sentiment is emphasized by the boldness with which the lovers broke all the ethical and religious rules.

Most of the available evidence of adultery concerns the upper level of Byzantine society. There are a few sources, however, concerning ordinary familial life and the position of woman within the family. A good starting point is the description of a woman's life in the tenth-century *Life* of Mary the Junior, for although Byzantine hagiography normally tended to minimize the difference between male and female saints (see Chapter 5), this *Life* is a register of the everyday life of a middle-class woman who never pretended to be a holy person.[63]

Mary was the fifth and youngest child of an Armenian family living on Byzantine soil. We know nothing about her upbringing, but like Psellos's mother, she was probably taught weaving and the elements of reading.[64] Education for girls was not very popular with the Byzantines. George Tornikes in his panegyric of the princess Anna Comnena, the daughter of Alexius I, remarked that her imperial parents did not make much of her education, regarding "supreme knowledge" with the same suspicion as children-loving mothers, who feared that matchmakers would inspire girls with amorous passion. Anna had no choice but to study her "beloved grammar" unbeknownst to her mother, in the same way that a girl (Tornikes continues to evolve the same line of erotic similes) stealthily, through cracks, looks at her future bridegroom.[65]

Consequently the position of women in both cultural and political life was restricted. The high rank and esteem that seems to have
been accorded to women in Anatolia during Antiquity, and even under the Romans,[66] disappeared with the advent of Christianity. Although the New Testament proclaimed that "there is neither male nor
female" (Galatians 3.28), masculine domination was particularly evident in church services. Only a few women participated in liturgical
activity as deaconesses, most of them chosen among widows, who
assisted at the baptism of women, as long as it was performed by im-
mersion. There were about twenty deaconesses in the church of Saint
Sophia in the sixth century, but later both their number and importance diminished, first in the West, then in Byzantium, where they
were still known to Balsamon in the twelfth century and where they
fulfilled the function of overseeing the discipline of women in the
church.[67] After the death of Hypatia, who was murdered by fanatical
monks in 415, little is heard of scholarly or literary activity on the part
of women. The poetess Kassia at the end of the eighth century and
the historian Anna Comnena are outstanding among them. More
women, however, were patrons of art and literature, and several
scholarly treatises were dedicated to them. Many empresses were
fond of power and tried both to wield political influence and to receive the external signs of imperial cult, and some noble ladies followed suit.

St. Mary the Junior continued to live with her mother after her
father's death. Many widows are found living with their children,
both male and female, in Byzantine sources of the fourteenth century,
and they obviously ran the household, for although the Byzantine
family was patriarchal, a widow could be the head of a household.[69]
As in all traditional societies, widows were usually more numerous
than widowers, mostly owing to the customary difference in age between spouses. Mary was probably about fifteen when she was married to a friend of her older brother.[70] Her husband, Nicephorus by
name, occupied the military post of *drungarius*.

She is presented by the hagiographer as an ideal of gentleness, temperance, piety, and mercy. Nobody had seen her angry, and she never whipped or scolded her servants. She was modest both in dress and in food and was generous to the church and the poor. Of course, not all the Byzantine women lived up to such a high moral standard. The vernacular verses of Prodromus conjure up the image of an ambitious housewife whose wretched husband was completely under her thumb and who deprived him of his dinner, until at last the poor devil, suffering from hunger, dressed as a beggar and thus was given a meal at his own house.[71]

Mary was unfortunate with her first offspring, since her son Orestes died at five, and her second son Bardanes also died prematurely. Soon after his death Mary had twins named Baanes and Stephen. This family history agrees with the figures for the mortality rate of children given by Laiou-Thomadakis, who calculated that half the babies died by the age of five.[72] Mary bore the death of her sons with fortitude. While others wept and wailed, she avoided any improper [ἄσεμνον] actions, such as tearing her hair or clothing, pouring dust on her head, or swearing. This fortitude, *semnotes*, or solemnity of behavior does not indicate that Byzantines lacked affection for their offspring. Psellos, who dedicated a passionate epitaph to his daughter Styliane, appreciated affection toward children in other people. When he sent some fruit to John Ducas, he wrote: "If you do not want to eat them, give them as toys to your two babies [grandchildren]. They will play with apples and pears, and you look at them and smile."[73]

Mary's husband Nicephorus distinguished himself in the war against the Bulgarians during the reign of Leo VI, and he was appointed for his military deeds a *turmarches* and sent to the town of Bizyae in Thrace. As a professional soldier, he was crude and ruthless. When his brother Alexius and sister Helen accused Mary of infidelity with a slave named Demetrius, he shut her up in an isolated room under the surveillance of a servant, whom he urged to calumniate Mary. When she refused, Nicephorus threw her on the floor and ordered her to be whipped. When Lent came, Nicephorus did not keep the fast but ordered the table to be set where the relatives of the host could also attend. Nicephorus's wrath rose as he ate and drank. He left the table and went to his wife's room, which was dimly lit by the light before the icon of the Virgin. Mary lay in bed with a baby in her arms. Nicephorus at once attacked her, dragged her by the hair, and started to beat her. Mary tried to escape and hide somewhere in the house, but she fell and injured her head. Suffering from grief and weakness, as well as from the blows, she died a few days later. On her deathbed she ordered her *chlamys*, or outer garment, to be sold in order to pay her creditors, whom she listed by name. These examples drawn from the *Life* of St. Mary the Junior show that Byzantine life and personal behavior were matched to the individualistic traits of Byzantine society and differed greatly from the ideal of behavior in Antiquity.

It was masked by an internal contradiction, however, between ideal behavior and actual practice. This contradiction may in part have been a result of the gradual development of social behavior and of the emergence by the eleventh and twelfth centuries of some elements of pre-Renaissance attitudes. But it was also owing to the typical ambivalence of Byzantine social relationships, which will be the subject of a subsequent chapter.

CHAPTER FOUR

Homo byzantinus before God

A LTHOUGH the two preceding chapters began with statements that scholars have until recently neglected various important aspects of Byzantine life, the opposite is true of Byzantine religious life. The importance of theology and religious controversy in Byzantine history has long been recognized, and it is commonly accepted that the church dominated political, social, and cultural life in Byzantium. Countless studies of this subject have been written, but most of them are to a certain extent biased by the fact that theology is divorced from human concerns. A good place to begin is with the historiography of the problem, not in order to pile up a myriad of names but so as to trace three main scholarly approaches to the subject.

The first approach to Byzantine religious history was made during the Enlightenment, and its principal purpose was to unmask Christianity. Those who took this approach considered the religious controversies to be pure nonsense, an expression of Byzantine stupidity and folly. They dismissed the Trinitarian disputes of the fourth century as squabbling over a mere iota, without making any effort to show why so many people were involved. To a lofty enlightened mind, mankind seemed foolish and its deeds seemed to lack any underlying reason. Voltaire's contemporaries watched, without surprise and even with satisfaction, the foolish Byzantines who spent their lives in senseless arguments.

The second approach was more serious. Its adherents tried to unveil the political interests hidden behind the religious controversies. For these scholars, the Trinitarian disputes were an expression not of eternal human stupidity but of the political claims of different groups and regions. They discovered under the theological surface a clash between the sees of Rome, Constantinople, and Alexandria, or the centrifugal aspirations of the oriental provinces, or the rivalry of the circus factions. This political approach to theological controversy raises the general question of the relation between the religious content of the dispute and the underlying political aims, because it differs from the first approach in associating human aspirations with theological conflict, but resembles it in arguing that the conflict did not in itself reflect human aspirations. Scholars thus continued to repeat that in the mid-fifth century the sees of Constantinople and Rome made common cause against Alexandria, but the Trinitarian disputes remained for them a struggle over a mere iota. In other words, the iota of controversy was not in itself assumed to be related in any way to human aspirations. It had no internal logic and was understood only as a token or hieroglyph of political struggles. '

According to the third approach, Byzantine theology was an autonomous system with its own inner laws of development that were seen as belonging to the sphere of pure thought and unconnected with any political or social aspirations. From this point of view, the Trinitarian controversy, far from being foolish, was a conflict of philosophical and religious ideas and a continuation and development of Greek philosophical thought. Its starting point, as Harry Austryn Wolfson defined it, was the rejection of the concept of the absolute unity of God that runs through everything said by the church fathers in support of the Trinity. But since the fathers were consciously opposed to antique polytheism, according to Wolfson, they constantly tried to explain that belief in the Trinity does not imply disbelief in the unity of God.[1] Being thus restricted to a philosophical dispute, and regarded in some cases even as outside the framework of the history of philosophy, the Trinitarian controversy appeared isolated both from political struggles and generally from the needs of the age and the society that had created it.[2]

It must be borne in mind that the Trinitarian controversy was a mass movement. Religious disputes were carried into the streets. For the men and women of the fourth and fifth centuries the conflict was of vital concern, as it could never have been had the points at issue been purely academic, designed either to reconcile biblical and Neoplatonic traditions or to refute Neoplatonic traditions in the name of the Bible.

According to each of these three characterizations of Byzantine religious controversy—human stupidity, a hieroglyph of political aspirations, a link in the independent development of religious and philosophical thought—Byzantine theology is considered to be without a social context and outside the framework of time. This is not to say that there is no reasonable basis for each of the three approaches, since the actions and opinions of the mob were often stupid, the ecumenical councils were constantly arenas of political claims and clashes, and the church fathers and their opponents used the teaching and language of Aristotle or Plato in their polemics. But all this, though true, was not the heart of the controversy, nor the most important aspect to be considered today, when it must be asked why *homo byzantinus* was so ardently involved in discussions that seem alien to mankind in this rationalistic age. What were people looking for in these theological disputes and how did they try to understand themselves and their world in theological terms and ideas?

In the final stage of Antiquity, Christianity created a language, a system of images and formulas, that later became the common language of both western and eastern Europe in the Middle Ages. The human world view could be defined only in Christian terms, and the most important social, political, moral, and aesthetic problems were posed and solved in Christian terms—that is, within the framework of the Christian ideological system. At the outset, therefore, it is necessary to define the essence of the new religion as it was established after its first troubled centuries at the threshold of Byzantine history, and to ask again, in a new form, the old question why Christianity won in the competition with other ideological currents of the time. Various answers have been given. Henri Grégoire gave two: first, that the empire needed a soul or core of religion, which Christianity provided; and second, that Christianity brought with it an organization in which the empire found a unifying factor.[3] Hubert Jedin stressed the first of these two elements, emphasizing not only the high moral level and ethical values of the Christians in contrast to the moral emptiness of pagan beliefs but also the attractiveness of the image of Jesus Christ.[4] Robert Browning, on the other hand, stressed the second factor, suggesting that the lack of a coherent doctrine had been one of the weaknesses of the traditional Greco-Roman religion.[5]

These two answers both sound convincing, but they do not stand up under thoroughgoing examination. Their weakness is that they aim at an abstraction rather than a historical explanation. For Grégoire, and especially for Jedin (as for many of their adherents), Christianity won because its organization, ethics, and imaginative system were better than those of paganism. Such an answer is in effect no answer, however—or is, rather, a circular answer: Christianity won because it was better and must have been better because it won. It won and was better, however, because it responded to the aspirations of man and of society. Many religions of the past had had strong organization and unifying effects. A cult of either Jupiter or the emperor might in theory have served as a unifying factor, but neither could in fact have done so at this particular time or in these particular social conditions. The same is true of the first element. The old religions had been for many centuries the souls of their societies and peoples. They had created high moral principles and lofty images that suited their societies and members but no longer satisfied the needs and desires of people in the new social, political, and cultural situations of late Antiquity. Although Christianity was not simply "a soul" or "a unifying factor," it acted as the soul and the unifying factor of this particular age. It met the challenge of these crucial times, when old social relationships were destroyed, traditional piety perished, and confidence in old ideas and institutions and in the power of man to control his own destiny, or even to understand the world in which he lived, had waned. Christianity served to transplant the ethical ideal beyond the boundaries of the earthly world, and the main aim of man became the search for salvation, expressed as an ascent to God.[6]

Jedin emphasized the significance of the image of Christ, his uniqueness, and both the tension and the undeniable freshness of the belief that He created. This image suited the human aspirations of this age perfectly. In order to understand the uniqueness of Christ, it is necessary to realize the differing concepts of the relation between God and man in earlier religions and in Christianity. Earlier Mediterranean religions had proposed two principal solutions to the problem of the relations between God and man. In Greek religious thought the gods were understood as the elder brothers of men. The differences among them were quantitative rather than qualitative. The gods were stronger, swifter, and wiser than men. They were immortal but not eternal. Even Zeus's age was counted. Since there was no clear boundary between gods and men, "mixed marriages" were normal, and the demigods born of these unions, the heroes, were the physical expression of the closeness of god and man.

The oriental notion of the relation between God and man was radically different. God was seen as the divine Almighty and man as a being who cringed before the godhead. No bridge across the gulf between man and god was possible. To some extent, the gap was filled by the strange beings who were later called angels and who acted as mediators, but since they were neither human nor divine, they could not tangibly connect the opposing parts of the cosmos. Other forms of mediation led to the title of Son of God, who was seen as an adopted son rather than as a real son and as the man beloved by god, like the biblical King David.

In other words, pre-Christian religious thought proceeded from two separate standpoints: either from that of an unbridgeable gulf between God and man—or between heaven and earth—or from that of their carnal and consubstantial proximity. Theologically, these two positions are referred to respectively as the transcendence and the immanence of God. For many people in late Antiquity the first of these was too pessimistic and the second too earthbound. Neither satisfied the search for salvation that characterized the critical times of the late Roman empire, when ancient social bonds loosened, then dissolved, and when men and women were increasingly thrown back on their own devices in religion as well as in society.

Accordingly, two different approaches to the problem of the relationship between heaven and earth were worked out in late Antiquity. The Gnostic solution—and later the Manichaean solution—was a consistent development of the idea of an unbridgeable gap. According to Gnostic thought, the deity is absolutely transcendent and alien to the universe. He neither created nor governs it, and it is understood as a vast prison, ruled by the lower powers, the archons. Both the body and the soul of man were shaped by the archons and are a part of this world, but within the soul is enclosed the spirit, the pneuma, a portion of the divine substance. The task of the spirit is to awaken the knowledge, the gnosis, of the transcendent God and of man himself in order to enable the soul after death to journey upward, dropping away, stage after stage, all the physical vestments, so that the spirit stripped of alien accretions reaches God to be reunited with the divine substance from which it originated.[7] While these Gnostic ideas stressed the individual way of salvation, the Manichaean world view, also dualistic, emphasized the cosmic nature of the drama, presenting history as a perpetual strife between good and evil. In the beginning, two distinct realms of light and dark existed side by side. The demons of darkness then launched an attack against the realm of light, and during the war part of the light was mixed with darkness, so that the spirit was imprisoned in matter. The war must continue until all the particles of light have returned to the realm of good and the cosmos is again separated into two independent spheres.[8]

Another solution, proposed by later Neoplatonists, was monistic rather than dualist in its core. According to Plotinus, the greatest Platonist of the third century, the original and prime transcendent being was the One or Good, and all reality proceeds from this in a succession of dialectical transformations. Intellect, the second hypostasis, proceeds from the One, and soul from intellect, in the same way that light is diffused from the sun or heat from fire. The life of intellect is that of eternity. Soul passes to a life in time and a life of flux and desire for movement. During this time of the soul, the material universe comes into being. Below the higher soul lies the world of pure forms, which is nature, or the image of soul. At the same time, this world produces the shadowy things of reality, which constitute the lowest level of the cosmos. But even the lowest level of bodies—and here the contrast to the dualistic world view becomes evident—is operated by nature and endowed with a soul so that individual souls come down and occupy bodies that are prepared for them.[9] This hierarchical structure of the cosmos opened the way for the carnal world of things and for man to ascend first into the sphere of souls and then, step by step, into the intelligible world. In the Neoplatonic conception there was no place for painful feelings of disjunction between good and evil, no tension created by the pneuma striving to reach its source. Good and evil were not understood as existing as cosmic entities in eternal conflict, but as distant links in a single chain. Matter is not a substantial evil but a lack of goodness, a passive receptacle of forms, a dark void.[10] Souls that are in constant contact with bodies rise from their own level up to union with the One.

Christianity began as a small Palestinian sect and was transformed by the fourth century into a strong political and social organization and a mighty ideological power. It did not accept either the Gnostic-Manichaean solution or the Neoplatonic solution but elaborated a distinctly new concept, which responded perfectly to the common search for salvation. In forming this ideology Christians drew on various sources, including Gnosticism and Neoplatonism, and used old formulas, presenting their new religion, as it were, in old clothing. There are obvious similarities between Gnostics and Christians on the one hand and between Plotinus and the contemporary Christian theologian Origen on the other. But the fact that the Christian fathers took over earlier interpretations does not mean that Christianity was merely a derivative ideology or a combination of oriental and Greco-Roman traditions. On the contrary, its intermediary place between the two main ideological currents of the age—between Gnostic-Manichaean dualism and Neoplatonic monism—created the uniqueness of Christianity and the originality of its response to the social and ideological problems of the diverse population of the late Roman empire.

Toward the beginning of the fourth century Christianity developed into a religion of what has been called resolved dualism, meaning that it preserved the gulf between earth and heaven, or man and God, and to that extent followed the oriental religious system and the Gnostics, but introduced the idea that this gap could be bridged.

Therefore, although Christianity did not abolish the boundary between man and God that typified the oriental concept of the godhead and although it never admitted a pagan consubstantiality of human and divine beings, it nevertheless both permitted man's ascent to heaven and placed this idea at the center of a whole theological system.

While the dualists dealt with the tragic effort of the particle of spiritual pneuma imprisoned in the material world and the Neoplatonists saw the soul as ascending to the One and Good by a series of dialectical metamorphoses based on calm contemplation, Christianity appropriated the Gnostic tension of unsatisfied volition and at the same time opened the way to God not in an eschatological would-be utopia but in the here and now. The Christian ascent to heaven was realized not by dialectical contemplation, as it was conceived by the Neoplatonists, but by a supernatural mystery, which abnegated and destroyed the humble physics of the lower world. God was not considered as dwelling outside the boundaries of the universe. He not only created the present universe—in contrast to the supreme godhead of dualistic thought, who left this job to a *demiourgos*—but also descended to Earth. Every step in this relationship of God to His universe was treated as a mystery.

If we now return to Trinitarian and Christological controversy, we can understand that it was not a dispute about a mere iota or a purely political conflict between the greatest sees, nor was it a contest of various philosophical tendencies. It had a broader human and social background, centered on the problem of man's ascent to God. Human thought looked for a structure of the Godhead that, while preserving the principal differences between God and man, still allowed man to ascend to God. Human thought, moreover, looked for vehicles or intermediaries to make possible this ascent, which had to be derived from the structure of the Godhead. "The Fathers," as John Meyendorff emphasized, "were actually preoccupied, not with speculation, but with man's salvation," and the implications of this wording are highly significant.[11]

The triune concept of the Godhead corresponded to the human search for salvation. According to the orthodox formulation, God consists of one essence in three hypostases. The term *homoousios* [consubstantial] signifies that God is a unity in His substance and therefore possesses a largely different substance from that of the created world and of man. But the Christian God is nonetheless not absolutely removed from the universe, because He revealed Himself as Father, Son, and Holy Spirit, and this numerical distinction, though within the framework of the consubstantiality of hypostases, creates divine openness to the cosmos.

The contradiction in the idea that a real distinction exists in the Trinity between the common essence and the Persons, or hypostases, could be solved only as a mystery, but mystery, as noted earlier, was a cardinal trait of Christian thought.[12] Formal logic could easily show the lack of consistency in the Trinitarian construction, but any attempt to deny the mysterious structure of the Triune God led to the abolition of divine openness to the world and therefore annihilated the hope of salvation.

It is not therefore fortuitous that the theological polemics of the fourth century centered on the Trinitarian problem. The orthodox formulation was elaborated as a middle way between two positions that were polar opposites: the Sabellian monarchism of the Godhead on one hand, which brought Christian theology back to the oriental concept of god as absolutely distinct from created man, and the Arian subordination on the other, which stressed the difference between the Father and Son so greatly that man appeared to be in touch not with the Godhead Itself but only with a lesser deity, the adopted Son of God.

The Christological disputes of the fifth and subsequent centuries reveal even more clearly the social background of the theological controversies. The Trinitarian structure of the Godhead created the openness of God to the universe and consequently the possibility of man's ascent to God. This possibility was realized in the incarnation of the Logos, the Second Person of the Trinity, who assumed the human shape of Christ. According to orthodox teaching, Jesus Christ united in Himself the perfection of both the human and the divine natures. In Him God and man became one hypostasis, and an unbreakable bond between God and man was made manifest. The hypostatic union of God and man in Christ was a mystery, like the Trinity, which could not be explained by formal logic. It was considered a unique and cosmic event, the central moment in human history.

The concept of the perfect God-man hypostasis was established, like the doctrine of the Trinity, during a long and acute struggle and formulated as a middle way between two different approaches, both of which denied the mysterious dual nature of Christ. For while the teaching of Nestorius emphasized the full and autonomous humanity of the historical Jesus,[13] and denied the title Mother of God [*Theotokos*] to the Virgin Mary, because she was the mother only of a human being, the Monophysites stressed the predominance of the divine principle in Christ. Especially for the Syriac Monophysites, Christ's unique hypostasis was the pre-existing hypostasis of the Logos [God-Son], which was assumed to have taken the place of the human soul in Christ, and so it was God Himself who was crucified in the flesh, a view that is called *theopaschism*. Various conclusions were drawn from this fundamental concept. Severus of Antioch stressed the notion of the basic goodness of physical creation and regarded the humanity of Christ as an iconic representation of the divinity; Philoxenus of Mabbug, on the contrary, rejected the idea of the natural humanity of Christ and natural participation of mankind in God and emphasized the complete dependence of man on God for good crops, health, and shelter.[14] But in both cases the Monophysite teachers rejected the orthodox concept of the contradictory unity of opposites of heaven and earth.

Despite the sharp theological dissent between the Monophysites and the Nestorians, their criticism was directed at the same end, since they both dissolved the connection between heaven and earth that was personified in the mystery of the Incarnation of Christ. The union of perfect and complete man with complete and perfect God in the unique hypostasis of Jesus Christ was a pledge that assured the ascent of man to the Godhead. By denying this union, the Nestorians and the Monophysites both returned to the pre-Christian idea of the unbridgeable gulf between heaven and earth and between God and man, and therefore created an unsurmountable obstacle on man's way toward heaven and salvation.

Beneath the Trinitarian and Christological controversies lay the issue of salvation and the search for a concept of the Godhead and of the relations between God and man that could, even as a mystery, secure man's ascent to heaven. This central problem was complicated by various political and ideological issues, of which some have been fully studied, such as the political rivalry between the most important sees and the conflict of philosophical currents and their dependence on ancient sources, and of which others remain unclear, including the possible connection between the Christological disputes and the strife of the circus factions.[15] Yet other questions in the great religious conflict of the fourth and fifth centuries remain to be studied by scholars.[16]

The fact that Monophysitism spread in the eastern provinces of the late Roman empire is often attributed to the alleged desire of the people in these regions for political independence. This explanation is doubtful, or at least one-sided, since the trend towards political independence was in fact even stronger in the West, where Monophysitism hardly existed and the Roman popes established their independence while defending orthodox theology. It must also be borne in mind that the Monophysites were among the most ardent missionaries of Christianity beyond the eastern boundaries of the empire,[17] and that this was an area where monotheism had strong roots, as is shown by the later rise of Islam. But the sympathy for Monophysites may also have been based on local religious traditions, since the idea that God Himself suffered on the cross was quite acceptable in an area where the worship of gods who die and rise again had been accepted for many thousands of years. The forerunners of the Monophysites in Syria and Egypt had worshiped Osiris or Adonis, and their descendants had no difficulty in believing that the true God had suffered, died, and risen again. While the idea of a suffering and dying God might seem strange and illogical to the sophisticated mind of an urban philosopher of the fourth century, who was acquainted with the Platonic traditions of a supreme being, it sounded natural to the inhabitants of villages, where local cults had survived, and perhaps even grown, after the internal collapse of the official Roman religion.

Another question that needs to be studied is the social distribution of the supporters of the various religious movements of the fourth and fifth centuries. While it is true that there is no clear-cut evidence concerning the social programs of the Arians or Monophysites and that their elevated theological views had no direct social implications, an answer can be sought in the prosopography of the adherents of the religious movements. It is known from Philostorgius, for example, that Arius addressed his *Thaleia* primarily to sailors and other craftsmen and that among his most famous followers were intellectuals, such as Eusebius of Caesarea, Aetios, and Eunomios.[18] Arius was endorsed by the bishops of the Pentapolis, Syria, and Palestine, regions where urban life was particularly well developed. This suggests that Arianism spread especially among city populations.[19] The forerunners of Monophysitism, on the other hand, such as Cyril of Alexandria, and the Monophysites themselves, such as the monk Isaias, found support among the desert monks, whose lives were based on a rejection of ancient urban civilization. Further biographical data must be gathered and summarized before any definite conclusions can be drawn, but it is possible that the Arian and Nestorian opposition to Monophysitism represented, to some extent, a confrontation between the city, with its remnants of ancient formal logic, and the countryside, which was traditionally bound up with the worship of agrarian cults. This suggestion raises new difficulties, however, such as the need to explain how Arianism, born in an oriental urban atmosphere, became a barbarian religion among the Germanic tribes on the northern frontier of the empire.

The Trinitarian and Christological controversies were at their height during the fourth and fifth centuries and continued into the seventh century. A new period of religious strife began in the eighth century, centered on the issue of the use of images. The historiography of this movement shows many of the same patterns as that of the Trinitarian and Christological disputes. Iconoclasm has been interpreted on the one hand as a purely political and economic movement, of which the rejection of icon worship was an outer sign or hieroglyph, and on the other hand as a purely philosophical and theological doctrine that repeated rather than developed the ideas of the ancient philosophers and early church fathers. About a hundred years ago Constantine Paparrhegopoulos expounded the view, which has recently been supported by Elena Lipšic, that Iconoclasm was a kind of enlightened ideology struggling against superstitions.[20] Konstantin Uspenskij treated it above all as an imperial attack upon the great estates and the growth of monastic property.[21] And Michael Sjuzjumov saw in Iconoclasm an attempt on the part of the landed aristocracy to seize the movable wealth of the monasteries and the precious metals and stones used to embellish icons.[22] None of these views, though different and even contradictory, takes seriously the religious content of the controversy.

Another group of scholars emphasizes the theological and aesthetic aspects of the controversy and in so doing tends to divorce the views of the opponents and supporters of icon worship from the actual problems of the time. For them the conflict would turn out to represent either an oriental influence or the continuation of Greco-Roman controversies. The hostile attitude of Leo III (717–41) toward image worship was attributed already by some of his contemporaries to both Muslim and Jewish influence, and many authorities have accepted this point of view. Milton Anastos put forward the counter-argument that an emperor who was engaged in a deadly struggle with the Arabs would not have adopted a typically Muslim attitude toward images;[23] it is questionable whether his argument is valid, since there are many historical examples of the influence of the ideology of an enemy on one people or another. Oleg Grabar went a step further: he examined the differences rather than the apparent similarities between Muslim and Byzantine Iconoclasm. He stressed the "striking practicality" of Muslim art, which not only disapproved of expensive possessions but also denied the possibility or value of trying to escape time by freezing a moment or idea in a work of art.[24] On the other hand, Leslie Barnard proclaimed recently that whereas the Iconodule position resembled that of the pagan defenders of statues and anti-Jewish apologists, and therefore showed "no sharp break with the Greco-Roman past," the Iconoclastic position "involved a clean break with the past and so had no hope of final success." Stephen Gero, on the contrary, emphasized the traditionalism of Iconoclastic ideology, arguing that the Iconoclasts in their doctrine of the eucharist depended on certain elements in patristic tradition.[25] It is true that the question of image worship was not new at the time that Leo III initiated Iconoclasm. The worship of images was opposed by various Christian writers from the fourth century onwards. Epiphanius of Salamis, in the fourth century, wrote a treatise against idolatry, and a number of churches with nonfigural decoration, which may have been inspired by hostility to images, date from this period. For Epiphanius and his contemporaries, however, the question of image worship was secondary, while in Leo III's day it became the center of the ideological struggles.

The time has come to assemble, as cautiously as possible, what is known for certain about the Iconoclastic controversy. As a social movement Iconoclasm was primarily an antimonastic reaction. It was not an attack against monastic property, since—as Sjuzjumov has pointed out—there are no traces of any considerable monastic property of this period. The monasteries at this time were still communities of people hard at work earning their daily living (see chapter 6). But Sjuzjumov's own theory that the confiscation of precious metals and stones formed the core of Iconoclasm does not seem convincing. When Byzantine emperors such as Heraclius (610–41) or Alexius I Comnenus (1081–1118) stood in need of gold and silver they would seize or "borrow" ecclesiastical treasures without embarking upon a reform of ritual. The assault on monks waged by the Iconoclast emperors was not an attack on monastic wealth but on the monastery as an institution, as a sort of community survived from late Antiquity.

By describing the persecutions of monks during the reign of Constantine V (741–75), Theophanes especially stresses that Michael Lachanodrakon, one of the most enthusiastic supporters of Iconoclasm, gathered a crowd of monks in a valley near Ephesus and forced them to put on white garments and at once take wives (Theoph, 445.3–9). The Iconoclast authorities were not satisfied merely to dismiss monks and convert monasteries into public buildings. They saw in marriage and the family unit, which were to become the cornerstones of Byzantine individualistic society, the negation of monastic communities.

It was just at this time that the ancient family changed its form: familial ties were greatly strengthened and possibilities of divorce restricted (see chapter 1). By this time, moreover, as André Guillou has demonstrated, the nuclear family had become the most substantial element of economic life, and according to John Haldon the burden of military service was attached to families.[26] The support of the Icono-clasts for the family, as opposed to monasticism, was not merely sym-bolic, since it was a sign of a conflict between two different forms of social organization.

Was this social contradiction somehow reflected in the Iconoclas-tic controversy itself? For Epiphanius's contemporaries the question of image worship was secondary, since they were principally con-cerned with the problem of salvation, which had to be worked out at the level of Trinitarian and Christological ideas. Iconoclasm as a large-scale movement emerged only after the end of the Christological dis-putes, when the search for salvation shifted to another level. The hope of salvation had been attached to the unique historical moment of the Incarnation of the Logos, and it was Christ who had made real the mysterious link between the human and divine principles and be-tween heaven and earth. Once the Christological problem seemed to have been solved, the problem of man's ascent to heaven moved from the level of cosmic event to that of individual experience within ritual activity, above all within the liturgy, which was understood as a means to reach the supernatural and to ascend for a moment from earth to heaven. The general trend of the time had changed from the idea of the salvation of mankind by Christ's death and resurrection to that of individual salvation through ritual.

Some profound changes in the Byzantine liturgy took place at the beginning of the eighth century. On the one hand, public processions were reduced, and the clergy developed rites that were performed be-hind closed doors. The prothesis was no longer a room where the faithful left their offerings, and the homily ceased to be a kind of pub-lic speech.[27] On the other hand, the mystagogical symbolism of the liturgy typical of Pseudo-Dionysius and Maximos the Confessor was replaced by a new kind of symbolism. Whereas the earlier fathers un-derstood the liturgy, as a whole, as a presentation of divine activity or of the saving acts of Christ's life, the Patriarch Germanus (715–30) at-tempted to show it as a reflection of the drama related in the individ-ual details of the actual ritual. These two developments—the reduc-tion in the public significance of the liturgy and the new view of the liturgy as illustrative symbolism rather than a universal cosmic drama—were part of the cultural atmosphere of the time that Leo III attempted to inaugurate Iconoclasm. In other words, the central question was how far society could move toward the individualisation of cult.

The Iconoclasts denied the possibility of depicting in an image the inconceivable and mysterious person of Christ, especially His divine nature, declaring that to depict His human nature only was to accept the Nestorian heresy. This kind of argument did not apply to the icons of the saints, yet the images of the saints were also prohibited by the followers of Leo III. The worship of images preserved more of the elements of public ritual, because the icon was supposed to address itself to the congregation as a group and not to any individual. The Iconodule leader Theodore of Stoudios even considered those who accepted images only as a means of explanation and recollection to be the enemies of icons, since they denied their significance as objects of worship.[28] Finally, the Iconoclastic opposition emphasized the role of man himself in the act of salvation. For them the true image of Christ was the saint—that is, the man endowed with Christian virtues, not paintings or sculptures or even the eucharist.[29]

Iconoclasm thus emerges not so much as a stage in the development of Greco-Roman thought or as an imitation of Muslim reforms but as an ideology that was associated with the social and political tendencies of its time. It reflected rather than covered or alluded to the social, political, or regional tensions of Byzantium in the eighth century. The search for an individual way of salvation that formed such a substantial part of the Iconoclastic concept was bequeathed by the defeated Iconoclasts to their victorious descendants and manifested itself even more clearly in the development of mysticism, which was of central importance in Byzantine spirituality.

The nature of mysticism was complicated. Even monastic asceticism has sometimes been identified with a kind of mysticism, though it was limited in reality by the *praxis* of behavior, in which the most substantial element was the principle of submission. For Evagrius of Pontus, in the second half of the fourth century, this *praxis* formed only the first stage in the ascent of man to God, of which the doors to the next two stages—the "natural *theoria,*" or religious contemplation of the cosmos and *theologia,* or contemplation of the divine Monas, who is at the same time the Trinity—would open only when man, following this way toward heaven, reached impassability and love. The Evagrian point of view was accepted and developed in the seventh century by followers such as John Climacus and Maximos the Confessor.

Another school of Christian mysticism was founded by the unknown author, usually known as Pseudo-Dionysius, who probably lived in Syria in the late fifth and early sixth centuries but was believed to have been Dionysius the disciple of Paul named in the New Testament. Scholars have argued over whether his sources were Christian or Neoplatonic, or even a reconciliation of the two, since the Pseudo-Dionysian treatises have been called the final rapprochement, after centuries of bitter conflict, between Neoplatonism and Christianity. Although Pseudo-Dionysius sometimes took passages word for word from the fifth-century Neoplatonic philosopher Proclus, a rapprochement with Neoplatonic doctrines is found in only a few isolated passages and concepts, such as his emphasis on the significance of the celestial hierarchy. His God remained above the celestial hierarchy, however. The universe was arranged hierarchically, but it was created and illuminated by God. Inasmuch as the Pseudo-Dionysian system of thought was dominated by the principle of antinomy, it is in contrast to the Neoplatonic attempt to see the universe as a consistent entity.[30]

The central idea distinguishing the teaching of Pseudo-Dionysius from the mysticism of Evagrius and his school was the doctrine of the hierarchical structure of the cosmos, which was reflected on earth in the ecclesiastical order. This element in the thought of Pseudo-Dionysius is acknowledged by all scholars. It is uncertain, however, whether any social content underlay the Pseudo-Dionysian idea of hierarchy. If so, what was it? Did his treatises mirror the prevalence of episcopal organization over the monastic system, as Hermann Goltz suggested,[31] or did they set forth in theological language the bureaucratic hierarchy of his age or the emerging hierarchy of personal dependencies in society?

In order to understand the social significance of Pseudo-Dionysius, it is necessary to recall that although he exercised a profound influence on medieval philosophy in the West, from Eriugena to Ficino, where his works were used in many important disputes, including that concerning the two swords, his influence in Byzantium seems to have been limited. Even Maximos the Confessor, who may have written a commentary on Pseudo-Dionysius, followed the Evagrian doctrine. It is also surprising that Symeon the Theologian, the greatest mystic of the middle Byzantine period, did not use the treatises of Pseudo-Dionysius. Hans-Georg Beck remarks tellingly that Pseudo-Dionysius came too late and that his effect on Byzantine mysticism was slight because the character of mystical enthusiasm was lacking in his hierarchy.[32] It may be, indeed, that the Pseudo-

Dionysian concept of hierarchy and arrangement of earthly and celestial powers in subordinate ranks remained alien to the Byzantines.

The ethical and theological doctrine of Symeon, on the other hand, was precisely suited to Byzantine social realities.[33] He emphasized an individual rather than ecclesiastical way of salvation and direct communication of man with God rather than a rapprochement through intermediary agents. Consequently he emphasized, as we have seen, individualism in social behavior. He denied not only the relation of friendship, as did Kekaumenos, but also the ties of family. The individualistic content of Symeon's ethics and soteriology matched the individualistic structure of Byzantine monastic life. Yet Symeon's individualism, typical in Byzantium, was an individualism without freedom, since it presupposed the submission of man to the authorities of God, his teacher, and the emperor. Symeon constantly repeated and illustrated the principle that there was no power on earth but the emperor, who was the source of all offices and who alone possessed the right to nominate judges.[34] In Symeon's works there is no place for celestial, ecclesiastical, or temporal hierarchies. The hero of Symeon's sermons and hymns stood naked, as in Byzantine reality, deprived of social links and directly subjugated to almighty authorities.

The individualistic features of monastic organization became more prominent in the later Middle Ages, when the so-called idiorhythmic type of monastic community developed. The monks in these communities formed small quasi-familial groups holding their property in common. Even private ownership was allowed.[35] The idiorhythmic system was endorsed by the Hesychasts who, following Symeon the Theologian, developed physical techniques of prayer intended to induce inner tranquility and holy silence as a way of personal ascent toward God. This direct, mystical communication with God was in apparent contradiction to orthodox worship, which was associated primarily with the sacraments of the Church and the veneration of icons—that is, with the remnants of public ritual. The Hesychast was pictured by contemporaries as sitting with his eyes fixed on his navel, which was regarded as the seat of his heart, and as reaching toward a vision of God through silent concentration on his own soul and body.

The theory of Hesychasm was elaborated in the fourteenth century by Gregory Palamas, a scholar of great learning and the author of several works on rhetoric and astronomy. His principal task was to explain the possibility of the deification of man—that is, the mystical

ascent of the individual to God. Palamas emphasized, in accordance
with ecclesiastical tradition, that God is in essence totally inaccessible.
In contrast to the Pseudo-Dionysius, according to whom the gulf between the knowable and the unknowable was bridged by means of
the cosmic hierarchy, Palamas maintained that the antinomy between
the transcendence of God and the ascent to deification of man could
be resolved by divine energies. These were not divine emanations
and did not in any way diminish God. They were considered to be
distinct from God's essence and a means through which mankind
could find access to God.[36]

The dogmatic resemblance between Palamas's doctrine and Hesychastic practice, on the one hand, and Symeon's teaching, on the
other, is beyond doubt, and the real question is whether the social
functions of both doctrines were similar. Is it by chance that Symeon
consistently stressed the authority of the emperor and that during the
troubles of the civil war (1341–47) Palamas was an adherent of Kantakuzenos, the leader of the aristocracy? Is it accidental, moreover,
that Symeon was closely connected, through his system of images,
with the world of the imperial court and of merchants and craftsmen,
while Palamas was opposed to the centralizing policy of Alexius Apokaukos and even more so to the urban revolt in Thessalonica? It
should also be noted that Symeon stood in opposition to the official
church of his day, while Hesychastic ideas were welcomed by the Byzantine church.

The religious confrontation between Byzantium and the West
was most clearly embodied in the schism that gradually developed
after the ninth century.[37] As in the case of the Trinitarian and Iconoclastic controversies, scholars have presented the schism as either a
senseless contest over insignificant matters or a manifestation of political contradictions. This religious controversy should be regarded,
however, as an indication of the social and cultural differences between East and West, rather than as a hieroglyph of political claims,
such as the ecclesiastical supremacy of Rome, the domination over
the Slavic world, or an unavoidable conflict between such men as the
Patriarch Michael Cerularius of Constantinople and the papal legate,
Cardinal Humbert. The controversy flared up in the mid eleventh
century at the time of the increasing Norman threat in southern Italy.
Pope Leo IX (1049–54) visited the plundered regions. Later he described their calamities in a letter to Constantine IX Monomachus
(1042–55) and entered into contact with the Byzantine general Argyros, who returned to Italy from Constantinople.[38] It is uncertain
whether the papacy and Byzantium disregarded their common needs

in the face of the Norman assault and sacrificed the political benefits of an agreement for the sake of dogmatic—that is, social and cultural—divergencies or whether Leo IX and his advisers were ready to dismiss an alliance with Byzantium because they realized that the Normans were their possible supporters. Whatever the answer to these questions, political considerations were not the only element in this dangerous conflict.

The central issue of the controversy was the use of the term *Filioque*, which—translated from theological into secular language—appeared as a problem of the hierarchical structure. Western medieval philosophy accepted and developed a picture of the universe as a continuously graded hierarchy of unequal beings. These hierarchical structures were of different natures, ranging from the hierarchy of the church militant to the hierarchy of the angels. All creatures returned to God by way of assimilation with the Trinity—that is, by way of submission to the hierarchy. Some attempts were made to describe even the Trinity as a hierarchical system or ordo. In the thirteenth century Bonaventura described the Trinity as an *ordo horizontalis*, in which the Father was the principle and the beginning [*primum*], the Son was the *productum et producens*, and the Holy Spirit represented the fulfillment of the *ordo divinus*, which he saw as reflected in the structure of the universe and in the ecclesiastical hierarchy.[39] The twelfth-century Byzantine theologian Nicetas of Maroneia, a staunch supporter of church union, expounded this idea in a simpler and less sophisticated form. He denied that the Latins had introduced two principles. In his construction, as later in that of Bonaventura, the Father remained the principle and the beginning. Like Bonaventura, Nicetas emphasized, in contrast to the usual Byzantine doctrine, that the intermediary role of the Son within the Trinity was directly connected with the Father, while the Holy Spirit was connected only indirectly with the Father and realized through the Son. In order to clarify the interrelationship of the Persons of the Trinity, Nicetas drew some parallels, one of which may reflect the social and earthly content of the *Filioque* dispute. In one of Nicetas's dialogues a Latin refers to the relationship in the Byzantine army between the emperor, the taxiarch (general), and a soldier and asks whether this kind of relationship proves the existence of a dyarchy. In no way, Nicetas answers, since the soldier is subordinate to both the emperor and the taxiarch. The taxiarch, though dependent on the emperor, is nonetheless for the soldier a power and a principle.[40] Nicetas, like Bonaventura, thus stressed that the Trinity possessed an order [τάξις] and that if this *taxis* really existed, the first, the middle, and the last were necessarily found in the

Trinity.[41] In other words, Nicetas had in mind not the political organization of the Byzantines, according to which the emperor was equally the father and lord of all his subjects, but the western hierarchical structure. Orthodox or Byzantine theology, on the contrary, by rejecting the term *Filioque*, refused to accept any possibility of a hierarchical notion of the Trinity and maintained the formula developed by Basil the Great that the Son and the Holy Spirit were the right and the left hands of the Father.[42]

Many other distinctions that emerged during this controversy were also connected with the hierarchical outlook of the medieval West, where the church was treated as an element of hierarchical society. The older division of society into the professions of monks, clerics, and laymen came to be replaced in the tenth and eleventh centuries by the hierarchical division into the first, second, and third estates of those who prayed, fought, and worked. Thus the monks and clerics were joined in a single ecclesiastical order and the laity were divided into two. There was a marked trend toward a more rigid separation of the clergy from the laity by such means as celibacy and a special form of communion. The bishop was more important in the ecclesiastical hierarchy in the West than in Byzantium, and the pope occupied an exceptional position. The relative uniformity of the Byzantine church, on the other hand, corresponded to the relative uniformity of the Byzantine population, with its weakly developed vertical social links.[43]

The church in the West seems to have exercised greater influence on political, economic, and cultural affairs, particularly education, than did the church in the East. It even claimed greater importance than did the Byzantine church in the system of relations between God and man. According to western teachings, there was no salvation outside the institutional and sacramental structure of the church, whereas the Byzantine mysticism of Symeon the Theologian and the Hesychasts, without denying any of the sacraments, icon worship, or other forms of public and ecclesiastical communication with heaven, allowed and even encouraged an individual way of salvation, albeit within the framework of ecclesiastical or monastic organization. If for the westerners the *mysterium* appeared to be the most important means of salvation, Symeon and the Hesychasts taught that the ascent to God was assured primarily by man's purification and subjugation to supernatural authority. The western church consequently exerted a greater influence on the fate of the dead, admitting the existence of purgatory and the possibility of the redemption of sins. In so doing, it stressed the solidarity of all members of the Body of Christ, a solidarity founded above all in the church itself.

Beyond these issues, other points concerned primarily with ritual practices (see chapter 3) became the subject of sharp dispute and aggravated the principal controversy, which was to a great extent rooted in the differing social structures of the two worlds. The idea that the controversy centered on the problem of the hierarchy of the universe helps to explain why the Pseudo-Dionysian concept of the hierarchy of celestial and ecclesiastical structures was more influential in the West than in Byzantium, where it did not correspond to social conditions.

In earlier chapters we have tried to demonstrate the individualistic and antihierarchical structure of Byzantine society. Here we have tried to show that the religious ideas of Byzantium were internally connected with the social self-awareness of the Byzantines, had their origins in the same circle of opinions, and mirrored to some extent the same antihierarchism. Beneath the religious controversies there lay not only political rivalry but also—perhaps above all—social and ideological diversity.

CHAPTER FIVE

Homo byzantinus in the History of Literature and Art

NO real history of Byzantine literature has yet been written. Karl Krumbacher's classic work and even Herbert Hunger's recent survey, though they are important reference books, are not literary histories in the modern sense of the term.[1] The prevailing view of Byzantine literature tends to condemn rather than to try to penetrate its nature or understand its historical significance. It is commonly regarded as "not a great literature," which should not be judged by purely aesthetic or literary standards.[2] "No literary value," according to Franz Dölger, "was attached [in Byzantine literature] to originality of content, freedom of invention, or freedom in the choice of subject-matter."[3] André Guillou refers to it as a *production littéraire* rather than as a true literature.[4]

It is certainly difficult to appreciate a literature written in a language no longer current, with allusions that are no longer comprehensible. Is it true, however, that Byzantine literature, though dead today, was in its own time really "a literature without a public and without problems," as it was described by Paul Lemerle?[5] Was it only a means of escaping reality, as Hans-Georg Beck proposed?[6] To put the question differently, who is at fault in looking at Byzantine literature in this way: Byzantine literature itself, or the scholars, for using the wrong criteria? We are in danger of applying anachronistic criteria and categories to the literature of a people who saw things differently.

The aim of most modern investigations of Byzantine literature has been classification, of which the principles were established by Krumbacher and were retained in the recent works of Dölger and Guillou. Hunger introduced some changes, but he did not break the tradition of classifying the entire body of texts first, on the basis of the language, into "pure" and "vernacular" literature, and then of sub-dividing the pure literature into theological and profane sections and the vernacular literature into prose and poetry. Basic to this classification are genres and subgenres. Historical literature is thus divided into histories and chronicles and rhetoric into speeches and letters.

There are many contradictions in this classification, of which only a few examples need be cited. Kantakuzenos's *History* is written in "pure," though relatively simple, language but incorporates a long letter in the vernacular, implying that the border between the two types was not unbridgeable. Gregoras's *History*, on the other hand, though acknowledged to be a secular work, is permeated with theological habits of mind and includes detailed theological disputes. The erotic romance must be classified as secular literature, but the Byzantines understood it as an allegorical description of the aspiration of the soul toward salvation—that is, as within the theological sphere.[7] Even the *Ars amatoris* of Ovid was given a theological interpretation in the Middle Ages.[8] Some Lives of saints stand in close relation to the chronicles, for which they had supplied material. Thus, there is no clear boundary between theological and secular literature.[9] The same is true of the distinction between prose and poetry. There are erotic romances and historical works in both prose and verse, and in such cases the question must be considered seriously whether works should be classified according to content or rhythmical pattern.

Contradictions of this kind are less a criticism of Krumbacher's system than a warning that it tends to dissect a living body and to lose sight of an author's personality as well as of literary development. From this standpoint it is impossible, as Dölger put it, "to consider each author as a whole in his own right, and literary figures have had to be split up according to their various works."[10] The same author may reappear in different chapters as a theologian or a secular writer, or as a historian, a rhetorician, or an epistolographer, and the unity of literary development is destroyed. One example will suffice to illustrate this. In the eleventh century Symeon the Theologian, Kekaumenos, and Symeon Seth, the author of "Stephanites and Ichnelates," all began to discuss the problem of moral responsibility and the aims of human existence. Though their approaches were different and their solutions did not always agree, their discussions marked an important new trend and showed an interest in human behavior. In works on Byzantine literature, however, Symeon the Theologian has been treated in the sections devoted to religious literature, Kekaumenos as a "pure" author, and Seth, for reasons that are obscure, as a vernacular writer, thus losing sight of an important aspect of the cultural development of the eleventh century. Scholars should therefore move away from the classification of Byzantine genres toward a real history of Byzantine literature.

It is necessary, first of all, to define the object of Byzantine literary history. Since Krumbacher's aim was to classify he tried to include all works written in Greek from the sixth century to the fifteenth, even military handbooks and juridical texts. To be consistent, other types of works, such as the so-called *praktika*, or peasants' inventories, charters, funerary inscriptions, and inscriptions on seals and coins must also be included, but the result of such all-inclusiveness would be to destroy literature as a cultural phenomenon and to dilute it with a mass of texts that lack any aesthetic value. The principle of comprehensiveness is certainly objective and apparently scientific, while the aesthetic principle points the way to loose definitions and personal taste. In order to avert this danger to some extent and to obtain a more precise idea of what constitutes a literary Byzantine text as contrasted with a nonliterary text, two passages can be compared. Though both were written in the same century and sound similar, one can be characterized as literature and the other as a document designed to impart purely practical information. The authors are two of those mentioned above, Symeon Seth and Kekaumenos, each of whom wrote about the properties of different kinds of food. Seth prohibited the eating of venison and Kekaumenos mushrooms, from which he said many people had died.[11] What is the difference between these apparently similar passages?

Kekaumenos's advice not to eat mushrooms must be seen in the context of the sentiments of fear and caution that penetrate his work. He is surrounded by an unstable world, in which poisonous mushrooms have a logical place. Whereas Seth in his *Syntagma* gives only dietary information, for Kekaumenos the idea was closely connected with an image of the universe and transcends the immediate content of his words. This passage presents not only information but what can be called superinformation, indirectly expressed or suggested.

This distinction forms the basis of the definition that we propose. Texts that present only practical information and of which the purpose is to be as precise as possible, such as mathematical and administrative treatises or lists of *paroikoi*, are not called literature, which begins when a text contains not only exact information but also unformulated elements that are only indirectly connected with information. This superinformation may appear as a general context, as in the work of Kekaumenos, or it may be an artificial or rhetorical embellishment of the narrative, such as metaphor, simile, rhyme, rhythm, or word play. This type of superinformation in Byzantine literature has been relatively well studied with regard to single works or authors, but even here the focus of scholarly attention has been on the preservation of ancient rhetorical techniques,[12] and the elements of the art of rhetoric are described rather than analyzed. Since most researchers do not try to reconstruct the artistic system of Byzantine authors, the attempt of Sergej Averincev to elucidate the vocabulary system of two writers of the fifth and sixth centuries, Pseudo-Dionysius and Nonnus of Panopolis, is particularly important. Though different in scope and content, they both saw the universe as an enigma, a view that is reflected in their enigmatic and consciously complicated sentences.[13]

Other kinds of literary superinformation are given by playing with real and imaginary worlds, by hinting at forgotten events, by indirect attacks on literary predecessors, by the inverted use of traditional images such as sacred utensils or well-known quotations, even from Holy Scripture, and by irony or the conflict of contradictory notions. This subject matter, with rare exceptions, has hardly been touched by scholars, and it is necessary to turn again to Averincev's book to show the internal possibilities of such a method. Averincev analyzes a *kontakion* or hymn on the slaughter of the Innocents written in the sixth century by Romanos the Melodist, who repeats, stanza by stanza, Herod's order to his soldiers and their reply. The cruel death of the small children is described in detail, and evil seems to dominate the world, but only seemingly, since in contrast to the superficial content of the *kontakion*, each stanza ends with a refrain that Herod's power will soon be destroyed. Had Romanos formulated this idea directly, his *kontakia* might have been poetical homilies, as they have been called by many scholars, but he in fact expresses his threat negatively as well as positively, since Herod's soldiers try to reassure him that his power will not be destroyed. They urge him, at the end of the fifth strophe, not to offend Bethlehem lest his power soon be destroyed. "Be not afraid," they say at the end of the sixth strophe, "that your power will soon be destroyed." The continual repetition of this phrase creates an impression opposite to its content and leads the listener to understand that Herod will in fact be punished for his misdeeds.[14]

In summary it can be said that literary texts are those in which methods of expression that do not convey information but that nevertheless influence the reader or listener are used. Seen from this standpoint some astrological or geographical works may belong to the sphere of literature, while many letters, lacking this superinformation, remain outside the framework of literature as we have defined it.

What is the main aspect of Byzantine literary history? The traditional approach has been to study the Christian, eastern, or Hellenic background and influences and especially to try to discover pagan or biblical sources and to show the literary legacy of the past. Such an approach can be called quantitative, because it considers Byzantine literary production as the sum of separate contributions in which previously created forms and ideas are employed. It would not be too much to say that most scholars see Byzantine literature as a combination of existing elements, a mosaic of ancient clichés, or an exercise in formal and technical skill. The only real change that has been recognized by modern scholars is the shift from the accentual pattern of classical literature, which was based on quantity (syllabic length), to that of Christian writers, which was based on accent (syllabic stress), but even this transition has been attributed to Syrian influence, and much work still needs to be done on the metrical systems of both prose and poetry in the Middle Ages. Approached from a different point of view, however, Byzantine literature can be regarded not simply as a collection of quotations, imitations, and repetitions but as an expression of creative human activity. From this point of view the main object of Byzantine literary history is *homo byzantinus* as creator, consumer, and subject of literary works. This approach presents three problems for investigation: the author, the audience, and the participant.

The problem of the author in its turn involves several elements. First, there is the question of the author's self-awareness, which was asked by Igor Čičurov in his study of self-awareness in Theophanes' chronicle.[15] Comparing the preamble of Theophanes with those of earlier Greek historians, including the church historians of the fourth and fifth centuries, Čičurov showed that Theophanes consciously kept his personality in the background and omitted any detail that might make it possible to evaluate him as a historian. Even the fact that he wrote his history is explained as the result not of an internal reason but of the deathbed request of George Syncellus that Theophanes continue Syncellus's unfinished chronicle. There are no remarks in the text, moreover, that reflect Theophanes' personal attitude toward the events related. Čičurov concluded that Theophanes tried to create an anonymous chronicle. This sense of anonymity is so marked that Mango has recently raised the question who actually wrote the chronicle.[16]

An analogous tendency is found in many contemporary hagiographical works, in which the author also tried to suppress his own personality and even stressed his inability to fulfill his noble task.[17]

George, the author of the seventh-century *Life* of Theodore of Sy-keon, called himself an unworthy serf and sinner and by this trite for-mula deprived himself of individuality. In order to stress his imper-sonality even more strongly, George placed the "preamble" in the middle rather than at the beginning of his narrative, so that his mea-ger self-qualification sounds particularly incidental and superficial.[18] But this apparent rejection of individuality and humility must be seen in the light of contemporary literary standards, since the author of a Life was considered not as a creative personality but as an impersonal tool in the hands of the Holy Spirit. This was a new concept, differing radically from the antique tradition, with its high appreciation of human individuality. In the eleventh century, beginning with Psellos, the author's self-interest revived and continued till the end of the em-pire. Theophanes' theory of incidental reasons that compelled him to accept his task even became the object of mockery. At the beginning of the thirteenth century, Nicholas Mesarites declared in his descrip-tion of the unsuccessful attempt by John Comnenus to seize the throne that he had taken up his pen because so many people had asked him about these events that his throat was sore and he was out of breath and unable to speak.[19] The anti-individualistic topos of Theophanes is here tinged with irony and transformed into a per-sonal premise to a personal story.

Another element in the problem of the author is the social origins of the Byzantine literary elite and in particular whether it was stable or changing. Beck argued that most Byzantine authors were drawn from the ranks of those accustomed to holding high political or eccle-siastical office,[20] but the real picture is not uniform. At the beginning of the ninth century most people who were active creatively were as-sociated with monasteries. Though no exact calculations have yet been made, it appears that almost all the great writers of this time were monks. Theophanes retired from the world soon after his mar-riage at the age of eighteen; Theodore of Stoudios was about twenty when his whole family took the habit; Joseph of Thessalonica, the au-thor of many speeches and homilies, had been a monk from the age of nineteen and Theophanes Graptos from twenty-two; Nicetas of Amnia, who wrote the famous *Life* of Philaretos, also entered a mon-astery in his youth. We can add to this list the future patriarch Metho-dios, the monk of the Chenolakkos in Constantinople, Michael Syn-cellus (who began his career as a monk in the Sabas-Laura and became later a *higumenos* in the Chora in Constantinople), the poetess Kassia (who entered a convent after her misbegotten attempt to marry a prince) and, somewhat later, the chronicler George the Monk, not to mention several less well known hagiographers, hymnographers, and other writers. In contrast, only a few writers of this period are known who belonged to the imperial or patriarchal bureaucracy. The future patriarchs, Germanus and Nicephorus, both began their careers in the imperial chancellery. Stephen, the author of the *Life* of St. Stephen the Young, and another hagiographer, Ignatius, were deacons of Saint Sophia.

From the middle of the ninth century, until the eleventh, however, most writers display the social characteristics postulated by Beck. Between George the Monk in the mid-ninth century and Symeon the Theologian at the end of the tenth, there was a long interval in the literary predominance of monks, and the major figures among writers were high-ranking officials, including both emperors such as Leo VI and Constantine Porphyrogenitus and patriarchs such as Photius and Nicholas Mystikus. Even the revision of hagiographic texts was undertaken by the logothete Symeon Metaphrastes, who was in all probability not the same person as Symeon the Logothete, the author of a chronicle.[21]

In the eleventh and twelfth centuries civil officials continued to dominate the literary activity of the Byzantine empire,[22] but from the twelfth century on the importance of a new social type of professional literati, characterized by such men as Prodromus or Tzetzes, was growing. The fate of this social type during the last centuries of Byzantium is a matter for debate. According to Hunger, the real promoters of literature and scholarship at this time were intellectuals from the lower social strata, the so-called poor,[23] but Ihor Ševčenko has stressed that most of the "begging intellectuals" lived in the twelfth century and were relatively rare in the fourteenth century. Ševčenko has shown further that just over half of all fourteenth-century authors were ecclesiastics and that twenty-eight of these were monks. Of the literati whose social and economic standing is known, three were landowners; three were of imperial rank, eleven came from noble or prosperous backgrounds, and four or five were of humble origin.[24] Igor Medvedev disagrees with both these views, arguing against Hunger, on the basis of a presumed analogy with conditions in Italy, that merchants were not alien to literature and scholarship and, against Ševčenko, that a significant number of late Byzantine literati were drawn from the aristocracy, but he presents no evidence for these arguments.[25]

The problem of the audience for Byzantine literary works has hardly been touched. The question itself seems vague and undefined and must be asked in another way if it is to be clarified. It must be decided whether Byzantine culture was oral or written. It has been said that the transition from late Antiquity to Byzantium coincided with the collapse of written culture and that books became rare and expensive as the great libraries of the Hellenic world were destroyed,[26] but the problem was not simply that of the availability of books, since although Greco-Roman society produced many books and established big libraries, its culture was fundamentally oral. The main element of mass culture in Antiquity was the theater, in which performance appeared as the incarnation of spoken words and books were rejected as elements in the performance. Books are not mentioned even in those scenes in Greek comedy in which they would be expected to appear, such as the derision of Socrates in Aristophanes' *Clouds* or the dispute between Aeschylus and Euripides in *The Frogs*. In the Middle Ages the main element of mass culture was the liturgy. The theater died out; the last voice in its defense grew silent in the sixth century, and Byzantine *dramatia* [short plays] were written to be read rather than performed. Even an attempt to use the stage for Christian propaganda was a failure. There is a Syrian version of a play dedicated to the mysterious conversion of several pagan actors,[27] but this genre found no successors. Likewise in the West, it is doubtful whether the Christian dramas written by Hrotswitha in the tenth century were ever performed, and the fact that they have been produced successfully in recent years is the result of the author's imitation of ancient models rather than of her experience in actually staging plays.

Although Christianity was founded by a Man Who belonged to an oral culture, wrote no books, and was treated by His followers as the Incarnate Word or Logos, it was based on the written word, and the Byzantine liturgy attributed a central place to the book, Holy Scripture, both in the service and in church decoration, as in the iconography of the Preparation [*Hetoimasia*], where the book represents the Lord Himself. In the fourth century a radically new form of book was introduced and the antique book, the roll, which was made to be read aloud and had to be held with both hands was replaced by the Byzantine book, the codex, which was suited for solitary reading and formed a perfect counterpart to the solitary and silent prayer that was alien to the public life of the Greco-Roman period. It was also in the fourth century that the new habit of silent reading became popular. Augustine describes in the *Confessions* how astonished he was to see Ambrose reading a book without a sound: "When he was reading, he drew his eyes along over the leaves, and his heart searched into the sense, but his voice and tongue were silent [*vox autem et lingua quiescebant*]."[28] This new fashion of reading already existed, but it impressed even a well-educated man such as Augustine as something remarkable. Silent prayer also was replacing the public recitation of prayers, especially in monasteries, on account both of the spiritual esteem and practical need for silence and of opposition to the tradition of pagan rhetoric. Although the term *legere* in the Middle Ages never entirely lost its ancient association with speech, and pages were still thought to have voices, it came to refer more often to reading silently, from a codex, rather than to reciting from a roll.[29]

Averincev drew attention to another difference between Greco-Roman and Byzantine attitudes toward the book. The ancient Greek poets preferred to sing about rather than describe their heroes, and the term ἀείδω stressed the oral element in their culture. According to Averincev, respect for the written word began in Byzantine literature with Nonnus of Panopolis.[30] In fact, even in Nonnus's vocabulary the classic ἀείδω [to sing] prevailed over the Byzantine γράφω [to write],[31] and as late as the seventh century the Byzantine poet and historian George of Pisidia used both expressions.[32] There was nevertheless a clear tendency—especially later, among the Hesychasts—away from a public, oral culture toward a private culture of the book and solitary prayer. This does not mean that oral exercises disappeared and that the country plunged into silence. Storytelling remained the backbone of popular culture, as it is today in the Balkans and the Middle East.[33] Most business, both administrative and commercial, was done by word of mouth, since the majority of the population could neither read nor write, and the majority of charters and other documents are records of oral agreements, which acquired legal force not by being written down but through a physical transaction of which the memory was preserved by witnesses. Reading aloud still formed an important part of the liturgy, especially in monasteries, official rhetors still recited their discourses before emperors and patriarchs in their courts, and letters were read aloud to recipients, often in the presence of many friends. But literature, as we have defined it, was addressed primarily to the solitary reader.

A certain dynamic tendency already existed in the ancient reverence for action and for the spoken word. The dynamism of aesthetic perception permeated every aspect of antique culture, from post-archaic sculpture to the virtual worship of horse racing in the late Roman period. The artistic dynamism that was typical of ancient drama appears particularly evident when contrasted with Byzantine semi-dramatic pieces. Although the literary drama *Christ Suffering*, which has been dated anywhere between the fourth and the twelfth centuries, was a compilation of lines from classical Greek dramatists, primarily Euripides, it is based on aesthetic principles quite opposed to those of Euripides. Action gave way to stories about action, and tension was built up not by dynamism and motion but by the expectation of miracles and by the radical transformation from grief to joy.[34]

The Byzantines rejected dynamism not only as an aesthetic principle but also as an ideal of behavior. Statues no longer imitated human originals; man, rather, tended to maintain a statuesque attitude (see chapter 3). Images, in their turn, were seen as reflections of eternal prototypes and therefore as essences more real and more stable than the changing forms of reality.[35] Ernst Kitzinger has suggested that a significant transformation in the imaginative system took place in the seventh century, when the holy figures ceased to participate in a drama, avoided action, and developed into the passive, motionless, isolated persons of portrait icons.[36] According to Kurt Weitzmann, Byzantine hieratic compositions were designed to express dignity and sanctity and represented "the greatest possible contrast" to the vivid action and dramatic sequence of scenes still found in sixth-century book illumination.[37] The ceremonies in churches and palaces were slow and solemn, and dignity became an ideal of behavior. This worship of solemnity was a mark of Byzantine literature distinguishing it both from ancient Greek and from medieval Latin literature. If the two descriptions of the uprising of Isaac Angelus in 1185—the one by the Byzantine historian Nicetas Choniates, the other by his younger contemporary from Picardy, the knight Robert de Clari—are compared, a sharp contrast can be seen between the dynamic Latin manner of narrating events, with plenty of conversation,[38] and the solemnity of Choniates' narrative, which was consciously slowed by the insertion of *ekphraseis*, classical quotations, and psychological observations.[39]

The lack of aesthetic dynamism was closely connected with the principal sociopsychological features of Byzantine society. On the one hand, dynamism was better suited to collective perception than to an individualistic world that cherished individual contemplation and compassion, since collective perception strengthened emotional effects, disturbed calm veneration, and placed the actors in a state of motion and mutual relationship. On the other hand, the Byzantines, morally exhausted by the instability of their life, strove to create a world of stable essences, eternal truth, perpetual principles, and solemn order. In this frozen imaginary world the beholder enjoyed a clarity and stability that were lacking in real life.

The third, and perhaps most complicated, problem of Byzantine literary history is *homo byzantinus* as a participant in literature, especially the image of the hero. For although Byzantine authors preserved the language of their classical predecessors, continuing to use traditional topoi, idioms, similes, proverbs, mythological names, and allusions to events of the Greco-Roman past, their representation of characters changed radically from that found in Antiquity. Let us look at the type of the Byzantine hero and its variations.

Just as in the Christian religion man appeared as the central figure of the created cosmos and as the crown of creation,[40] so the human image remained the center of both Byzantine literature and Byzantine art, including not only painting and book illumination but also small enamels, silver vessels, and painted pottery. Writers dealt primarily with the so-called epic character, who appeared not as a real human being but as an incarnation of moral virtues. Characters were presented as signs of qualities linked with human names and the external features of real lives. That does not mean that they were deprived of individuality. On the contrary, they had to display unmistakable attributes that identified them with their roles and that showed the virtues and vices they represented. The idea of the complexity of human nature, which reached its peak in the works of Tacitus, was consciously rejected by Byzantine authors, who aimed at the creation of a paradigmatic ideal. Theophanes had found it in the past in the person of Constantine the Great. Attaleiates, on the other hand, found it embodied in his own time in Nicephorus III Botaneiates (1078–81). Both writers showed their heroes as almost superhuman beings, endowed with an unattainable harmony of virtues. This unattainability was demonstrated in contrast with other characters, who, even if praised, possessed the same qualities insufficiently or in underdeveloped form.

In opposition to the epic hero in Byzantine literature stood the antihero, the allegorical incarnation of sin. The relation between the hero and antihero is shown as a struggle between good and evil, virtue and vice, or light and darkness, but since the participants in this struggle were complete in their qualities and could not change, their struggle lacked internal tension and became in effect a draw. The distinctive type of tension found in Byzantine literature was created by the perpetual striving of man toward an unattainable ideal rather than by the conflict between contradictory tendencies. Suffering and pain are frequently portrayed in Byzantine literature, but not the tragedy of doubt and hesitation. Thus, though the Virgin suffered in anticipation of the crucifixion of her Son, there was no choice, either for her or for Him. Occasionally the hero in the Life of a saint seems to have felt some hesitation when faced with alternate courses of action, but the problem was quickly solved by a vision, dream, or other form of divine guidance, showing the right thing for the saint to do, and there is no real choice if the eternal values are to be preserved.

In the historical writings of the tenth century the same dichotomy is sometimes presented as two characters stand in contrast to one another, such as Basil I, the founder of the so-called Macedonian dynasty, and his predecessor and benefactor Michael III, whom Basil ordered killed. Basil is represented in tenth-century histories as the embodiment of all possible virtues and Michael as the embodiment of all possible vices. The artistic and moral victory was from the start won by Basil. Even more notorious for Byzantine aesthetics is the much criticized poem on the capture of Crete written in the tenth century by Theodosius the Deacon, who is regularly called an imitator of George of Pisidia, and who did, in truth, follow George in many formal elements.[41] But whereas for George the hero was Heraclius, for Theodosius the Byzantines and the Arabs stand against one another and the individuality of the actors was lost in the concept of *ethnos*. The Arabs were called a bad, wicked, bloodthirsty people, who marched into battle with horrible noise, while in the Byzantine ranks order, silence, and solemnity prevailed. The stars rejoiced and the angels danced in celebration of Byzantine victories. The war took on a cosmic character as a contest between light and darkness. Theodosius consistently stresses that the shields of Byzantine soldiers shone and that their scale armor and lances glittered. The Arabs, on the other hand, were successful only at night and turned and fled with the dawn.[42]

Byzantine virtues differed from those of the ancient heroes not only on account of Christian piety, which figured prominently even in the Mirrors of Princes, but also because many of the most important classical virtues and standards either disappeared or lost their earlier significance.

Physical vigor, beauty, and even reason were not accepted as actual virtues in Byzantium until at least the end of the tenth century. Theophanes, although he hated the Iconoclastic emperors, described in detail their martial deeds and successes, and in order to explain this anomaly some scholars have suggested that he drew this information from a lost Iconoclastic source.[43] Theophanes could easily have suppressed this information, however, if he had really considered military activity as admirable, and the real explanation is that for him the military prowess of the Iconoclastic emperors was not praiseworthy.

In Byzantine social theory, the family appeared as an earthly ideal and celibacy as a heavenly ideal. Likewise in literature, the hermit appeared as the heavenly counterpart of the secular hero of Byzantine tales. The hero of hagiographies was a complete denial of all classical virtues and of all human activities.[44] His very power over social and political events, over the forces of sea and earth, and over time and distance was a reward for his determination to stand outside secular society and to devote himself to God rather than to man. Even the conscious dirt and ugliness of his body stood in antithesis to the ancient worship of harmony and beauty.

This treatment of character changed radically in the eleventh century with the appearance of the so-called romance type of hero. Psellos, and later Choniates, introduced actors who were neither perfect emperors nor absolute villains but combined the qualities of hero and antihero. Such, for instance, in Choniates' *History*, was Andronicus Comnenus, who was at the same time a ruthless tyrant and an incredibly talented and charming man.[45] An even more complicated approach to the image of hero is found in the *History* written by Kantakuzenos in a monastery after he had been forced to abdicate in 1354. In it he tried to refute the accusations brought against him by his adversaries and to win the confidence of his readers by including in detail the speeches of his opponents, emphasizing his own defeats and mishaps and using many terms and expressions that were in contrast to the alleged virtues of his hero. In other words, he presented himself as a true hero in the epic style but against a background that pointed up, by contrast, the main content of his book.

Even in the finest works of Byzantine literature written after the eleventh century, however, this psychological approach to human character did not lead to a real change in the external presentation of human beings.[46] Individuals were not portrayed by revealing their inner feelings or the inner strife between opposite tendencies that were discovered by writers in the eleventh and twelfth centuries. Even in Psellos the portrait remained traditional: it consisted of a list of various isolated traits rather than a synthetic account of an individual. There were a few departures from this method, however. Byzantine writers usually abandoned the traditional technique of portrayal, for instance, when they described an ill or dying person, whose normal appearance had already been distorted by suffering. To the description by Psellos of Romanus III before his death, quoted by Ljubarskij in the book mentioned above, can be added the description of Prodromus himself, after recovering from small pox, as having a bald head with a huge beard covering his cheeks,[47] the description of a dying friend whom he could not even recognize,[48] and particularly the portrait of the usurper John Comnenus the Fat by Nicholas Mesarites, who saw him just before his downfall, after the unsuccessful rebellion of 1200. Contrary to the strict rule of Byzantine frontality, the rebel is pictured from the rear, with wiry black hair, fat shoulders, and the back of his head swollen. When Mesarites came closer, he saw that John was limp, half dead, and unable to answer questions and that his head drooped. At the very end of his work Mesarites returned to John's appearance; already beaten, the usurper was sitting on the floor. He had taken off all his imperial garments except the crown, was out of breath, sweated, and constantly used a towel.[49]

Actual portraits in Byzantine art are even rarer. Byzantium begins with symbolic or allegorical representations of power, solemnity, piety, and other incarnate virtues and their opposites. The image was conceived as epic, and the artist tried to show the hidden essence rather than the changing and unstable appearance. Though sculpture did not vanish entirely in Byzantium,[50] its importance was clearly diminished in comparison with that it had had in ancient Greece and Rome, and it never experienced a revival comparable to the brilliant upsurge of sculpture in the medieval West. Sculpture remained closely bound to the world of palpable things, while the mosaics and frescoes that dominated Byzantine church decoration presented an ideal vehicle for contemplating the supreme essence.

Although designed to reflect eternity, the epic character of Byzantine mural painting did not create entirely uniform images.[51] In spite of consistent frontality and a limited series of available clichés, the Byzantines distinguished the heroes of their legends and used specific attributes for each of their saints. The images are thus in a certain way connected with the earthly world. The emphasis by the Byzantines on the imitative power of the artist was not simply an account of their adherence to the tradition of Antiquity. The image stood between the two worlds, having its roots on the earth and yet reaching toward the supreme essence unattainable by the human mind.[52] Its supernatural aspect as a ladder by which to ascend to God, ardently defended by the Iconodules, originated precisely in this ambiguity.

Byzantine art had to deal not only with the relation between the original and the image but also with a three-tiered system in which the image occupied a place between the essence or archetype and the earthly world, to which its relation was consequently not restricted simply to that of an image or imitation. The Byzantine image was seen as having a magic power. Just as the icon of the Virgin defended the Byzantines on the battlefield,[53] the old Roman statues in the streets and squares of Constantinople magically influenced current events. It was no accident that Andronicus Comnenus, when he seized the capital, had the portraits of the executed widow of Manuel I, the Empress Xenia, repainted so as to depict an old and decrepit woman rather than a beautiful lady.[54]

The character of Byzantine portraiture was determined by all these factors and brought together various artistic tendencies, including an approach to essence that accounted for the idealization of the portrayal, a connection with the earthly world that in some instances approached a conventional imitation of nature,[55] and an idea of the social function of the image that generated both functionally specific types of portrait and the representations of social roles, as of an official or a donor (the votive portrait).[56] In the twelfth century Byzantine portraiture seems to have undergone a development analogous to that in literature, which can be seen, for instance, in the portraits in Saint Sophia of the Empress Zoe in the middle of the eleventh century and the Empress Irene, the wife of John II (1118–43). The plump, rosy, unwrinkled face and the slightly heavy nose of Zoe's portrait is conventional, though it recalls both the features of her Macedonian ancestors and the description by Psellos, who stressed that she preserved until her final years a face without wrinkles—although he also described her shaggy eyebrows and slightly hooked nose, of which there is no sign in the mosaic. Irene looks less idealized. The highly raised eyebrows, deep creases, pursed lips, and sidelong glance all give an impression of constraint and tension.[57]

When Byzantine artists tried to depict human emotions, especially sorrow, they were not simply influenced by sermons elaborating the theme of the mother's embrace[58] but also by the general concern in Byzantine literature with the depiction of illness and death. The frescoes at Nerezi in Macedonia, dated 1164, are notable for their attempts to portray the human form and especially for the artistic tension attained in the moving scenes of suffering and death.[59] These attempts were developed further in Constantinopolitan painting of the fourteenth century.

An examination of the social stratification of Byzantine literary characters brings out two relevant points. First, the broad social spectrum found in hagiographic literature may reflect the loose structure of early Byzantine society. Second, warriors and noblemen begin to appear extensively in Byzantine literature in the tenth century. There is a clear contrast between the descriptions of the protagonists in the *Life* of the Emperor Basil I and in the *History* by Leo the Deacon, which were written only a few decades apart. The author of the *Life*, who was either Constantine Porphyrogenitus or someone of his circle,[60] consistently stressed Basil's justice and equability while only vaguely mentioning his military successes. The author reports some unsuccessful sieges and describes in detail how Basil helped to build a bridge over the Euphrates and carried a load equal to that of three soldiers. Leo, on the contrary, depicted his hero, Nicephorus Phocas, as a genuine warrior, and his tale is concerned primarily with the victories of this gifted general.

The image of the noble knight was introduced into Byzantine literature with Nicephorus Phocas. In the middle of the eleventh century John Mauropus still contrasted the triumphant piety of an emperor with the reckless military energy of barbarians and rebels (see chapter 3), and a little later Kekaumenos still praised the traditional aspects of the imperial ideal, including the concept of the emperor as a father of his people[61] and his piety and justice, without mentioning imperial glory on the battlefield. It was Attaleiates who added to the list of imperial virtues the new qualities of noble origin and military courage.[62] By the end of the eleventh century, indeed, the image of the noble general began to overshadow even that of the emperor. The last part of Skylitzes' *Chronicle* concentrates not on the fate of the emperors but on the cunning military actions of Katakalon Kekaumenos, and the *Commentaries* of Bryennius, written at the beginning of the twelfth century, relate above all the feuds and agreements of some mighty and noble warriors.[63]

The militarization of portrayals in the visual arts appeared at almost the same time. In the middle of the eleventh century some attempts were made to create a new type of imperial effigy on coins. Isaac I Comnenus (1057–59), a close friend of Katakalon Kekaumenos, had gold coins struck on which he was shown wearing chain mail, with his left hand on the hilt of a sheathed sword. This new coin caused a kind of social shock, and the rumor spread that by this effigy Isaac had tried to emphasize that his power came not from God but by the sword.

A specific group in the Byzantine hagiographic galaxy is formed by the so-called military saints, George, Demetrius, the two Theodores, Procopius, and Nestor. In the earlier legends of these saints there is no reference to their military deeds. Only later did Demetrius, like many others, acquire particular social characteristics and begin to appear as a warrior of noble stock.[64] Effigies of saintly warriors appear on coins only during the Comnenian dynasty: Demetrius under Alexius I, George under John II, and Theodore under Manuel I.[65] They are also often found on seals in the eleventh and twelfth centuries,[66] usually the seals of individuals belonging to the military nobility, while the civil aristocracy preferred the Virgin and the figures of John the Baptist, St. Michael, and St. Nicholas. The images of military saints became very popular in the minor arts of the eleventh and twelfth centuries.[67] To a great extent, indeed, the figure of St. George the Warrior replaced that of St. George the Martyr after the tenth century.[68]

A parallel development took place at about the same time in the West, where ancient saints appeared in military garb and new saints with a military character emerged.[69] St. Martin, who had figured primarily as a monk and a bishop, was now often portrayed as a soldier. Erdmann, and more recently Peter Brown, have drawn attention to an interesting passage in the *Ecclesiastical History* of Orderic Vitalis, who died about 1142, telling about Gerold, a clerk from Avranches, who "made a great collection of tales of the combats of holy knights," including not only western holy knights, such as Sebastian and Eustace, but also warriors, such as Demetrius, George, and Theodore.[70] Brown may go too far in suggesting that Gerold's catalogue was dominated by Byzantine saints, since the legends of military saints were popular and even intermingled with epic elements in the eleventh- and twelfth-century West. A French version of the legend of St. Eustace is preserved in the form of a *chanson de geste*. But the text shows that Byzantine military saints were known in the first half of the twelfth century to a writer in Normandy, who may have heard about them from the Normans in South Italy and Sicily.

The role of women and the topic of sex and love in Byzantine literature present a special problem.[71] Women were often the heroines of hagiography, but in this genre they remained without specific sexual attributes and resembled their male counterparts in their actions and efforts. Hagiographers sometimes emphasized that at first sight it was impossible to distinguish the sex of the saint.[72] The androgynous quality of many early saints has been remarked upon by several scholars, and it was not unusual for a female saint to pose as a man in order to lead a holier life.[73] Only in the tenth-century *Life* of Mary the Younger (see chapter 3) is a genuine female tragedy found in the story of a woman killed by her ruthless and jealous husband. Women are still shadowy figures, however, in tenth-century historical works, such as the *Life* of Basil I or Leo the Deacon's *History*, although the stories of Eudocia Ingerina, the mistress of Michael III and the wife of Basil I, and especially of Theophano, who was involved in the plot against her own husband, offered excellent opportunities to depict romantic affairs. Psellos was the first to introduce an erotic topic boldly into his narrative, and the next century saw the revival of the erotic romance, of which the embryonic plot can be found in the *Commentaries* of Bryennius, where the center of the narrative is formed by the marriage of Alexius Comnenus and Irene Doukaina, who as representatives of two rival aristocratic families succeed, as in a romance, in surmounting various obstacles.

There is a difference between images of women found in Byzantine literature of the eleventh and twelfth centuries. The heroines of eleventh-century writers bear the stamp of the gynaeceum. Even Zoe, around whom much intrigue was woven, looked forward to a calm life and the preparation of aromatic unguents. Sklerena, the mistress of Constantine IX, was praised for her beauty and for her mildness, but Psellos did not mention her political ambitions. Twelfth-century authors, on the other hand, created a series of female images of another kind: fond of power, ambitious, and bold enough to emulate men. The obscene words put by Choniates into the mouth of Anna Comnena blaming her husband for weakness (see chapter 3) are typical of the new self-confidence of the Byzantine woman or of her image in contemporary writings. In a courageous poem addressed by Pseudo-Prodromus to Manuel I, the *sebastokratorissa* Irene was presented as an arrogant and indomitable person who knew her rights and defended them.[74] In an analysis of the development of Byzantine literature, therefore, from the triple standpoint of who created it, for whom it was created, and whom it created, a greater connection between literature and real life can be found on the one hand and a greater difference between the Byzantine literary world and its Greco-Roman forerunners than is usually supposed on the other. The Byzantines were not simply the heirs to a great past that had produced literary models to which authors had to adhere as best they could. Self-awareness on the part of the author, a changed attitude of the reader to the text, and the image of the hero were all new features, following in the steps of Byzantine reality and changing and shifting in the stream of time.

The very attitude toward Antiquity changed. The initial period of neglect and oblivion was followed by the age to which Paul Lemerle has given the name *encyclopedism*, which is preferable to the customary and questionable *Renaissance*. This was a period of accumulation and arrangement of the classical heritage. The first steps in this movement were the introduction of the minuscule script at the beginning of the ninth century and the creation of Photius's *Myriobiblon*. It reached its height at the court of Constantine Porphyrogenitus and coincided with the revival of the classicizing tendencies in Byzantine art.[75] The antique heritage was appropriated formally and without any clear internal understanding. The imperial reality around Photius, for instance, who was one of the most learned scholars of the ninth century, distorted his comprehension of the ancient past, and Herodotus remained for him primarily a historian of the Persian monarchs and usurpers.[76] Greek mythology and history simultaneously attracted and alarmed the Byzantines. They used classical images in order to contrast them with their heroes rather than to compare the two. Even so classicizing a writer as the author of the *Life* of Basil I timidly stressed that his hero was not an Achilles, though he did not hesitate to compare his antihero with some figures in Greek mythology. This negative attitude toward Antiquity appears even more clearly in the poem by Theodosius the Deacon, in which Greco-Roman images are frequently used but only in order to stress that the Byzantines are better, stronger, and cleverer than their ancestors. He addresses Demosthenes, exclaiming that Philip of Macedon was not powerful enough, and addresses Dio Cassius, announcing that Sulla was only a hollow demagogue. These classical politicians and generals are ciphers compared to the actual hero, the Emperor Romanus II.[77] Only from Leo the Deacon onward did Greek myth and history cease to be an alien, if charming subject. Direct comparison with antique personages then become customary, and Anna Comnena unhesitatingly compared her father with Heracles.

A new period of assimilation of the classical legacy began in the eleventh century. Robert Browning in his article on the Homeric tradition in Byzantium showed that beginning with Psellos there was a new freedom in the handling of traditional material, which can be seen clearly in the work of the twelfth-century writers Eustathius of Thessalonica and John Tzetzes.[78] Homer was no longer an alien. He belonged to the same world as Eustathius, who made use of peasant customs, popular beliefs, and the spoken Greek of his time in order to explain the content of the epics.

Attitudes toward Antiquity were more complicated and active than simple imitation or linguistic borrowing, and antique reminiscences were more than ways of avoiding governmental control over literature and escaping into emptiness, as Beck suggests. The active and changing use by the Byzantines of their literary and artistic legacy implies that it was an important tool for understanding themselves and the surrounding world.

The Byzantines are often blamed for obstinately clinging to stereotyped biblical and classical expressions that seem boring and trivial. This was a conscious position, however, not a sign of incapacity or lack of creative activity, since the use of antique reminiscences had important social and aesthetic functions. They gave an illusion of a close connection with a brilliant past, which was regarded at first as attractive though dangerous, then as a synonym of order, and later as a treasury of wisdom and artistic elegance. Finally, in the fourteenth century, Theodore Metochites remarked elegiacally that the grandeur of the old Greeks had formed an insuperable obstacle to the advancement of Byzantine thought.[79] Stereotyped expressions also created the illusion of stability that was painstakingly sought in the unstable society of Byzantium. At the same time, clichés were a significant means of artistic expression, since they brought out the intricate range of images and ideas implied in a brief and trivial sentence. They provided a means for indirect references, hints, or allusions of various kinds. A single word or quotation could raise a whole range of considerations and imply a concealed sense that was clear to learned Byzantines but is often beyond understanding today. Choniates relates an eloquent scene in which the patriarch of Constantinople, Theodosius Boradiotes (1179–83), when he met Andronicus Comnenus, quoted only a brief line of Psalms 47.9, of which, Choniates said, "the ambiguous sense . . . did not escape the tyrant and pierced his soul like a two-edged sword."[80] Cliché was a formidable weapon in political struggle, not an innocuous or tedious literary game. The best Byzantine authors, moreover, such as Psellos and Choniates, used stereotypes and quotations in combination with fresh images and expressions. The conjunction of the emptiness of a cliché and the originality of a courageous statement could produce a particular emotional tension and an unexpected effect.[81] It must not be forgotten that the stiff figures on Byzantine mosaics and frescoes appeared to medieval observers as moving and vivid. In his description of the church of the Holy Apostles in Constantinople, Nicholas Mesarites speaks of the Pantokrator as "looking forth through the windows, leaning out down to his navel through the lattice which is near the summit of the dome, after the manner of irresistibly ardent lovers."[82] For a Byzantine these images were truer and more real than living persons, and they filled the space of every church.

It has often been said of Byzantine literature that it could never become a means of expressing genuine emotion. This mistake stems from the traditional evaluation of Byzantine literature as a deterioration from the classical system of description and consequently as a cluster of long rhythmic periods full of antiquated terms, supported by far-fetched comparisons and allusions to Greek mythology and to the Bible. In fact, Byzantine literature was concerned with real issues and was able to express them. Its main problem was the value of man in a dehumanizing society and the unstable world of autocracy, in which the earthly virtues of man were not highly prized. In order to survive, man had either to be lifted above the lower world or plunged into the glorious past. Artistic media were consequently designed either to create a stable duplicate of the earthly world or to reveal the hidden movements of the human soul. In both these aims the Byzantines were successful. The point of view from which we have evaluated Byzantine culture may be unexpected, even paradoxical, but it is based on an effort to ascertain whether it was in fact as sterile as is often said. As far as Byzantine visual art is concerned, we can point not only to the present scholarly interest in this topic but also to a trend among modern artists to apply Byzantine characteristics in their work. The Byzantine icon is the object not only of aesthetic admiration but also of imitation. Even Byzantine literary works can be regarded as a live literature capable of influencing contemporary writing. There is a completely "Byzantine" portrayal of the heroine in Vladimir Nabokov's novel *Ada*. Each of her features is isolated and described, ranging over "Her forehead area . . . eyebrows . . . eyes . . . nose . . . neck . . . shoulders . . . nipples . . . [and] lovely strong legs." [83] Everything from top to bottom is described separately and according to a Byzantine order. We also find there a conglomeration of puns, including many based on proper names—"Ada, our ardors and arbors"—most of them designed to show the author's extraordinary vocabulary and capacity for putting words together. Yet another feature of Nabokov's technique that can be called Byzantine is the retardation of the narrative by means of scientific—mainly entomological and botanical—deviations, ekphraseis, or literary allusions. In Nabokov as in the Byzantine *Christ Suffering* the recollection of actions often replaces the actions themselves. Nabokov's proficiency is obviously not restricted to Byzantine techniques. He has the experience of centuries, the boldness of sexual images, and psychological subtlety. But while the differences are obvious, his works show that Byzantine literary principles are closer to modern fashions than many historians of Byzantine literature have realized.

CHAPTER SIX

Continuity or Change:
Byzantium through the Years

THE most conspicuous feature of Byzantine civilization is often said to be conservatism, that is, traditionalism and immutability. "If one were to ask any educated modern Westerner," wrote Arnold Toynbee in his book on Constantine Porphyrogenitus, "what was the first idea that associated itself in his mind with the word 'Byzantine,' his answer would probably be 'conservatism.'"[1] Is this the opinion of the scholarly world as well as of the general public? In order to clarify this problem, we must distinguish two aspects. First, to what extent did Byzantine social and cultural life depend on the legacy of Antiquity? Second, did Byzantium in fact change in any considerable way in the course of its long existence? These two aspects do not necessarily coincide. Toynbee, in the book cited above, tried to distinguish between the lives, both spiritual and political, of the Hellenic and Byzantine worlds and referred to the antithesis between the Byzantine and Hellenic spirits, but he did not consider Byzantium itself as a developing and changing body.

There is no doubt that Byzantium was the heir of Antiquity. The people used the same language and learned by heart the same epics. The question to be answered is the extent and depth of this heritage. Can it be said that the keynotes of Byzantine culture were the same as those of Antiquity and that we are dealing with a continuous civilization which underwent only slight and insignificant changes? Two possible solutions to this problem can be proposed.

The first is to deny any basic distinction between the society of Antiquity and that of Byzantium. This point of view was maintained by Günter Weiss in the article mentioned in the introduction. After a thorough investigation, Weiss concluded that Byzantium underwent no serious structural alterations [*Strukturwandel*]. The position of the emperor, the work of the state officials, the functions of the church and the monks, and technology did not undergo any considerable change, though Weiss admitted that there were some insignificant changes [*unwesentlicher Wandel*] in the position of the ruling group, in urban life, in the rights of the dependent peasants, and in the social attitude toward trade. He nonetheless insisted that all the innovations of importance, including Christianity and feudalism, had already taken place within the framework of the Roman empire and that the transition to the medieval world was entirely different in Byzantium from that in the West because the eastern empire overcame the crisis and preserved the state bureaucratic machine.[2]

The same view, with some modifications, is found in Soviet historical research. Two versions of the so-called theory of synthesis are popular among Soviet historians. According to Sergej Averincev, Byzantine civilization was born out of a mixture or union of the cultures of the Near East—that is, of the Bible—and of the Greeks and Romans. Whereas the world of Greek philosophy and poetry was a cosmos, a regulated and symmetrical structure of space, the biblical world existed as a history, a current of time, carrying all things within itself. This antithesis reappeared in the differences between the Alexandrian and Antiochene schools, of which the first developed Hellenistic traditions and the second "the oriental ideology of the holy empire." Averincev finds the victory of the Alexandrian tendency over the Antiochene ideology in the seventh and eighth centuries.[3]

A different understanding of synthesis is found in the writings of Zinaia Udal'cova, the official representative of Soviet historical studies, who distinguishes three historical models for the development of so-called feudal society in various parts of Europe. The first postulates a feudal society that grew out of barbarian tribal organization, without any synthesis; the second, a feudal society that originated from a balanced synthesis between the feudal elements generated both within the framework of the slaveholding system and at the last stage of tribal organization; the third, a synthesis of the same elements from the crippled slaveholding system and prefeudal tribal organization in which the antique principles inherited from the Roman empire were predominant. The third type of social development, which came about without a barbarian conquest or any radical dissolution of the state machine, was characteristic of Byzantium.[4]

Three different approaches to the theory of continuity have thus been presented: one stressing the complete continuity of the Greco-Roman social structure through Byzantine history and the other two postulating a synthesis or mixture, in varying degrees, between either

Greco-Roman and barbarian social structures or between Greco-Roman and Near Eastern, or biblical, civilizations. It is important to stress that the theory of the Roman-barbarian synthesis suffers from the lack of evidence concerning barbarian influence on Byzantine civilization, where almost no trace of barbarian culture can be found.[5] The cultural shift in Byzantium must be attributed to influence from another direction.

The second solution to the question of the extent of the Byzantine debt to Antiquity is to acknowledge that Byzantium was different from the world of the Greeks and Romans. According to Vasilij Vasil'evskij, whose opinions were examined in the introduction, the Slavic ethnos, the village community, and Orthodox Christianity were the hallmarks of Byzantine society, distinguishing it from that of Antiquity, but it is now known that the Slavic settlements and village communities did not introduce any basic alterations into the social life or structure of Byzantium. We tried to show in the introduction that the concept of the village community as the principal buttress of Byzantine Orthodoxy and the national monarchy was rooted more in the Russian experience of the late nineteenth century than in Byzantine conditions. If this is true, Orthodox Christianity remains the only hallmark of the new state. This viewpoint is found especially in the above-mentioned *Reich der neuen Mitte*, by Herbert Hunger, for whom the formation of Byzantium was a transition from pagan to Christian beliefs and customs. Toynbee proposed a broader range of differences. For him the keynote of Byzantine spiritual life, in contrast to Hellenic rationalism, was in the administrative system as well as in religion. The resemblance between public administration of the Roman empire in the East and the Diocletianic-Constantinian system created at the threshold of the fourth century seemed to him superficial, and the special character of Byzantine social structure was expressed in the ceremonial act of *proskynesis*, in which a subject acknowledged his servitude to the emperor, and also in Byzantine dress, architecture, and visual art.

A more general attempt to underline the antithesis between Byzantine and ancient Roman societies can be found in the theory of Byzantine feudalism, but the theory is questionable and can be understood in at least two different ways. If feudalism is understood as a system of relationships within the framework of the ruling class, and as a kind of hierarchy and interdependence, it certainly appeared only toward the end of Byzantine development, and it can be considered not as a feature of Byzantine society at its height but only, as George Ostrogorsky argued, as a sign of its disintegration and collapse. If, on the other hand, feudalism is identified with any great landed property based on the exploitation of dependent peasantry, it can be found in the Roman period and brings us back to Weiss's concept. The introduction of feudal relations even in this sense has been dated quite differently. For Elena Lipšic, it came at the time of Constantine the Great, while for Sjuzjumov the victory of feudal landlords was delayed until a later period.[6] Owing to these confusions and ambiguities in the meaning of feudalism, it may be wise to avoid the term and to restrict discussion to the specific social and economic institutions, such as dependent relationships and the tenure of land in return for military service, to which collectively it refers.[7]

Even the most prominent exponents of the concept of the novelty of Byzantium recognize and emphasize the importance of Greco-Roman traditions. For Ostrogorsky, the main elements that determined the development of Byzantium were Roman political concepts, Greek culture, and the Christian faith, and he asserted the continuity of urban life in Byzantium.[8] Hunger frequently stressed the continuity of Greek culture in the Byzantine empire.[9] And although Sjuzjumov criticized the theory of synthesis, he nonetheless insisted that ancient cities and the Roman bureaucratic system were preserved in Byzantium.

The picture of the distinctive nature of the development of Byzantium is likewise far from absolute. Most of the scholars who recognized the antithesis, as Toynbee called it, between Greece and Byzantium considered that aside from its territorial reduction Byzantium hardly changed after the establishment of Christian society there. For other scholars, whether or not they considered Byzantium as the direct heir of the Roman empire or as a new Christian or feudal state, it remained stable and mighty until the eleventh century and then suffered from steady decline and decay, which are often attributed to foreign—that is, western—influence. Another kind of theory of limited development was presented by Hélène Ahrweiler, who argued that Byzantine society, especially Byzantine political ideology, was constantly changing but that this ideological shift took the form of a wave or sinuous curve, according to which Byzantine society oscillated between the poles of universalism or imperialism at one end and of nationalism or patriotism at the other.[10]

The study of the problem of Byzantine continuity is hampered by the consciously antiquated language of the sources. The Byzantines believed themselves to be the *Rhomaioi*, the Romans, and their capital, Byzantion, and country to be the Roman empire. In about the thirteenth century they may have begun to emphasize their Greek origin, but even then they considered themselves to be the direct descendants of Antiquity and the heirs of ancient language, law, and terminology. Was this Greco-Roman self-image correct? Byzantine terminology is a distorting mirror and a snare, according to Paul Lemerle, who wrote that "To represent Byzantium as unchanging for eleven centuries would be to fall into the trap that it itself prepared." [11] The Byzantines always exaggerated their dependence on Antiquity, and whether new forms and relations were concealed under antiquated legal terms must continually be questioned.

In several Greek acts from the archives of the monastery of Saint Mary of Messina the terms of Roman law were used to describe purchases of land. The vendor was said to hand over the "perfect and full [τελείαν καὶ πλοιρεστάτην] property," as it was called in a document of 1076/77. But the appearance of the new term *fief* [φίον] in a document dated 1175 suggests that new forms of tenure may have been hidden under the classical terminology.[12] Another example of the potentially confusing use of Roman legal terminology is found in the document of 1081 by which the monks of Kosmidion announced that they had granted "perpetual freedom from care" [ἀμεριμνία καὶ ἀφροντισία] to the monastery of the Amalfitans on Mount Athos in accordance with the *stipulatio Aquiliana* and *acceptilatio*,[13] which are Roman terms for extinguishing an obligation and operate as a special procedure, such as questions and answers, for bringing about the release of a debtor without the payment of his debt. In the act of 1081 they are used repeatedly in a distorted form and bear no relation to the content of the legal act described there, since the document refers not to a contract, stipulation, or release from debt, but to a transfer of ownership, and the scribe specifically mentioned that money was conveyed to the alienator in the presence of two *tabullarii*. The terminology of Roman law in this document has preserved none of its earlier meaning and is used only as a rhetorical shell, the purpose of which is to strike the imagination of the recipient and to emphasize the indelible links with the glorious past.

The legal code issued by Leo VI (886–912) and known by the name of *Basilika* is a representative example of Byzantine legal thought, into which old juridical texts were incorporated almost without alteration. Did this indicate that the social, political, and legal relations treated in these texts—and consequently in the *Basilika*—still corresponded to the realities of Byzantium in the ninth and tenth centuries? To some extent it did, for the *Basilika* regulated buying and selling, crimes and punishments, and lending and borrowing, with which Byzantine judges therefore dealt, or could deal, in accordance with the Roman law reflected, for better or worse, in the *Basilika*. Leaving aside these self-fulfilling correspondences, however, and turning to the social, political, or geographical information included in the *Basilika*, we can see that many of the offices no longer existed in the time of Leo VI, that some oriental provinces had long been lost by the Byzantines, and that the terms for the peasantry had become incomprehensible to the legislators of the ninth century. The work of Constantine VII, *On the Themes*, though different in content from the *Basilika*, is parallel to it in method, since Constantine inserted into his work, alongside the contemporary information, some authentic fossils. At this point it should again be emphasized that this attitude of the Byzantines toward their heritage was more than a learned game or an attempt to escape reality and that it had a deeper social significance as part of the constant search for stability in an unstable world. But this peculiarity still creates for the researcher the situation that Lemerle called a trap.

Before pursuing this point, however, we must define what we mean by continuity. Weiss, in the article cited above, asks whether there was "a transformation of the substantial forms and functional lines in the social relationship" and denies that any such transformation took place during the Byzantine period.[14] Since Weiss did not define what he meant by a "transformation of substantial form," we must attempt to do so. First, the classical structure from which Byzantium is said to have departed must be understood. Second, it must be decided whether the moment of change or transformation, if it existed, came at the time when the new social or ideological system was engendered or only when it emerged as a considerable power, and especially whether the transformation or radical change of Greco-Roman urban life occurred during the Hellenistic period, when the first signs of crisis appeared, or only in the seventh century A.D., when most of the ancient cities ceased to exist. With regard to religious life it must also be asked whether the transformation or radical change took place in the first century, when Christ preached to a little community on the outskirts of the Mediterranean world, or in the fourth century, when Christianity won the day. An analogous inquiry for modern history could be formulated on the question whether the crucial point in modern Russian history was the publication of the *Communist Manifesto* or the creation of Stalin's state in Russia. Third, we must examine impartially whether the transition from the ancient world to the medieval in the West was radically different from that in Byzantium or whether this process had common traits in both parts of the Roman empire. Did Weiss simply transplant from the West to the East the concept developed by Friedrich-Karl Savigny in the nineteenth century? Assuming that there was a caesura or break, in the West, can its main features be found in the early Byzantine age?

It seems to us, unlike Weiss, that there was a basic difference between the social system of Antiquity and that of Byzantium. Antiquity created a social structure that was based upon the city and had developed social links, above all of a municipal kind. Man was understood as—and to some extent really was—a citizen of an urban community and remained closely connected with his native city in spite of the territorial openness of the Roman empire. This principle, as we have said before, was not absolute. Many exceptions can be found, and social mobility was a common feature of society in Antiquity, but the municipal associations were nevertheless both close and strong. The number of Roman inscriptions dedicated to citizens offering grants to the city until the beginning of the third century would otherwise be incomprehensible.[15] A natural relation between man and power grew out of this situation, since both earthly and celestial power were understood by man as his own and as intimately linked with him. Even if in reality the society was far from being free, equal, or just, and the majority of the population were subject to authority, people were not really estranged from society and from power. The public character of the outward expression of culture, the recognition of man as the measure of all ethical and aesthetic values, the high value placed upon individual human behavior and on personal honor and responsibility toward the city or state, the harmony of ethical and aesthetic ideals, and the monism of the world outlook, either materialistic or idealistic, all were the result of this relation between man and power, as was the pluralism both of political forms—monarchy, aristocracy, and democracy being in theory equally admissible, and an ideal monarchy always appearing in republican garb—and of philosophical currents.

This system of social links decreased in the West so gradually that it is useless to try to fix a date for its final disappearance. No special significance can be attached to the traditional year 476, when the Herulian or Hun Odoacer was proclaimed king by his soldiers and deposed the nominal emperor in the West, the youth Romulus Augustulus. The ancient system of social links was replaced in the West by a new one of which the roots can be found in Germanic society, with its kindred, primitive retinue, and various bonds to landholding and village, as well as in the aristocratic society of the western Roman provinces. M. T. W. Arnheim has shown the difference between the structure of the ruling class in the western and the eastern parts of the empire in the fourth century. In the West, nobles were regularly appointed to high office, while the East continued to be governed by persons not of noble origin.[16] The amalgam of economic, social, and political forces in society, aristocratic in tone, distinguished the western half of the empire from the territories that later formed Byzantium. But it took centuries for this difference, reinforced by the invasions, growing linguistic divisions, and religious discord, to be recognized as an established contrast between the two different worlds.

It was not until the eleventh century that a recognizably distinctive system of social links was established in the West, where a new network of territorial, professional, and personal ties grew out of the disorder of the early Middle Ages. These ties can be divided into two groups, vertical and horizontal. The vertical ties—primarily, the system of vassalage and fiefs—united people of different social levels, while the horizontal ties formed links between socially equal strata by means of cooperative structures such as villages, guilds, and towns. Western society thus succeeded in creating the complicated system of small but tightly united microgroups that were able to resist superior authority in various ways and to defend their property and their liberty, in the medieval sense of restricted and graduated freedoms.

The development in the West helps to elucidate what was happening in the East, where the old system of social links disintegrated to a perhaps even greater extent than in the West.[17] Whereas the old nobility in the West tried to preserve the Roman traditions, its counterpart in the East was loose and incoherent. The western medieval system of social ties never developed in Byzantium, or, rather, existed only in an embryonic form. The looseness of Byzantine social links accounted for the type of individualism that we have mentioned before and of which the special features need therefore only be summarized.

The nuclear family became the most important social unit and was accompanied by "closed," as contrasted with "open," houses and clothes. Little by little the old public character of everyday life disappeared, and the town took on an increasingly medieval shape. Trade in the late Roman cities moved from the centrally located market squares to the main streets covered by porticos. In medieval Corinth and Cherson, to take the best-excavated centers, ateliers and shops were placed in private houses built on curved and narrow streets. Worship came to be conducted inside rather than outside religious buildings. The first step was to admit the people into the temple, which thus resembled a secular public building or basilica. The public processions that in the sixth century were still important in the Constantinopolitan church service decreased, the whole service was celebrated inside, and the central section of the liturgy was taken into concealed rooms and became inaccessible to the common people. As the axis of the temple space gradually became vertical rather than horizontal, the vision of the believer was carried upward from earth toward heaven, which was symbolized by the church dome. Books acquired the new shape of a codex, adapted for individual use, and cultural life as a whole, in contrast to the ancient public culture of the spoken word, began to be concentrated on the written word.

This loss of public life was associated with the estrangement of man from society and power. Eremitical life and celibacy were proclaimed as the ideals of human behavior. Power was regarded as an alien, superimposed force. Man stood alone, like a real hermit in the surrounding world, defenseless before both heavenly and earthly power and before God and emperor, whose omnipotence seemed to be unlimited and supernatural. The Byzantine cult remained focused on the image of God as the ruler of the world or Pantokrator, while western ritual and church decor came to be concentrated on the image of Christ, especially in His shape of a suffering man on a crucifix. The exact date and place of the replacement of the living and royal Christ on the cross by the dead and suffering man is uncertain, but after about the year 1000 the two images in East and West grew more and more different as the Byzantines clung to the traditional representations while the westerners moved along the road that culminated in the pathetic and terrible crucifixes of the late Middle Ages. May not this difference have been the result of or connected with the sociopolitical divergences of the two worlds?

The break with Antiquity also led to the disappearance of the harmony that had characterized the sphere of ethics and aesthetics in Antiquity. The development in Byzantium followed two main directions, of which the first could be called an adjustment to the circumstances of life in Byzantium, leading to what may be called the ethical concept of groveling. Kekaumenos showed this attitude in his worship of power and his belief that the ruler of Constantinople would always win. Submission and entreaty were the only possible attitudes toward power and the only hope of man. Out of this attitude grew the endless laudations of imperial power, which bore no relation to the real qualities of the ruler. The imperial virtues were understood not as personal qualities but as an eternal essence, tinted by the colors of semidivinity, and the fact that the reality of princes did not always correspond to the ideal was looked upon by the Byzantines with a mixture of bewilderment and a kind of subconscious triumph. From this position also arose the lack of fidelity, since loyalty to the ideal could sometimes be shown only by disloyalty to the person who for the time being wielded power. Treachery, which was of course not unknown either in Antiquity or in the medieval West, became in Byzantium a principle of human relationship.

In addition to fostering this attitude of groveling, Byzantine ethics and aesthetics also attempted to rise above the wicked reality and to establish an illusory world of unparalleled stability. The tendency is seen in the immutability of aesthetic norms, terminology and grammar, juridical tradition, and the like. The importance of clichés in Byzantine literature and visual art, the stubborn adherence to the antique heritage, the worship of *taxis*, or order, the tendency to depict human beings as statues, in majesty rather than action, were all specific marks of the Byzantine concept of cosmos and man. This tendency should not be attributed to lack of skill, to the decline of Greco-Roman artistic techniques, or to the simplifying influence of eastern or biblical traditions. It had social meaning and represented a tendency, as we have said, to construct in the artistic imagination a stable duplicate of the unstable reality, to escape the dangerous world, and to find secure peace among eternal values and images.

This brief survey of some of the principal features of the Byzantine world view allows us to look at Byzantium as a particular type of society, distinct both from Antiquity and from the society of the West. It was also distinct from its eastern neighbors, but much work still needs to be done on both the similarities and the differences between Byzantium and the Muslim and Arabic world.[18] Even more important are the differences between Byzantium and its northern neighbors, despite their common adherence to Orthodoxy. Robert Browning almost alone has tried to point out the divergences between the civilizations of Bulgaria and Byzantium, of which the common features have until recently been stressed by most scholars.[19] The social and political structure of ancient Russia was likewise very different from that of Byzantium. The Russian princes began consciously to use Byzantine political models and terms only later, when the tendency toward centralization prevailed in eastern Europe.[20] To call Byzantine society Christian is only half an answer, since western society, though different from Byzantium, was also Christian. Christianity accounts for only some of the distinctive features of Byzantium, which in our view are better covered by the concept of individualism without freedom.

If, then, Byzantium can be seen as the result of a transformation of ancient society, the second important question to be asked is whether Byzantine society changed in the course of time. Did *homo byzantinus* change and develop or did he remain the same? And can we, on the basis of this development, establish periods in the history of Byzantine civilization? By this we mean periods based not on the facts of political, military, or dynastic events but on changes in society itself, of which the stages do not always coincide with the divisions that are based on conventional history, since social and cultural developments are often not directly connected with dynastic changes and military endeavors. The defeat at Myriokephalon in 1176, the capture of Constantinople by the Latins in 1204, and even the fall of Constantinople to the Turks in 1453 were less obvious milestones in social and cultural history than is often supposed. The political regime and the official religion may have changed, but the mass of people continued to live and think and conduct their daily affairs in much the same way as they had before these great events, and basic changes in society and culture emerged only with the passage of time. Division into periods on the basis of such inner characteristics has therefore the practical drawback that the distinctions between social and cultural periods, in contrast with those based on rulers and battles, are often vague, because the transition from one to another could not be completed in a day or even in a year.

An initial period, running from the fourth century to the middle of the seventh, has been called protobyzantine by Paul Lemerle.[21] Its main features can be described as still within the framework of ancient history, since it was a transitional period, and the pace of transition differed in different branches of life. The empire at this time was a Mediterranean state facing the sea. The city remained the core of its social structure, even though some cities diminished in size or decayed.[22] Evelyne Patlagean has emphasized the contrast between the inner stagnation of urban life and the external prosperity of the polis, where building activity, a money economy, handicraft production, and trade all continued.[23] The continuous growth of the great estates has also been traditionally regarded as a feature of the epoch but has been questioned as a result of recent research. Excavations in northern Syria, for instance, suggest that during this period smallholders increased in importance at the expense of the great landowners, and Peter Brown has argued that the early monasteries in the East were supported less by great landowners or their dependent peasants than by "the more ambiguous, but no less influential, class of 'comfortable farmer.'"[24] In this connection it should be stressed that the surviving early census records from various places in western Asia Minor and the islands of the Aegean show that the average agricultural unit was very small and that even rich landlords owned scattered farms rather than single great estates, a phenomenon later referred to as *Streubesitz* in the West. It is quite possible that in the early fourth century most of the land in Egypt was in the hands of peasant proprietors.[25] Although great estates certainly existed from the fourth to seventh centuries, it is still uncertain whether these should be regarded as the remains of the old Roman latifundia or forerunners of the new features of seigneurial landownership. The private power of landowners at this time could have originated in Roman times, when the aristocracy possessed significant jurisdiction over the slaves and dependent classes on their latifundia.[26]

Certain elements that foreshadowed the future social structure and culture seem to have emerged during this period, but as a rule they took the form of a reaction against Antiquity rather than of distinctively new institutions. The study of these elements is often hampered by the existence of analogous, though not homologous, forms, such as the undeniable similarity between the late Roman colonate and medieval serfdom, which should probably be seen as two parallel responses to similar economic and political situations rather than as historically connected institutions, since the colonate vanished in most parts of the Mediterranean world before villeinage was established.

In this connection the peculiar character of the autocracy at this time needs special consideration. On the surface Justinian (527–65) seems to be omnipotent, and it is hard to draw a clear distinction either in essence or in ceremonial beween the protobyzantine monarchy and its later heirs. Weiss and other scholars have indeed insisted that the position of the emperor did not change between the late Roman period and the Byzantine.[27] Dvornik, on the other hand, called Justinian's concept of imperial power "Hellenistic ideology in Christian garb"[28] and argued that the Byzantine political system was made up of various elements, including Jewish, Greek, and Roman ideas of kingship. J. B. Bury developed the theory that the assumption of kingship by Heraclius (610–41) reflected Iranian influence,[29] thus recognizing that after Justinian there was an important shift in the political system, which he attributed to Iranian influence. Irfan Shahid has gone a step further, affirming that the assumption by Heraclius of the title of *basileus* marked a change in Roman constitutional history but that this change was the result less of outside influences, either Hellenistic or Iranian, than of factors inside the Empire.[30]

Imperial power in the times of Constantine and Justinian differed from the later Byzantine *basileia* not only in isolated constitutional features but also, more important, in an apparent lack of internal cohesion during the earlier period between imperial power and contemporary sociopolitical structures. The autocratic regime seems to have been superimposed on a society that was not yet ready for it. Thus the outwardly autocratic appearance of the state was in contradiction with the inner centrifugal forces. Not only were the familiar and effective political and ecclesiastical movements inconsistent with the principle of centralization, but the empire also had to face a constant tendency toward cultural regionalism and independence. After the fourth century the previous uniformity of everyday life began to diminish, and even cities took on more variegated shapes. The emergence of regional cultural particularity can be seen in the flowering of Syriac literature, in Coptic fine arts, in the science of Alexandria, and the jurisprudence of Berytus. Little by little, linguistic diversity grew stronger.

The inner political life of the empire was also far from uniform, as is shown by the continued activity of the Byzantine circus parties until the beginning of the seventh century.[31] This problem has long been discussed, and the conflict between the Blues and the Greens has been attributed by various scholars to economic, social, and religious factors as well as to the rivalry between the various regions of the city. None of these explanations is satisfactory, however,[32] and there has been a tendency recently to return to the old view that these parties were simply associations of sports fans, whose most important traits, according to Alan Cameron, were hooliganism and the system of claques and whose factions were not an expression of political divisions among the people. They were directly inspired by the excitement of the games themselves and were the natural escalation and culmination of the sporting rivalries between factions, whose riots normally took place in or near the Hippodrome.[33] While it is true that simple hooliganism was an important element in these riots and even in some church councils, particularly those at Ephesus, in 431 and 440, political, economic, and religious issues frequently became involved in the disturbances at the games. When the "prasinorum . . . et venetorum turbae" united against the Emperor Anastasius I in 512,[34] the cause of the riot was primarily religious; the Nika riot in 532 followed demonstrations against unpopular taxes and ministers; and the people who raised the hue and cry in the Hippodrome in 556 demanded an abundant supply of corn from the emperor.

The circus parties must be seen in a broader historical perspective. Even if they were not social, religious, or regional factions, they seem to have been a traditional element in the Roman world, going back to the early days[35] and aimed at the creation of a system both supported by and supporting a certain balance of forces. The competition of the parties was not simply the quarreling of claques of fans but also an indispensable element in the political structure. The two-faction system was a quasi-constitutional principle, apart from and contradictory to a normal autocracy, and it vanished in the seventh century, when the circus parties were transformed into a means of imperial ceremonial. Religious controversies were a prime source of political confusion and regionalism from the fourth century to the seventh. In some cases the emperors tried to suppress these disputes; in others they looked for a compromise, but they were faced with strong organizations that were capable of maintaining and defending their opinions. The regime, alleged to be autocratic, was too weak to suppress the struggling groups and to establish an obedient ecclesiastical instrument.

In summary we can say that the society of this early period was far from being internally uniform. It was an urban society that displayed a fractious and impassioned polity with a complex interplay of interests. The monarchical superstructure appears not as organic and arising from inside but as a feature imposed from above, perhaps in an effort to surmount the crisis that the Roman empire faced in the third century and that continued during the period of the barbarian migrations.

Another important feature of society at this time was monasticism, which arose in the third or fourth century and is often assumed to have existed without change throughout the history of Byzantium. Without hesitation Weiss included monasticism among the established elements of Byzantine social structure.[36] The issue is not a single one, however, since it is necessary to consider whether early and late Byzantine monasticism were homologous institutions, fulfilling the same social function, or whether they were only superficially analogous, with common traits and a common name, but differing in their essential character.

The early monastic communities offered a means of escape from secular society. The life of the first monks was based on a consistent denial of urban life with its conveniences and of traditional ethics and social relationships. A typical figure of this early period was the Egyptian monk Or, who inhabited a small hut in the desert, did manual work, and lived off wild herbs and roots. His long beard was a mark of his repudiation of conventional appearances.[37] Even when such monks intervened in worldly affairs, either as arbitrators in land disputes or as consultants of kings, their influence derived precisely from their noninvolvement in society and their contacts with higher, invisible powers.[38] When some groups of monks were organized within society, they formed communities like those reflected in the *Asketikon* of Basil the Great, but the members of these communities or *koinobia*, were in theory no less cut off from the world than the hermits, and Basil preserved, with certain restrictions, the antiurban ideal of poverty.[39] The early monks appear in the pages of contemporary sources as in constant conflict not only with traditional morality and behavior but also with the government and the official church, which attempted, as at the Council of Chalcedon in 451, to subordinate monks to the authority of the local bishop.

The early monasteries did not own big estates or control dependent peasants, and their members supported themselves by handicrafts and agriculture as a matter of economic necessity. Although some scholars have argued that the policy of Iconoclasm was inspired partly by an effort to abolish monastic property, the theory of the monastic principalities of the seventh and eighth centuries was created by Konstantin Uspenskij in the early twentieth century on the basis of later sources,[40] and subsequent research has shown that there is no real evidence for monastic principalities on the eve of the Iconoclastic strife.[41] Monasteries gradually became landed proprietors and received lavish imperial grants only after the ninth century. Their position in the Byzantine establishment thus changed from a form of social retreat into an indispensable element of the Byzantine ruling class. Monks functioned as the counselors of emperors and patriarchs, and many monasteries were founded by nobles as a convenient way of arranging and governing their lands and chattels.

The vigorous cultural activity of this early period has often been connected with eastern influences. According to Cyril Mango, however, the artistic vocabulary of the early sixth century, primarily as represented in the decoration of the church of Saint Polyeuktos at Constantinople, was not the result of "the slow infiltration coming from the East" among the highest strata of the ruling class and in the imperial government.[42] Whatever their origins, these new tendencies appear to have involved contradictory elements, since they were to some extent a genuine negation of Antiquity and yet coexisted side by side with clearly traditional forms. The intellectual and artistic creations of those days, however, though of great repute in the following centuries, found virtually no successors. Justinian's Saint Sophia, the masterpiece of early Byzantine architecture, was surrounded by many legends concerning the history of its building and was regarded as divine by posterity, but neither it nor the other churches of the sixth century, including Saint Polyeuktos, Saint Irene, and Saints Sergius and Bacchus, served as examples for later ecclesiastical architecture, which was based on the special type of church building that can be seen as a cross inscribed within a square.

The literary and intellectual activity of early times likewise remained practically without successors, in spite of its high reputation. John Chrysostom, for example, was held in unparalleled esteem in later tradition. His works were repeatedly copied and republished, and he was continually praised as the greatest Christian rhetor. Later Byzantine rhetoric did not follow his example, however, and his writings belong with late Hellenic rather than Byzantine literature, in the ranks of which he found no real successor. The most popular Byzantine rhetorical genres, such as progymnasmata, enkomia, and monodies, were not influenced by his works. The same is true of Procopius, whose works were known and used by Theophanes, who followed, however, different principles of writing history. Even church historiography in the fashion of Eusebius was not continued after this early period. And in the field of law, the code of Justinian, which dominated Byzantium and was considered a living body of legal rules, in fact served as a final summing-up of Roman law rather than as a starting point for a new period of legal history. The legislators of Byzantium continued to venerate the *Corpus juris civilis* long after they had abandoned its spirit.

The final representatives of the so-called pagan culture, in spite of their hostility to Christianity, nonetheless contributed greatly to the development of the political thought and aesthetics of their time. Walter Kaegi pointed out the contradictory elements in the political ideology of Zosimus, who criticized Constantine I while also declaring that Constantinople had become the greatest and most prosperous city of the empire, greater even than Rome itself.[43] Gilbert Dagron showed how another pagan writer, Themistios, developed the idea of internal links between the autocratic power of the emperor on earth and the omnipotence of God in heaven.[44] And Sergej Averincev emphasized that the Emperor Julian, known as the Apostate, stood at the cradle of Byzantine literary aesthetics.[45] These examples show that even in its contradictions this period produced innovations that contributed to the formation of Byzantium as it emerged in the seventh century.

The second period of Byzantine history started with the collapse of the empire in the middle of the seventh century, when urban life declined not only in the Balkans but also in Asia Minor. The city, the main unit of provincial society (see chapter 2), lost its significance, and even in Constantinople economic activity was limited. The decline of urban life has been connected by most scholars, particularly Clive Foss, with the invasions of the Slavs into the Balkans and of the Persians and Arabs into Asia Minor. These invasions appear to us to have been the precipitating factor rather than the basic reason for the economic and political downfall, since the real question is not why the cities were destroyed but why, after being destroyed in the seventh century, they did not recover till the tenth century and at that time arose in a new medieval shape.

The breakdown of the polis was followed by a decline in creative activity that encompassed both fine arts and literature. Relatively few churches are known to have been built in the seventh, eighth, and ninth centuries, and not many examples of painting from this period are known. The greatest Greek thinker and writer of the age, John of Damascus, lived outside the frontiers of the empire. Even the hagiographers, as Ihor Ševčenko has shown, were silent through the eighth century.[46]

It is hard to judge the character of other changes in view of the scantiness of the sources for this period. A simplification of social structure probably took place. The hereditary nobility and the urban upper class declined, and the importance of slavery and the dependent peasantry diminished. The population became more uniform than before, and vertical mobility dominated. The principal social groupings of this period were the shifting bureaucracy, the relatively uniform population of the countryside, if the Farmer's Law gives a true picture, and the privileged inhabitants of the imperial capital, since Constantinople acquired an unparalleled significance in the early Middle Ages, particularly as the provincial centers declined and the territory of the empire shrank.[47]

The imperial administrative machine was severely shaken although not destroyed by the barbarian invasions. Throughout the seventh century the central power was disrupted and weakened by family feuds. The fear for the throne was so pressing that the normal fate of a prince was to be executed or mutilated.[48] This period of interfamilial strife came to a climax in the bloody reign of Justinian II, which in many respects resembled the struggle for power in sixth-century Merovingian Gaul. At the beginning of the eighth century the commanders of local troops become the masters of the country, proclaiming and deposing emperors in rapid rotation. The ideology of the emperor was rivaled by the image of the holy man, and the worship of the ideal of the independent monk had to be destroyed before the omnipotent Byzantine monarchy could be established.[49]

The Iconoclasts prepared the way, but the full results were apparent only after the final restoration of icon worship in 843.

The character of popular movement also changed. During the preceding period the city was a natural center of popular violence, and the most important and frequent riots, aside from ethnic revolts such as the Samaritan rebellion in 529, took place in large cities such as Constantinople, Antioch, Alexandria, and Milan. In the eighth century little or nothing is heard about urban movements, and social violence was dominated by the themes and by local and military units. In 713 the Opsikion theme revolted against Philippicus-Bardanes; in 715 the Opsikians, this time with the support of the so-called Gothogreeks, compelled Anastasius II to withdraw from Constantinople; in 717 Leo III entered Constantinople with the support of the Anatolikon and the Armeniakon; and in 742 Artabasdes was backed in his revolt against Constantine V by the themes of Opsikion and Armeniakon. The two principal revolts of the ninth century, those of Thomas the Slav in 820–23, and of the Paulicians, who were put down in 872, likewise originated in the countryside.

The third period can formally be dated from the restoration of the worship of icons in 843, but this date is drawn from the history of the church rather than of economic and cultural affairs, where the revival, of which the first signs appeared at the end of the eighth century, reached its peak only after the middle of the ninth century. This period, which could be called that of the Byzantine establishment, coinciding with the encyclopedism described by Lemerle,[50] lasted until the beginning of the eleventh century. It was a time of slow economic revival in Constantinople and in the Aegean basin, including Thessalonica. While the revival of urban life was clear, the town regenerated in a new medieval shape. There was a marked tendency toward *taxis* in this period. Many books aimed at the establishment of order were written, including works on military tactics, *taktika* for officials, treatises on taxation, and collections of fragments concerning various political, geographical, diplomatic, and even agricultural purposes. A somewhat clumsy adaptation of Roman law was likewise made at this time.

The imperial government tried to establish strict control over society and the economy. An official social stratification was introduced, classifying the three groups of peasants, *stratiotai*-warriors, and the "powerful," in whose hands both wealth and the administration were concentrated. This is in contrast with the situation in the West, where there emerged at about the same time the classification of society into those who prayed, those who fought, and those who worked, though vestiges remained for some time of the earlier classifications into clerics, monks, and laymen or simply into the clergy and the laity. In Byzantium, the clergy did not constitute a separate order, and the "powerful" were distinct from the *stratiotai*. The *Book of the Eparch*, issued by Leo VI, was designed to control trade and industry. The Constantinopolitan corporations, or guilds, were placed under the sway of the imperial government. Leo VI's father, the Emperor Basil I, tried to abolish usury, and after Leo's death the government attempted to introduce controls over the sale of land. The legislation of the tenth century attempted to apply the principle of the just price by allowing only limited sales outside the village community and set up a sophisticated hierarchical system in order to regulate the preference [προτίμησις] in purchasing allotments. Peasants were bound to their fiscal assessments and obliged to pay taxes for fugitive neighbors or even for abandoned lots.

These controls over trade and industry and over the sale of land and the freedom of peasants were the first step toward proclaiming that the whole imperial territory was the property of the emperor. The Byzantine government, apparently under the influence of the norms of Roman law, never issued a law of this kind but tacitly assumed the right of confiscation. Neither the powerful nor the monasteries could escape imperial control, which often led to the forcible exchange and even seizure of estates by the government. In contrast to Justinian, who devised various stratagems in order to force people to sell him the land on which to build Saint Sophia,[51] Basil II (976–1025) confiscated without scruple the immense estates of Eustathius Maleinos in the provinces of Charsianon and Cappadocia.[52]

This was also a period of cultural unification. The formative period of Christian worship was over, and a unified liturgy was introduced alongside the unification of church building and decor. A high-ranking imperial official, Symeon Metaphrastes, drew up a collection of uniform Lives of the saints, which formed an important element in the church services. The tendency to impose order embraced the slowly developing scholarly world, as well as administrative and ecclesiastical spheres of human activity. Some scholars have referred to this period as the Macedonian Renaissance, but its main task, as has been seen, was to gather and set in order, not to re-express creatively, the remnants of its classical heritage. The ninth and tenth centuries thus saw the transmission of manuscripts in minuscule and the creation of various anthologies and lexicons, including the *Myriobiblon* of Photius and the series of reference-books issued at the court of Constantine VII. It was in this period that the Byzantine autocracy finally came into harmony with the social and cultural uniformity of the empire, where the social atmosphere of individualism without freedom prevailed and where the nuclear family was the most prominent form of social grouping.

The following period can be labeled the Byzantine pre-Renaissance and covers the eleventh and twelfth centuries and perhaps also the first decades of the thirteenth century. It was marked by two outstanding socioeconomic traits: the development of new provincial towns and the predominance of the new aristocracy. Both these forces took root in the second half of the tenth century, but their growth coincided with the first emperors of the Comnenian dynasty, and they were among the main supports of the Comnenian rule.

The alliance of medieval towns and the new aristocracy, which seems strange to western medievalists, arose from the struggle against the economic and political system established by the middle-Byzantine autocracy and against the traditional type of control over economic and social life. The main internal problem of the empire was not feudal disintegration, as Fedor Uspenskij and his successors thought, but the crisis of the traditional bureaucratic system, which could no longer fulfill its function. The eleventh century saw a violent struggle between the traditional monarchy and the new forces,[53] during which Constantinople retained its economic and cultural monopoly; but in the twelfth century, some of the provincial cities began to emulate the capital successfully, and military nobles of provincial origin penetrated the Comnenian ruling elite.

The significance of the short and dramatic reign of Andronicus I (1183–85) has been variously assessed by scholars. For some he was a peasant king and a supporter of democracy, while others see him as a cruel tyrant. He seems to us to have been determined to destroy the two main supports of the Comnenian regime, the military aristocracy and the provincial towns. He broke, if he did not utterly destroy, the alliance of the Comneni and related families, which directed the economic and political revival of the twelfth century, and he brought the economic life of the provincial cities, which suffered more from Andronicus than from enemy raids, to the verge of collapse. This opened the way for the reestablishment under the Angeli, at the end of the twelfth century, of the traditional powers, especially the civil functionaries who had been pushed aside by the Comneni and who now again were leaders among the ruling elite. Even the eunuchs, typical of the previous period and despised under the Comneni, reappeared in the fore.

This was the situation on the eve of 1204. The capture of Constantinople by the crusaders must be attributed not only to the military predominance of the West but also to the sociopolitical weakness of Byzantium and the revival of the traditional bureaucratic regime, rather than to any feudal disintegration. The bureaucracy, still effective in the early eleventh century, was unable to keep up with the progress in other areas, and the Comnenian attempt at adjustment failed. The loss of Constantinople, however, and the destruction of the bureaucratic center of the empire ultimately proved to be a source of strength for the Greeks, who established out of the ruins of the empire a number of more or less independent principalities which became almost up to date by following the main lines of the Comnenian reforms, flourished economically, and created a strong system of defense against their neighbors to the west and east.

The ideological strife of the so-called pre-Renaissance age was penetrated by strong attacks, originating with different groups, on the traditional system. From inside the system, Symeon the Theologian criticized the strict *taxis*, fought against extreme ecclesiastical uniformity, and stressed the idea of individual salvation. The curious alliance of the towns with the new nobility was reflected in the half-historical and half-panegyrical work of Attaleiates, who idealized the chivalric nobility and took an interest in urban history. Yet another current directed against traditional society came from the intellectuals, whose ranks included not only the despised imperial panegyricists but also some severe critics of imperial power. Prominent Byzantine historians, such as Psellos and Choniates, came to the unexpected conclusion that the ruler himself was corrupted both morally and physically by imperial power and that the lack of an aristocracy was one of the most serious problems of contemporary Byzantine society.

The issue of human behavior was hotly discussed at this time, and a new image of man was shaped. The new ideal of the noble, military, and chivalric hero penetrated literature and to some extent also visual art. The new topic of love was introduced, sometimes interwoven with spiritual vision, and sometimes associated with indecent themes, obscene language, descriptions of physical functions, and rude laughter. Even more important, the traditional epic approach to human actions, represented as white and black, began to give way to a more complicated picture of human beings. These developments show many parallels with those in the West that have been summarized in the chapter entitled "From Epic to Romance" in R. W. Southern's well-known book *The Making of the Middle Ages*, and much work needs still to be done on the cross-cultural intellectual and literary influences, especially in the twelfth century.

Vernacular literature was born at this time and a new social type of professional literati appeared just when the genres especially connected with the traditional order, such as hagiography and hymnography, virtually died out. The attitude toward the heritage of Antiquity changed from one of simply collecting to an active effort of appropriation and from the transmission of manuscripts to a scholarly commentary on texts. A kind of new theology was developed on the basis not only of the authority of Holy Scripture and the church fathers but also of rationalistic logic. A contemporary of Alexius I, Eustratios of Nicaea, proclaimed that Christ Himself used Aristotelian syllogisms in His speeches.[54] In theological discussions Byzantine philosophers followed some of the same paths as Abelard in the West and began to come into touch with their western colleagues, who were themselves taking a new interest in the works of Origen, John of Damascus, and other Greek fathers.

In summary, this period can justifiably be called a pre-Renaissance if the term *renaissance* is taken to mean not simply a repetition or imitation of ancient Greek and Roman ideas and images but a re-expression of classical ideas and images in the form in which they served as the background for modern civilization. Byzantium, like Italy, was engaged in rebuilding its culture on new principles, but unlike Italy Byzantium did not succeed, since the Comnenian pre-Renaissance did not lead to a full renaissance.

Byzantium was faced with a dilemma after the Latin conquest of 1204. It might have developed into a series of small and independent principalities, towns, and islands of mixed Greek, Latin, and Slavic population with developed agriculture and prosperous industry and trade. Michael Angold has described the form of government that came into being in the thirteenth century as a household government, that grew out of developments that were already apparent in the twelfth century,[55] and survived in spite of the setback caused by the despotic and antiaristocratic regime of Andronicus I. The defeat of 1204 may indeed have delayed the progress of these tendencies. The development of the household government in Byzantium was interrupted, however, less by the Ottoman invasion than by the suicidal success of 1261, when the Greek army from the Nicaean empire entered Constantinople and the Byzantine government returned to a "great power" policy, for which it lacked both the human and the material resources. The old ethnos and language remained, but Byzantium developed a new social system. The upper hand belonged to the lay and ecclesiastical landlords in the fourteenth century, when in the West the urban population rose to predominance, at least in economic affairs.[56] The weak effort to establish a communal movement in Thessalonica in 1342–47 was suppressed, and the Byzantine tradesman could not live with the triple threat of native landlords, Italian rivalry, and Ottoman inroads.

A Renaissance society could hardly have developed under these circumstances, but some features of Renaissance behavior can be found in the late Byzantine empire, including scholarly circles with philosophical conversations, an interest in geography and engineering, and a search for new information about both the Latin West and the Muslim East. Byzantium never achieved the dialectical method of thinking that characterized the Italian mentality of the fifteenth century, however, and its world view, owing in part to political misfortunes, was tragic in comparison with that in Italy. The opinion of Theodore Metochites that the country's cultural potential was exhausted and that all problems had already been resolved (see chapter 5) was typical of the outlook of late Byzantine intellectuals.

Byzantium appears in this light as less traditional than it is depicted by many historians. Certain features in its social structure and culture were traditional; others followed a sinuous curve of appearance and reappearance; still others, including some of the most important, changed and developed. This development resembled in many respects that of western Europe. We can find in Byzantium a break between the late Roman and middle Byzantine periods, a regeneration of urban life in a new and distinctively medieval shape, elements of a hierarchy of personal dominance and dependence, and even pre-Renaissance traits of cultural life. But it was the medieval autocracy, based on an individualistic social organization, that determined the special character of the Byzantine world and hindered its development along the same lines as that of the West.

CHAPTER SEVEN

The Ambivalence of Reality

THE term *ambivalence* has become fashionable. Although many terms used by scholars remain only words, without promoting the perception of reality, ambivalence is a word of another kind. While it is not a new word, it reflects a new attitude toward Byzantine society and represents a new idea. Hans-Georg Beck, in his lecture at the Byzantine Congress in Athens, showed the fertility of this idea.[1] But what does it mean? In order to clarify this concept, we must again turn to historiography. The linear, one-sided perception of the past that typified Byzantine studies in the nineteenth and early twentieth centuries was closely tied to the idea that historical development is purposeful and is directed by the spirit of history or by the interests of a particular class or of a group of important historical figures. In all these cases, the interests were considered to be conscious and clear-cut: the spirit of history, great men, or classes knew in what direction they had steered mankind.

Consider the traditional view of the character of Basil II (976–1025), which is perfectly summarized by Romilly Jenkins. Basil saw, according to Jenkins, how much influence was wielded by military magnates and understood that under such conditions "the legitimate emperor could never be master of his own soldiers and his own revenues." He therefore built a "noble structure in order to hold in check by his own power the internal forces which threatened disruption," and he subjected the nobility "to the iron discipline of his imperial military machine."[2] The character of the same emperor was depicted differently by Gennadij Litavrin, who saw Basil not simply as a man of unswerving resolution, practical talent, and physical toughness but above all as a staunch and faithful leader of the high-ranking Constantinopolitan officials. Acting in their interests, Basil forced the provincial aristocracy to surrender and subjected the clergy to his will.[3] In the first portrayal Basil himself knew what had to be done; in the second he acted for the upper class of the capital, which knew what had to be done; but in both the results were attained by a clear and conscious effort.

Which portrayal is correct? Was the structure built by Basil really as noble as Jenkins thought and Basil himself is said to have believed? Recent research has shown that about a quarter of the aristocratic families that played such a great part in the political life of the following two centuries arose during Basil's reign, which suggests that his policies may have damaged the military aristocracy less than was once believed.[4] The personal policy of Basil II and the social policy of the bureaucracy may have sought to weaken the nobility, but these tendencies were effective only on the surface of social life, below which there was a growth in the political significance of aristocratic families rather than a decline.

Recent historical research, moreover, perhaps under the influence of psychology, has begun to make clear the importance of unconscious tendencies and of actions that are without personal or social gain and may even be self-destructive. Wars could be purposeless, either real conflicts interwoven with pure hooliganism or political actions fitted into the traditional role of *homo ludens*. This does not mean that human activity was always or exclusively without meaning or consciousness, but the role of the irrational in human culture must be kept in mind.

The process of history seems less purposeful now than it did some years ago. From a simplistic point of view, every significant event was necessarily followed by a sequel and was connected with its cause by the ties of necessity. The spirit of history thus led mankind from slavery to freedom; the feudal lords tried to despoil the peasantry; and even Caesar had no choice but to gain imperial power. He carried from his youth a marshal's baton in his bag. This edifice of causality is now shaken, and an effort is being made to understand the complexity of the past, stressing that the way toward a glorious future did not seem inevitable and that leading personalities did not necessarily have clear aims, either exalted or base. We can no longer afford to declare lightheartedly that one event was progressive and another retrograde, even though we may sympathize with an autocratic regime or, on the contrary, with disorder and riots. Owing largely to modern experience, many events of the past are now seen to have had more than one consequence, sometimes to have involved contradictory elements, can be variously viewed, and were—to use the aforementioned new word—ambivalent.

Ambivalence was not a peculiar attribute of Byzantium. Poetic apperception of the world is constantly opposed to common morality, with its supposedly clear and simple distinctions between good and evil. A single example, drawn from English Renaissance literature, Spenser's Sonnet 21, will demonstrate the point:

> Was it the work of Nature or of Art,
> Which tempered so the feature of her face,
> That pride and meekness, mixt by equal part,
> Do both appear t'adorn her beauty's grace?

The mixture of opposite qualities "by equal part" is the essence of the notion of ambivalence. Since poetic apperception usually deals with the exceptional, Spenser naturally recognized the ambivalent character of rare beauty and of the exceptional. In Byzantium ambivalence was less used as a vehicle of poetic expression and was a normal trait of reality. It was found at every step and was realized with unparalleled consistency in the various spheres of Byzantine social, political, and cultural life.

While we have touched on this idea in earlier chapters, it is now time to gather the scattered evidence concerning this aspect in order to understand how deeply Byzantium was permeated by signs of ambivalence. In the sphere of economic life we have already seen in chapter 2 the contrast between individualistic modes of production and centralized forms of appropriation. The ambivalence of the Byzantine economy was expressed in the union of barter with a monetary system, which was itself ambivalent, since currency in Byzantium was a means of accumulation as well as a medium of exchange. The fact that hoards of coins were gathered and that coins were used as items of personal adornment shows that their monetary function had disappeared or had at least declined. Coins were also a tool of imperial propaganda and as such had a particular significance apart from their economic function. We have also discussed the ambivalent attitude of the Byzantines toward their geographical environment. Mountains were both dreadful and holy; the sea was both threatening and attractive. The surrounding world seemed to be confined within the narrow limits of a village or monastic community and at the same time to be boldly open, since it included countries populated by marvelous monsters and holy men.

The ambivalence of social relationships was even broader. Historians have long asked whether Byzantine society was aristocratic and have until recently given two seemingly contradictory answers. One position was formulated by Pavel Bezobrazov, who insisted that the

Byzantine Empire had neither an aristocracy of noble origin nor a recognized nobility with strict privileges.[5] Rodolph Guilland, on the other hand, argued that the Byzantines throughout their history made a clear distinction between the old hereditary nobility and the nobility of rank and title.[6] It would be wrong to assume that one view is correct and the other false, since both reflect a part, but only a part, of the truth and therefore are unbalanced and misleading. The contradiction is real as well as historiographical, and its solution must be sought in evidence both of chronological diversity and of structural ambivalence. The concept of nobility was used in a variety of senses in both East and West in the early Middle Ages and changed in the course of time.[7] It was only gradually that the familiar features of succession and inheritance, occupational rules, chivalric culture, and class symbols, such as coats of arms, emerged as characteristic features of the nobility as a distinct group in society.[8]

To look first at the diversity in time and space, it is possible that small landholders came to the fore and the old aristocracy disappeared in the East in the seventh century[9] and even that the landed wealth and local influence of the aristocracy became concentrated in the West at a time when the East remained more highly urbanized.[10] It can in any case be assumed that there was hardly any hereditary nobility in Byzantium from the seventh century to ninth. A significant comparison in this respect can be made between the historians Theophanes, at the beginning of the ninth century, and Nicetas Choniates, on the threshold of the thirteenth century. Theophanes in his account of the events from 717 to 811 mentions ninety-seven people without second or family names and only twenty-two with family names, most of which are nicknames or sobriquets, such as Michael Lachanodrakon, Vardan Turk, or Leo "called" Kulukes, rather than real family names. Except for the two brothers, Nicetas and Sisinnios Triphyllioi, the same sobriquet is never applied to two different persons. Choniates, on the contrary, mentions only twenty-three people without second names, including some eunuchs or foreigners, and 105 with family names, many of whom belonged to the same families. The same distinction is found on Byzantine seals, of which the majority from the eighth century to the tenth are without patronyms, while names with patronyms are found on many seals of the eleventh and twelfth centuries.[11] The significance of this evidence is open to debate, and the lack of patronyms may be owing to differences in the organization of society, and especially the existence of families seen as clans rather than as genealogical trees, but it suggests that society began to redefine itself in several important ways sometime in the tenth and eleventh centuries, especially in the direction of lineal families with known names.

Several texts of the tenth century show that the Byzantines considered the nobility at that time as a new and unstable institution. The Emperor Leo VI (886–912), in his *Tactica*, for example, emphasized that the *strategoi* should be appointed on the basis not of their ancestry but of their deeds and achievements and that the *strategoi* from families not of noble origin fulfilled their duties better.[12] Even more important is the Novel of 996 of Basil II, who expressed surprise and indignation that several families had maintained a high position for seventy or a hundred years.[13] These relatively short periods of prominence, as well as the indignation of the emperor, are signs that the new Byzantine aristocracy was becoming established in the tenth century. The beginning of the custom of using patronyms at this time is another sign of the increasing consolidation of an hereditary nobility.

The Byzantine aristocracy was structurally ambivalent as well as chronologically diverse, since a constant vertical movement of social life coexisted with the hereditary possession of power, wealth, and reputation.[14] There were many examples of upward social mobility, not least of them the Emperor Basil I (867–86), who was born in a peasant family, earned his living as a groom in a rich household, and became famous after his victory over a Bulgarian wrestler. Subsequently he rose rapidly, and in 867 he ascended the throne. Byzantium had no law or custom defining nobility and regarded all subjects as in theory the servants and serfs of the emperor. The position of every Byzantine magnate was unstable, as the story of Maleinos clearly shows (see chapter 6). At any time his career might be ended, his estates forfeited, he himself flogged or exiled. Whether this threat was in fact realized, it existed, hanging over the heads of the Byzantines and engendering a sort of universal Kekaumenian fear. Nonetheless, the aristocracy was a real presence in society from at least the tenth century. A few families, especially those of the military aristocracy, maintained a high position from the reign of Basil II until the end of the twelfth century, and under the Comneni a specific kind of aristocracy developed out of the families related to the imperial house. Even the Latin capture of Constantinople in 1204 did not entirely destroy the nobility, since at least ten of the sixteen noble families listed by George Pachymeres in the thirteenth century had been prominent during two preceding centuries.[15]

Analogous ambivalence can be seen in the Byzantine concept of property, concerning which there are two apparently opposite historical views. According to the first, Byzantine ownership of land was regulated by the norms of Roman law, and the holdings were regarded as in the absolute dominium of the owner, who had the full right to sell, bequeath, lease, exchange, or otherwise convey the property.[16] According to the second view, land in Byzantium belonged to the emperor or to the government, which permitted its subjects to cultivate it on lease in return for a sort of rent and was entitled to take it back if the rent was not paid.[17] This direct or eminent domain was shown by the rights of the emperor or government to evict the holders of land without trial, on the basis of administrative decisions only, or to compel them to exchange or cede their holdings and also by the control of the emperor over private allotments, especially over the relation of the real size of the holdings and number of dependent peasants to the numbers assessed in the government inventories. A solution to this apparent contradiction can again be found in the concept of the ambivalence of Byzantine property, in its contradictory unity, and in the curious combination of private ownership with the imperial direct domain, which could at any moment cancel the effectiveness of private ownership.

The structure of Byzantine landed property became even more complex as the idea of hierarchical and conditional landownership gradually became established, not in the law but in practice, which was dominated by the principles of absolute ownership of the individual and the imperial *dominium directum*. Since the end of the last century scholars have considered the Byzantine *pronoia* to be a benefice bestowed by the emperor as a conditional property by right.[18] This opinion has been questioned in some recent works on the grounds that until at least the thirteenth century the *pronoia* seems to have been a grant of a quota of state taxes rather than a benefice in land.[19] Some embryonic forms of conditional or relative property, however, are found in the eleventh and twelfth centuries.[20]

Even the nature of Byzantine imperial autocracy was ambivalent. At first sight it appeared to be all-powerful, since the Byzantines saw in the imperial power the terrestrial image of the omnipotence of God. The emperor was seen as a representative of the heavenly Lord and as a ruler crowned by God, and he was surrounded by sumptuous ritual and semidivine cult.[21] The emperor's power was in theory unrestricted, since he was the supreme commander, senior judge, head of government, and sole legislator. He possessed full executive powers over all people, could put anybody to death without trial, and could arrest, banish, discharge or demote from office, mutilate, blind, take real and personal property, and impose divorce. No one was so important or so rich as to be beyond the reach of the emperor's hand.

Nobility, wealth, rank, or reputation was no defense against the imperial will. There were at the same time, however, striking limitations on imperial power in Byzantium. Since there was no familial succession to the throne, imperial power was never considered as belonging to a particular family, thus automatically excluding all outsiders from accession to the throne. This was also the practice in the West among the barbarian tribes in the early Middle Ages, but it was later replaced by succession within a family and by strict hereditary succession. The peculiarity of Byzantium in this respect was noted by several neighbors of the empire, including the Bulgarian writer John the Exarch, who mentioned the Bulgarians and Khazars, but not the Byzantines, as peoples with a strict order of succession to the throne.[22] The *Life* of Constantine the Philosopher says that the Khazars criticized the Byzantines for not choosing their rulers according to the principle of blood and kindred.[23] These observations took on a hyperbolical, almost fantastic cast in the work of Marvazi, writing at the end of the twelfth century, who claimed that Byzantine rulers who failed to achieve their ends were deposed and other persons elected in their stead.[24] To overcome this lack of a regular method of succession, a Byzantine emperor had to proclaim a coemperor during his lifetime and thus secure the throne for his would-be heir. The legitimist sentiment strengthened in the eleventh century, and the throne was occupied after 1081, with some brief exceptions, by members of four aristocratic families, the Comneni, Angeli, Lascarids, and Palaeologi, but even then no law of succession was issued, and the way to the throne remained open to anyone except a eunuch or a monk.

As a result, there was an extraordinary instability of individual imperial power. Half the Byzantine emperors were forcibly removed from power. Except for the hundred-year domination of three members of the Comnenian dynasty from 1081 to 1180, the reigns of Byzantine rulers tended to be short. Beck calculated that whereas during the thousand-year history of the German empire in the West there were about fifty rulers from five noble families, Byzantium during its thousand-year history was ruled by about ninety emperors from thirty different families.[25]

Another restriction on imperial power in Byzantium was the conservatism or traditionalism of the Byzantine administration. The burdensome ceremony, of which the rhythm and order were thought to reflect the harmony of the celestial sphere, made most of the emperors into puppets of ritual, and the cult that was intended to divinize the emperor and raise his authority in reality limited the area of independent activity. At the same time, the silent and stubborn resistance of the bureaucratic machinery prevented the emperors from making serious changes in the existing system. Even the brightest minds, such as Michael Psellos, considered conservatism to be an asset in an emperor and a reforming tendency to be a liability. Psellos wrote that Isaac I (1057–59) "wanted to change everything and hastened to trim away the Empire which had grown up for many years." "Had somebody," he continued elsewhere, "kept a tight rein on Isaac, he would have run through the *oikumene* winning victories everywhere, and none of the emperors of the past could have emulated him"; but although the Lord had taken six days to create the world, Isaac could not put up with the slightest delay.[26]

The ambivalence in the nature of imperial power is shown by the contrast between the omnipotence of the emperor when dealing with individuals, over whom he exercised complete power, and the weakness of his position as a crowned head. Put another way, it could be said that Byzantine imperial power was omnipotent when it was conceived as the collective will of a mobile ruling class but that the power of individual emperors was restricted and weak.[27] A significant sign of this ambivalence is the so-called caesaropapism, a term that was invented by scholars of the nineteenth century to describe the absolute and unrestricted control of the emperor over the church, including matters usually reserved for ecclesiastical authority.[28] It implies that the Byzantine church functioned as a department of the government, and André Guillou consequently describes the church as an element of the Byzantine administration, following finances, justice, diplomacy, and the army.[29] The theory of caesaropapism was used to express the hostility of the West toward eastern Christianity, since it emphasized the subjugation of the eastern church to secular authority and was contrasted with the theory of separation of ecclesiastical and secular affairs that prevailed in the West after the eleventh century. The caesaropapistic theory has been sharply criticized, partly in connection with the Orthodox tendency to defend the Byzantine church, but this criticism has tended to be superficial and theoretical, stressing that the Byzantine emperor never intended to function as a supreme priest and that the Caesar had no desire for the rights of the pope. The real core of the problem lies not in this formal distinction, but in the question to what extent, if at all, the emperor in fact controlled the church.

The answer given to this question in most recent works sounds rather elaborate and differs from both the western and the Orthodox points of view. In the words of Deno Geanakoplos, the emperor possessed a "gradation of powers, from the absolute to the virtually nonexistent, in the various spheres of the church-state complex."[30] There were many signs of imperial control over the church. The emperor had the authority to appoint the ecumenical patriarch of Constantinople, for instance, and in many cases forced patriarchs to abdicate. He both summoned and presided over ecumenical councils. The church was under the jurisdiction and tax administration of the emperor, who could confiscate ecclesiastical estates and property. As a sacred personage, the emperor had various liturgical privileges, including imperial coronation and unction, which emphasized his mysterious prominence and corresponded to his monopoly of the colors gold and purple, with his ritual progresses and exits, and with the quasi-celestial atmosphere of the imperial Great Palace. This imperial cult, however, as has been seen, in fact limited rather than enhanced imperial authority, which was restricted to the sphere of the inner aspects of ecclesiastical life. Only a few emperors seriously tried to influence the dogmas of the church and as a rule without success. Justinian leaned toward Monophysitism, perhaps in order to curry favor with the Christians in the eastern parts of the empire, and Manuel I Comnenus (1143–80) tried to placate the Muslims by modifying the wording of the so-called anathema of the God of Muhammad, which immediately evoked opposition in the church and exposed the emperor to the charge of heresy. Many imperial attempts from the thirteenth century to the fifteenth to attain union with the western church failed, moreover, in spite of the hope that the union would provide means of resisting the Ottoman threat.

Here again, therefore, is an ambivalent situation. Byzantine emperors were both omnipotent and powerless with regard to the church. They were signally successful insofar as they dealt with ecclesiastics or churches as individual subjects, but they were practically powerless whenever they had to cope with the church as an institution.

The effect of Byzantine autocracy on the structure of society was also contradictory and ambivalent. This issue has been particularly debated by historians, whose views of the imperial effect on Byzantium have changed many times and in each instance have obviously been colored by general historical, philosophical, and political principles of various scholarly schools of epochs. In order to clarify the problem, we shall reject vague ethical evaluations and avoid the extremes either of proclaiming that the monarchical power was the chief pillar of Byzantium or of condemning it for all the defeats and misfortunes of the empire. We shall restrict ourselves to the more limited and concrete question of the role of Byzantine imperial power in the interplay of centralizing and decentralizing forces. This question may seem at first to be unnecessary and even perverse, since the imperial authority has always been assumed to favor centralization, and a powerful monarchy, whether praised or blamed, has always been considered a bulwark against the rising decentralization of feudal elements.

The tendency to identify Byzantine imperial power with centralization, though simple and seductive, is biased. The idea that any kind of decentralization is bad derives from the German historiography of the nineteenth and twentieth centuries, which was influenced by contemporary political goals.[31] Stalin's idealization of Ivan the Terrible followed the same model. But this view fails to take sufficiently into account the geographical, social, and political realities of the medieval world in which Byzantium existed.

The Byzantine empire represented the principle of centralization within the decentralized, personalized, and tribal world of the Middle Ages. The other medieval empires, including those of Persia, the Caliphate, the Seljuq Sultanate of Rum, and Charlemagne, were all relatively short-lived. Even the so-called Holy Roman Empire, which lasted as long as that of Byzantium, lacked most of its centralized institutions and centralizing tendencies. This special situation had significant advantages, above all in the efficiency of taxation and the extent of military reserves. In the eyes of both western and Arab authors of the eleventh and twelfth centuries, Byzantium was an empire of great wealth and immense armies. This situation had naturally changed as Byzantine history neared its end, when the fifteenth-century chronicle of Tocco counted Greek troops in tens and Ottoman armies in tens of thousands.[32] The Emperor John V Palaeologus (1341–91) suffered the humiliation of being in effect held captive by Venice when he lacked money to return to Constantinople and to pay his debts to the city.[33] Until at least 1204, however, Byzantium controlled, by contemporary standards, large revenues and enormous armies, which were reckoned in the sources of the ninth and tenth centuries as being between ten thousand and a hundred thousand.[34]

The disadvantages of this situation need further study.[35] A centralized government in the Middle Ages was unable to keep in touch with its provinces. The enormous distances of the empire, which were doubled by the difficulties of traveling in a mountainous country and by the increasing dread of travel by sea, made the links between the capital and the provinces weak and tenuous. It took a long time for information to reach Constantinople or for an order to be received on the frontiers. The disadvantages of far-flung connections were aggravated by the instability of the political situation. Provincial officials were slow to react to dangers and out of fear of the central authority often preferred waiting for imperial orders to acting on their own initiative.

When Manuel I sent Andronicus Kontostephanos with an army against the Hungarians, according to Choniates, he prescribed not only the military tactics to be used but also the precise terms of engagement, type of weapon, and disposition of the troops. Just as Andronicus was facing the Hungarian army and preparing his soldiers for battle, moreover, a messenger arrived from the emperor with a letter declaring that the day, July 6, 1167, was unpropitious and prohibiting an engagement. But it came too late, and without a word Andronicus concealed the imperial message and ordered the attack.[36] Fortunately he won and was thus saved from an awkward situation, but Choniates' story clearly shows the dependence of a Byzantine commander-in-chief on the central authority even when this authority was far from the battlefield.

The information sent by provincial governors and their staffs to Constantinople was frequently influenced by private interests and was therefore inaccurate, false, or biased. A typical example of such selfish provincial administrators was the governor of Thessalonica David Comnenus, who consciously sent to the capital doctored information concerning the siege of the city by the Normans in 1185 and by so doing contributed to the defeat of the Byzantine forces.

Another weakness of a centralized government in the Middle Ages was the high cost of supporting the imperial court, the ritual of the church and, above all, the enormous armies. Whereas in medieval England the principal object of criticism was the system of justice, in Byzantium the main targets of public hostility were the characteristic figures of the tax collector and the usurer. This contrast even appears in the differing views of the disposition of souls after death, since in the West the fate of the deceased was settled by a trial before a judge or by a balance on a scale of vices and virtues, while in the Byzantine *Life* of St. Basil the Younger the soul is depicted climbing a celestial ladder and paying taxes at various customs stations.[37] The main function of Byzantine usurers was to lend money to peasants who were unable to pay their taxes, especially at the time of levy.

It would be useful to study the demands made by the participants in the various Byzantine riots and revolts. The riots of the fifth, sixth, and seventh centuries seem to have been the result of political and ecclesiastical controversies, demands for grain, and soldiers' complaints, in addition to the struggle between the city factions of the

Blues and the Greens. From the ninth century on, fiscal issues seem to have been crucial in popular discontent, which originated mainly in the countryside (see chapter 6). They had already appeared in the civil war led by Thomas the Slav, when tax collectors are said to have been suppressed in the rebellion, and when the government tried to gain the support of the people in Opsikion and Armeniakon by reducing the rate of the tax called *kapnikon*.[38] In 915–16 the inhabitants of Athens and Hellas, suffering from frequent vexation [συνεχῶς ἐπιηρεαζόμενοι], revolted and stoned the governor of the theme, whose greediness had grown unbearable.[39] The Emperor Romanus I Lecapenus (920–44) was constantly blamed for oppressing the population with high taxes, and his successor had to alleviate the heavy burden.[40] When Nicephorus II Phocas (963–69) came to power, the people were filled with hope that he would cancel the arrears owing to the inspectors of taxes.[41] Opposition to imperial taxation likewise figured prominently, according to Litavrin, in all the important eleventh-century revolts, in which the peasant masses were involved,[42] and it may well be that the apparent decrease of peasant movements in the twelfth century[43] was connected with the partial shift from governmental to private exploitation of the peasantry.

The Byzantine administration and army were paid directly from the treasury. Even many monasteries in the tenth to twelfth centuries received money directly from the exchequer or from the revenues collected by provincial financial officials, and the clergy were normally supported by stipends rather than, as in the West, by benefices of income-producing properties.[44] Military commanders and high officials were, as a rule, rewarded not with grants of land but with portions of state income. A considerable share of an official's income was made up of private payments from people who were obliged to pay, including litigants in trials and students in state schools. These payments were specific forms of recognized bribery rather than regular fees established by custom or law. Ordinary soldiers were required to provide their own horses and weapons, and for great expeditions arrows, spears, and shields were collected in the form of a levy.[45] The fact that the court and army in Byzantium were mostly supported by noneconomic means helps to account for the limited impetus they gave to economic development.

Many scholars, assuming that large armies directed from a single center must have been more effective than the decentralized forces of the medieval West, have associated the revival of the empire with the establishment of the military zones known as themes, where an effective native army was built on the basis of small holdings of land held in return for military service. Vasilij Vasil'evskij attributed this reform to Leo III and Constantine V, who fought successfully against both the Arabs and the Bulgarians. George Ostrogorsky, on the other hand, dated the establishment of the system of themes a century earlier, in the reigns of Heraclius and his successors, despite the fact that the successful attacks on Byzantium by the Arabs and other neighboring peoples showed the ineffectiveness of its army. The weakness of the Byzantine "centralized" army was first pointed out by Walter Kaegi.[46] Farmers whose agricultural tasks kept them from giving full time to military training were not very effective as soldiers and were probably not a decisive factor in the resistance to the Muslim invasion. The unprofessional and badly organized hordes that fought side by side with the mercenaries in the ranks of the Byzantine army were severely criticized by Theophanes.[47] The themes, moreover, were not interchangeable units, blindly obedient to the emperor.

The peasant-soldiers, or *Soldatenbauer*, as Ostrogorsky called them, were known as *agrarii milites* in the West, where they more or less disappeared after the tenth century. They continued to occupy a special place in the Byzantine social system and military establishment, however, and Muslim observers in the twelfth century were still struck by the great size of the imperial armies. Some steps had already been taken in the tenth century, however, to reorganize the military system and to introduce the type of trained and mounted knights who were so effective as fighters in the West. Nicephorus Phocas contributed greatly to the introduction of heavy armed cavalry by raising the required value of a soldier's property from four gold pounds to twelve, thus ensuring that a *stratiotes* would have sufficient means to support a horse and proper arms. The armed and mounted knight, or *kataphraktes*, of the tenth century was largely responsible for the remarkable victories on both the eastern and the western frontiers of the empire.

In spite of this reform, a western observer such as Liutprand of Cremona was struck by the lack of mailed cavalry in Byzantium in the tenth century, and two centuries later the Byzantines still envied the effectiveness of Latin knights. Byzantium never developed the characteristic military ideology of the medieval West, with its stress on fealty. Only a few embryonic elements of chivalric ethics are found in some Byzantine panegyrics. The weakness and disadvantages of the centralized Byzantine army in contrast with the more individualistic forces of the West are clearly shown by the events of 1204.

In theory the entire Byzantine population, like the army, was a homogeneous mass of subjects gathered around a single emperor and bound together by a common creed. In fact it was split into various ethnic groups, each with its own language, habits, costumes, and even religious beliefs. Ethnoreligious diversity led to mutual distrust, abuse, and hatred. The Jews, whose religious beliefs and observances were the object of derision and refutation, were deprived of certain civic rights. Except for a single physician in Constantinople, for instance, they were forbidden in the twelfth century to ride horses. They were debarred from most public functions, although attempts at forcible conversion were prompted only by special circumstances and never systematically carried out, and Byzantine Jewish communities may have been less isolated than those of the West,[48] at least after the Crusades. The Armenians, who preserved the Monophysite creed, were regarded with suspicion and accused of perfidy.[49] Communication with them was sometimes prohibited.[50] The Latins were considered arrogant and greedy, the Arabs treacherous, and so on.

Until the seventh century the empire was a multinational country in the full sense of the word. It was populated by many different nations and tribes, including Italians, Syrians, Copts, Thracians, and various Germanic peoples, and it is probable that the linguistic and cultural independence of these ethnic minorities grew during the sixth century. The Arab invasion of the seventh century deprived Byzantium of its eastern and southern provinces, with their heterogeneous populations, and most of the western lands were soon conquered by the Germanic tribes. Although the Greek element dominated in political and cultural life, Byzantium did not become a Greek realm. The Armenians were particularly numerous, and in the ninth and tenth centuries several emperors, such as Basil I, Romanus I Lecapenus, and John Tzimisces, came of Armenian stock.[51] In the eleventh and twelfth centuries about fifteen percent of the upper class were probably of Armenian origin. This Armeno-Byzantine elite as a rule rejected Monophysitism, and some members even occupied important episcopal sees, including that of Constantinople. Armenians were particularly significant as members of the Byzantine army, forming separate contingents, and there were Armenian communities in various towns over the country.

Slavic tribes settled in Byzantium from the seventh century on.[52] They were baptized and unlike the Armenians lost much of their ethnic particularity, though independent Slavic villages persisted in mountainous regions of the southern Peloponnese until the thirteenth century. The conquest of Bulgaria by Basil II had by 1018 increased the Slavic population within the empire. Although many prominent Bulgarian families moved to inland regions of the empire and merged with the Byzantine ruling class, Bulgaria remained pre-dominantly Slavic, with its own language and cultural traditions, and after several abortive attempts attained political independence at the end of the twelfth century.

The Arabs and Syrians formed a considerable part of the population in the eastern part of the empire and helped form the mixed and frequently bilingual society that produced, and was mirrored in, the Byzantine epic of *Digenes Akritas*. After the eleventh century the Turks also appeared within Byzantium and in the twelfth century were granted considerable lands in the Balkans and provided a series of generals for the Byzantine army. Various Caucasian peoples, the Georgians, Abasges, and Alans, entered Byzantine service, and from the eleventh century on the Pečenegs, Uses, Polovcy, and other nomads lived in Byzantine territory. Most of the emigrants from the West appeared as merchants, mercenaries, and diplomats and seldom formed a permanent population, though their numbers seem to have been significant. Eustathius of Thessalonica counted 60,000 Latins in Constantinople alone, and Abu al-Faraj estimated that there were 30,000 "Frank" merchants in the Byzantine capital.[53]

The conditions of these ethnic minorities varied. Some of them had their own regions and formed communities; others were settled among the Greek majority, for the most part in towns. Some appeared for limited periods as mercenaries or merchants; others had relatively strong roots in the country. Some belonged to the elite, others were herdsmen or average soldiers. Some accepted the dominant orthodoxy; others followed their own observances. In short, their very existence challenged the concept of Byzantine uniformity. Even their attitude toward the empire was ambivalent. On the one hand, many of them, as random passers-by or newcomers in Byzantium, needed the approval of the emperor or government and therefore tended to be particularly faithful servants of the regime. On the other hand, as aliens among the native population they frequently sought independence, longed for their own fiefs or principalities, and raised riots. They thus formed both the most loyal and the most turbulent part of the populace.

The ambivalence of the Byzantine polity is shown by the fact that outlying towns, many ethnic minorities, and provincial nobles had no place in the autocratic system and were compelled to stand in opposition to the empire. Various elements of society preferred to break the ties with Constantinople. The tendency toward decentralization in Byzantium originated not with the so-called feudal disintegration but with the steady resistance to the extreme degree of centralization, which was not suited to medieval circumstances.

The problem of decentralizing forces can also be approached from a chronological standpoint. It is plausible to suppose that some elements of late antique civilization survived into the early Byzantine period, after the decline of the urban system in the mid-seventh century, and helped to preserve forces that buttressed the demand for trade and handicrafts and promoted elementary education and the use of Roman law. Byzantium, like the West, underwent a crisis in the early Middle Ages but surmounted it more quickly than the Latin West. After this crisis, however, the relationship of forces changed— and we have here another example of ambivalence—since as new social and economic forms developed, provincial towns, medieval in character, began to expand, the military aristocracy tried to acquire power, and Byzantine autocracy became a progressively greater hindrance to further development. The West, although politically disrupted, was socially and ideologically united. There the crucial period of the tenth, eleventh, and twelfth centuries was marked by inner consolidation and the establishment of new social forms, a new ideology, communal and hierarchical links, monastic orders, papal organization, and intellectual unity. The Byzantine order that was revived in the ninth and tenth centuries, on the contrary, was based on a loose social organization and turned artificially toward a glorious past. In spite of its lush external appearance, it contained serious inner weaknesses. By clinging to its universal and ecumenical pretensions Byzantium failed to find a place in the Christian commonwealth of Europe and gradually came to be the target of repeated incursions and attacks from the West.

Byzantium was still amazingly rich in the twelfth century. It had at its disposal great armies of mercenaries and manipulated its foes with marvelous diplomatic skill, but it was still defeated by the West. This defeat owed less to feudal disintegration, as Vasilij Vasil'evskij and his followers thought, than to the centralized order that hindered the development in Byzantium of the type of urban life and nobility that elsewhere proved a source of cultural, economic, and political strength. The embryonic developments that were promoted to some extent by the first Comneni and by the Lascarids were brought to an end, first by the bloody regime of Andronicus I Comnenus (1183–85), later by the spectacular but dangerous restoration of the empire by Michael VIII Palaeologus (1259–82) in 1261. From the fourteenth century on, decentralizing trends were ubiquitous, and the Byzantine government kept only some sonorous names and ceremonies. By then it was too late, for although in the thirteenth century the Byzantines were still able to compete with the feudal lords from the West and in the autumn of 1259 at Pelagonia inflicted a crushing defeat on the armies of Manfred of Sicily (1251–66) and William Villehardouin of Achaia (1245–78), by the fourteenth century their main rivals in the West were the flourishing maritime republics of Venice and Genoa. Byzantium suffered at the same time from the constant pressure of the Ottoman Turks in the East. Small but strong republics such as Dubrovnik were able to survive the Ottoman invasion, but artificially centralized Byzantium gave in. After first becoming an obedient vassal of the Turks, it was finally conquered and ceased to exist.

From the ambivalence of the Byzantine social and political system we shall pass now to the ambivalence of Byzantine morality and psyche. Although modern historians have occasionally praised the imperial administrative system, they rarely have a good word for Byzantine intellectuals. Emperors could be gifted and monks honest, but Byzantine intellectuals are commonly seen as wallowing in moral depravity, flattering the rich, and groveling before the powerful. The truth was much more complex than this conventional picture suggests.

Byzantine intellectuals were certainly members of their society, and they were among the first to suffer from its instability. The known professional literati of the twelfth century had a particularly unstable position, since they were supported by an occupation for which there was no steady demand or established market in the capital. They sought a Maecenas, not because they were morally depraved, but because their only other choice was to perish. Prodromus, for instance, had to live off his influential patrons, because he was neither an employee nor a teacher.

There is nevertheless extensive evidence of both concealed and open criticism and opposition by Byzantine intellectuals. There are many examples in official Byzantine literature of imperial praises of which the exaggerated terminology might seem tasteless to anyone who was unmindful of the political experience of the nineteen thirties and forties; but even a panegyric of an emperor could be a means of criticism, especially if the emperor praised was dead and his example could serve as a reproach to his living successor. The *History* by Attaleiates, for instance, which presents an idealized image of Nicephorus III Botaneiates (1078–81), was until recently thought to have been written in honor of Nicephorus while he occupied the throne but was in fact, according to Eudoxos Tsolakis, published after his deposition.[54] This new dating changes the whole interpretation of the *History*, since to praise the deposed emperor was doubtless to offend the new one. The same could be said of the *Alexias* by Anna Comnena, whose aim was not only to glorify her father but also to criticize, in a more or less disguised way, the reigning Emperor Manuel I.[55]

The reign of Manuel I was especially rich in intellectual opposition. In addition to Anna Comnena can be cited the examples of Glykas, who reproached the emperor for his reliance on astrology,[56] Pseudo-Prodromus, who wrote a poem in defense of Irene, the accused and banished widow of the *sebastokrator* Andronicus,[57] and Eustathius of Thessalonica, who criticized Manuel's religious innovations and had demanded earlier, in the camouflaged form of a laudation, an improvement in the water supply of the capital.[58] In an analysis of a *Dialogue* concerning the heresy of the Latins between the Patriarch Michael III (1170–78) and Manuel, who finally recognized his defeat, Jean Darrouzès argued that the text must be forged because there is no evidence of a dispute between the two men, who seem to have worked in close collaboration. He also pointed out that the *Dialogue* is found in one manuscript (*Vaticanus* 1409) between two letters, one by the Patriarch Germanus II and the other by Hagiorites to Michael VIII, both written in the thirteenth century.[59] These arguments are weak, since neither an argument ex silentio nor the position of the text in a single manuscript can refute the strong manuscript tradition ascribing it to Manuel and Michael, which is further corroborated by the examples already cited of intellectual opposition under Manuel I. The *Dialogue* may well therefore be authentic.

The behavior of many intellectuals has to be reinterpreted in the light of what we know about Byzantine ambivalence. Under the flattering and coaxing surface of their writings they concealed an ability to express candid ideas and opinions, to defend their friends, and to criticize not only single representatives of the imperial power but also the very essence of Byzantine autocracy. The history of Byzantine intellectual opposition has yet to be written.

The general world view of the Byzantines was likewise ambivalent. Their cosmos was strictly divided into the two opposing spheres of the celestial and earthly worlds which, though not divided by an eternal dualistic strife, stood in a constant tension established by the dominance of the celestial world and the submission of the earthly (see chapter 4). The connection between heaven and earth was realized in the mysteries of the Trinity and Christ and in church services, icon worship, and the system of images. The imperial court and ecclesiastical institutions, particularly monastic life, were seen as images or reflections of the celestial world, and their existence was consequently turned into a *mimesis*, or imitation of eternal ethical principles, such as the good or the stable. The idea of *mimesis* spread over the whole range of social and cultural relations. The emperor had to imitate Christ, the subject was supposed to resemble the emperor, the writer followed the pattern of classical texts, and the liturgy repeated the mystery of Christ's birth, death, and resurrection.[60] The Byzantines were surrounded by images and symbols, and they regularly ascribed a hidden significance to paintings, architectural monuments, and literary texts as well as to natural events ranging from earthquakes to migrations of locusts.

The heavenly *taxis*, the order of the true world, was mirrored first and foremost in the ceremonies of the imperial court and in ecclesiastical services and church decoration. Pomp and solemnity were essential elements in connecting men with the heavenly order. The sumptuous imperial garments, the splendor of the emperor's chambers, the brilliance of church interiors, and the ritual of stately processions were all in the eyes of the Byzantines not ostentatious vanities or luxuries but a genuine image of the divine world.

God was expressed in the imperial and ecclesiastical magnificence and order, which were universally regarded as divine and holy, but His presence was less clearly seen in the realm of everyday human relations, apart from order and splendor. God for the Byzantines was in principle incomprehensible, and His will was beyond human reasoning. This gap between divine will and human reason created a moral problem, since no one was certain of the righteousness of his own way. Perfection might turn out to be evil; what seemed promising might turn out inglorious. Locusts and mice, earthquakes and hostile attacks might unexpectedly serve the noble task of human edification, and wealth and success might on the contrary forebode divine wrath. Even a supernatural capacity to predict the future, typical of the abilities of a saint, was no guarantee of proper behavior, since the Devil often deceived human beings by apparent foreknowledge. Although Nicetas Choniates scoffed at predictions by false oracles, he was also amazed at how often these false predictions came true.

This general attitude led to a double ethical scale. The Byzantine mentality was split, because it had different yardsticks. It led at the same time to a lofty moral system based on the covenant with God and to a reliance on human reason in practical activities. An apparent incongruity existed between the stable principles of religious ethics and the day-by-day behavior, adapted to circumstances, of the Byzantines. We referred in the first chapter to the conflict between Psellos and Cerularius, each of whom represented, we now see, a different side of this ambivalent ethics, Cerularius standing for the rigid heavenly principles and Psellos for the tendency to adapt one's behavior to circumstances. Since this contradictory situation had long existed, the novelty and audacity of Psellos lay in his attempt to transform a latent and disregarded tendency into a recognized mode of human behavior.

The ambivalence of Byzantine ethics can also be seen in an ambiguous attitude toward labor. What mattered for Symeon the Theologian was not the creative and productive activity but only the fact that the labor served to deter human laziness and instill obedience.[61] Labor was at the same time a humiliating trial and an elevating honor. The hagiographers praised the dirtiest drudgery performed by their heroes, and the writers of the twelfth century praised Manuel I for personally carrying stones when his troops built a fortress on the Turkish border.[62] The golden sweat of the emperor was a cliché among Byzantine poets and rhetors. Michael Choniates and Eustathius of Thessalonica, on the other hand, positively approved of productive labor. People like their tools not for their own sake, according to Michael, but for other ends;[63] Eustathius said that people have to work both to overcome the menace of famine and to acquire eternal goods. Man is created to toil, and it was simply a joke for a wise man in Antiquity to promise to feed mankind without any labor.[64]

The Byzantine attitude toward poverty and wealth was also contradictory, since poverty meant a lack of power and social esteem as well as a dearth of worldly goods.[65] Wealth was a basis for social stratification from the early period onward. In legal documents, the whole population was divided into the poor and the rich,[66] and Alexios Makrembolites in the fourteenth century considered the distinction between the poor and the rich as a major social conflict of his time.[67] In the imperial novels of the tenth century wealth appeared together with power, and the main division in society was that between the poor and the powerful, since power was regarded as tantamount to wealth. But it was not wealth alone that mattered, since Byzantine wealth was classified, and some forms of wealth were held in contempt by elevated minds, as is shown by the story of the Emperor Theophilus (828–42) ordering his wife's shipload of merchandise to be burned.[68] A salary from the treasury or an income from one's own estates was considered the noblest forms of wealth, while the profits from private service or trade, not to mention usury, were despised.

Wealth in all its forms was only of worldly value, however, and was as nothing, in spite of its significance for social importance on earth, on the scale of heavenly values. The poor were expected to be blissful in paradise and were often the heroes of hagiographic legends. Charity was given to Christ in the form of the poor, and the emperor himself had, once a year, to wash the feet of twelve Constantinopolitan beggars.

Even the attitude toward almsgiving was ambiguous. Side by side with the traditional view of *philanthropia* as a significant virtue and the mandatory duty of an ideal ruler,[69] there was a skeptical attitude and a concern whether almsgiving could lead to salvation. Symeon the Theologian insisted that unless people dedicated themselves completely to contrition and the care of the holy poor, they would gain nothing by giving away their money and property, and he cited the example of Mary of Egypt, who did not feed the poor, clothe the naked, or give drink to the thirsty and yet who was listed among the saints.[70]

The Byzantine notion of marriage was ambivalent, since marriage was regarded not only as the highest aim in human relations—God's means of creating the family, and the most important social institution—but also as unimportant in comparison with celibacy. The original meaning of the term *monachos*, in both pagan and Christian sources, was separation in the sense of not marrying, and celibacy remained the single most distinctive mark of the monastic state in the Byzantine church.[71] Countless saints established their claim to holiness by their efforts to preserve their chastity in the face of their parents' desire that they should marry and have children (see chapter 3). Secular wisdom and military courage were similarly considered high virtues on the earthly scale of values from the tenth century on but remained of no importance on the celestial scale of values.

The Byzantine world, the world of individualism without freedom, was contradictory in itself. There were social links, but they were relatively loose, and this contradictory ambiguity contributed greatly to the phenomenon of Byzantine ambivalence. Good and evil, light and darkness were at the same time radically distinguished from and flowed into one another, and the border between them remained shimmering and vague. The consistent ambivalence of Byzantine life and mind more or less reflected, or at least coincided with, the instability of Byzantine social and political life, since there was no place for stable, clear-cut values in an unstable society. The more unstable the sociopolitical situation, the more contradictory and ambivalent were the norms of human behavior and morality and the more insistent was the desire of creative thinkers for immovable ethical and aesthetic principles. Out of the indulgence and tolerance of the Romans the Byzantines created as their final denial both the idea of epic character and its visual counterpart, the frontal and steadfast hero of Byzantine monumental painting, individualistic, secluded from the noisy market crowd, concentrated on an internal world—a live negation of Byzantine reality. This stunning visual contrast between the lives of the imagination and of real existence was perhaps the most substantial and all-embracing evidence of the ambivalence in this ambivalent realm.

The same Byzantines who followed strict dogma in religious and political matters, who observed the cult of the emperor in the strictest manner, and who preached obedience to rule and *taxis*, at the same time created the concept of *oikonomia*, or dispensation, which was very close to permissiveness.[72] The rules were apparently fixed, but the borderlines between the extremes unexpectedly turned out to be vague and osmotic. The fact that many of the surviving sources are prescriptive, recording what ought to be done under various circumstances, should not lead to any assumption that the rules were always followed or that individualistic behavior was always condemned. The orders sounded solemn and all-embracing, but the average person knew how to escape the seemingly mandatory network of rigorism. The law was strong and severe, but enforcement was indulgent and practice was compliant. Doomed to weep, the Byzantine laughed time and again.

CHAPTER EIGHT

In Search of Indirect Information

IN the foregoing chapters we have tried to show that Byzantine studies are now at a turning point, of which the central feature is the replacement, only recently begun, of the history of political events, institutions, and monuments with the history of the men and women who actually lived and worked in the Byzantine world. This new direction of Byzantine research is not an artificial invention but follows the trail of the so-called New History of the school of historical research founded by Marc Bloch and Lucien Febvre and now concentrated primarily around the French periodical *Annales*.[1] The tendency to take a new direction originated simultaneously and independently in several branches of Byzantine studies, and we have tried to summarize these researches and present them as a coherent system, which had clearly been influenced by recent research on the West in the Middle Ages.

The statement that these tasks of Byzantine studies require new methods of investigation may sound odd. Is it not enough to discover, publish, and summarize new sources that will by themselves enlarge our knowledge of Byzantium? In the opinion of most Byzantinists, historians need only gather, understand, and comment on the facts in order to attain the truth and if the facts that they collect and explain are correct, they can approach the reality of the past. The cult of historical facts has been passionately developed by positivistic historiography, and the collection, scrutiny, and explanation of facts were declared to be the ultimate aim of historical investigation. This point of view has recently found strong support in the application to historical research of mathematical methods, because mathematics was thought to be objective in its very nature. The use of computers, mathematical language, and complicated formulas therefore gave scholars the sense of security that they sought. The editing of texts is likewise highly esteemed by positivistic historians, and for many Byzantinists the most honorable scholarly task is to find, publish, and describe a source. The high value placed on editorial work is supported by the obvious fact that it enjoys a longevity that strikingly outlasts the duration of historical theories. Editions of Byzantine authors and legislative acts made in the nineteenth century by Karl-Eduard Zachariae von Lingenthal, Carl de Boor, and Immanuel Bekker are still in use today, while almost no one now turns to even the most original works of nineteenth-century Byzantinists, except as part of the history of scholarship.

Neither the accumulation of facts alone, however, nor the editing of sources can change our image of Byzantium. Hans-Georg Beck, in the provocative book cited earlier, raises the question of how important the discovery of a new type of gold nomisma is for Byzantine economic history.[2] One lead seal more, one late Byzantine letter more, one poem more: all these will only lengthen the chain tying the researcher to traditional points of view. In order to meet contemporary demands, it is necessary not only to gather more facts but also to develop new skills in order to make the sources, including those already available, respond to the challenges of today.

Different attitudes toward sources have prevailed at various times. Simple narrative, in which historians restricted themselves to summarizing the sources, prevailed until the beginning of the nineteenth century, and in the Byzantine field this kind of attitude lasted until less than a hundred years ago. In the nineteenth century the critical principle was introduced into historical research. Historians stressed the need to check the sources, to compare evidence from different sources, and to verify the inner coherence of texts. This type of historical criticism, in fact, helped to overturn many traditional narratives. Among the most celebrated achievements of textual criticism were the denial of the Trojan War, the rejection of the reconstruction of early Roman history, and the development of the mythological concept of the origins of Christianity. Not all these hypercritical views have stood the test of time, but they sharpened the investigator's skill and contributed to the elaboration of new historical techniques.

The difference between narrative history and critical investigation is clear in theory if not always in practice. In the former the material needed for the narrative is put together from available sources; in the latter information is collated and the attempt is made to prove and justify the choice. The source is the focal point, and the critical study of sources [*Quellenkunde*] is the true—even the firstborn—child of nineteenth-century historical criticism and is embodied in the sciences of paleography, diplomacy, numismatics, sphragistics, and other disciplines concerned with particular types or aspects of sources.[3] The studies of Heinrich von Sybel on the sources of the history of the Crusades are an example of the work of this school in the area between medieval and Byzantine research,[4] while Ferdinand Hirsch's book is a perfect attempt to apply this technique to Greek medieval chronicles.[5] The critical investigation of sources led to the creation of the useful *Regesta* both of imperial and patriarchal documents,[6] to the thorough analysis of the inner structure of imperial *diplomata*,[7] and to a series of masterful commentaries on the texts or events of Byzantine life. This method, presented in the carefully prepared articles of Vasilij Vasil'evskij, may be said to have reached its peak in some of the studies by Paul Lemerle containing a text—in the original Greek, with a translation or summary—a commentary on the details, and a general evaluation of the text and of the events presented in it. Among the outstanding examples of this technique are Lemerle's studies of Kekaumenos, of the agrarian legislation of the Macedonian dynasty, and of the relations of Byzantium with the Seljuqs in the first half of the fourteenth century, which is treated in the form of a detailed commentary on the so-called *Deeds of Omur pasha*, the second part of the *Book of Instructions* by the fifteenth-century Turkish historian Enveri.[8] Each chapter begins with some lines of Enveri, followed first by a critical commentary, then by a reconstruction of the events. In his latest monograph Lemerle uses this technique only in the first part of the book, where he analyzes three Greek texts of the eleventh century— the will of Eustathius Boilas, the *Typikon* of Pakurianos, and the *Diataxis* of Michael Attaleiates—and devotes the last two chapters to a general consideration of Byzantine cultural and socioeconomic development.[9]

The approaches both of narrative history and of critical commentary, in spite of their differences, have an important feature in common, since they are both based primarily on direct and explicit evidence from the sources. In each the subject of the research is the fact found in a source or directly deduced from a comparison of several sources, such as the description of a war, revolt, plot, or other political event, the contents of a law, letter, speech, or other document, or the biographies of writers as summarized on the basis of different lemmata of their works and statements, and of references to them by their various contemporaries. Source material consciously and intentionally conveyed by an author is understood as direct or explicit information. Narrative history was restricted to the presentation of selected information and to its political and ideological interpretation. The method of critical history is more sophisticated.

Byzantine historians of the time of Constantine VII (913–59) praised Basil I (867–86) and scorned Michael III (842–67), and this example was regularly followed until Henri Grégoire, checking the inner coherence of these texts and comparing them with other sources, showed that the traditional picture of Michael III as a drunken sot was unbalanced and reflected the official views of the Macedonian dynasty.[10] A comparable situation in the West can be seen in the attitude of the Carolingian court historians toward the last Merovingian rulers, who as a result have gone down in history as do-nothing kings trundling around in oxcarts. The change of attitude toward Michael III is the result primarily of a change in evaluation. No important new facts were discovered by Grégoire; he simply reassessed the facts given in the surviving accounts, compared them with some occasional references in inscriptions and epics concerning Michael III, and explained why the historians of the tenth century tended to present a biased picture of Michael. He revealed the prejudices of those who surrounded Constantine VII by examining closely their intentions and statements. By looking at the other side Grégoire transformed a drunken sot into a great emperor.

Sources can also be asked questions that their creators never intended to be asked, and they can thus be compelled to give evidence about facts that stood outside the interest and imagination of medieval authors, who in this way unconsciously and unintentionally provide a type of information that we shall here call indirect. It not only permits the study of many problems not directly discussed in the source but also helps to satisfy the interest of modern scholarship in phenomena that were hidden from the Byzantines themselves. As long as political history was the principal end of Byzantine studies and scholars concentrated on political events, critically examined on the basis of a variety of sources, the descriptive and exegetical method by and large satisfied the needs of scholarship and the public. Now that historical investigation is more concerned with the problem of Byzantine civilization and culture—or, more explicitly, of Byzantine people—the tasks have changed. We want to know, for instance, whether Byzantium was a society with or without classes, although the Byzantines themselves never addressed this problem. The answer to this question cannot be found in imperial legislation; it must be squeezed out of indirect information in the sources. Such indirect information is used in many recent works by Byzantinists, and it is now time to look at several efforts of this kind and to show that they are coherent and purposeful and must be understood as part of an investigation reflecting an approach to the new needs and tasks of modern historical science.

The distinction between direct, or intentional, and indirect information is illustrated by numismatic evidence. Byzantine coins were struck as a medium of exchange, as a means of hoarding treasure, and as political propaganda, and these functions dictated their external qualities, of which the most important were the effigy, the legend, the purity of the metal, and the weight. These conscious creations met diverse political and economic purposes and reflected the taste and fashion of the age. They convey direct information, which has been studied by both numismatists and art historians. Numismatists have affirmed, for instance, that the function of silver coinage in the Byzantine monetary system was different in the sixth century from its function in the seventh, when the hexagram was introduced by Heraclius (610–41), and that the debasement of the Byzantine gold coin began in effect under Michael IV (1034–41). It is important for art historians that most of the effigies of emperors on coins of the middle Byzantine period are conventional and that the so-called Pantokrator image of Christ, usually found filling the summit of the dome in churches, is also found on coins.

The situation changes radically when coins are used as evidence for economic history, for which their external features and the direct information that they offer are less important than the geographical and chronological distribution of coin finds. Cécile Morrisson has shown on the basis of indirect information of this type that the debasement of the Byzantine gold coinage in the eleventh century should not be considered as evidence of an economic crisis (see chapter 2). On the other hand, it can now be assumed that there was a decline of minting from the end of the seventh century to the beginning of the ninth and that the pace of monetary revival in different regions of the Byzantine empire was uneven. Neither the emperors nor those in charge of minting were responsible for the geographical distribution of coin hoards or the number of coins that survive. This kind of information is indirect. Some of the best catalogues of Byzantine coinage, however, including the systematic work of Wolfgang Hahn,[11] overlook the importance of evidence concerning the location of coin hoards and the number of coins in circulation. Many scholars, indeed, question the possibility of using coin hoards as a source of Byzantine economic history. The indirect information from Byzantine coins is often mistrusted by Byzantinists, who prefer to deal with the direct evidence of narrative texts, however slight, even though coins provide relatively extensive material, and narrative texts describing the events of economic life tend to be particularly biased.

Students of Byzantine terminology are continually baffled by the vagueness of legal definitions, which present a direct and consciously formulated point of view. Byzantine law thus preserved the Roman definition of poverty, as formulated by Hermogenianus, that anyone whose property was worth less than fifty gold coins was recognized as being among the poor.[12] This legal definition did not correspond to social realities, however. Social rank depended on many factors other than wealth, but the criterion of Hermogenianus remained unchanged through the ages, and no account was taken of the difference between Roman *aurei* and Byzantine nomismata. In spite of the considerable debasement of the nomisma by the fourteenth century, this definition was repeated by Constantine Harmenopulus, following the *Procheiron* of the late ninth century.[13]

It would be useful to collect all the references to "poor" and "poverty" and to "rich" and "riches" in various Byzantine sources. Most of these references were incidental, made with no intent to define the terms, and they therefore as a rule convey an unconscious image of poverty and wealth. For this reason, as well as their freedom from legal presuppositions, incidental references provide us with an image of Byzantine poverty that changes with time and is adapted to social reality. Evelyne Patlagean concluded on the basis of evidence concerning poverty from sources between the fourth and sixth centuries that the ancient contrast between citizens and aliens was replaced at this period by a new contrast between poor and rich. She also showed the difference between active and passive poverty at this time.[14] These developments are not reflected in contemporary legal sources; they emerge only from indirect information.

The concept of nobility likewise is not defined in Byzantine legal sources and can be reconstructed only from indirect information— that is, from the incidental references to noble origin and parallel concepts that are scattered through various kinds of texts. This method gives an idea of the Byzantine aristocracy as it was seen by the Byzantines themselves and by their neighbors. From this evidence it is possible both to gain an insight into the structure of the Byzantine aristocracy and its difference from the nobility in the West and to trace some changes in the Byzantine notion of nobility.[15]

Byzantine legal textbooks contain precise definitions and present a unified picture, with a few negligible exceptions, of the law that survived practically without change from the early Roman empire. The picture would have been different had scholars attempted to collect the incidental information scattered in private acts concerning property, social stratification, obligations, and succession. Although the Roman distinction between *traditio* [transfer of ownership], *locatio rei* [letting out a thing by a simple agreement to hire], and *emphyteusis* [a special type of contract that allowed the holder to deal freely with land granted for a long term, provided he returned it unimpaired if the interest ceased][16] is preserved in the Byzantine legal textbooks, the term *emphyteuma* in late Byzantine practice in fact signified house rent and was used synonymously with ἐνοίκιον,[17] while the term ἔκληψις, or lease, was applied to perpetual transfers of land (under some special conventions)[18] and even to transfers without payment of rent.[19] The precise distinction between *traditio, locatio,* and *emphyteusis* was lost in real life; it existed only in the theoretical exercises of Byzantine jurists.

The many types of formulas that appear in Byzantine texts are a valuable source of indirect information. Repeated clichés can serve to reconstruct the social mentality, and even the slightest changes of emphasis can show important changes in the style of thought. Byzantine tax inventories, the so-called *praktika,* consist of standard items, listing in addition to the tax the name of the proprietor, the members of the family, the size of the allotment, and the number of cattle.[20] These inventories were drawn up for the purposes of taxation, since the tax collectors needed to know the number of *paroikoi,* the size of their property, and the sum total of their obligations. This was direct information that was consciously included by the officials who compiled the lists and used by the scholars who first used the *praktika* to calculate the size of the lord's demesne and the peasants' holdings to study the kinds of taxes and the amount of the lord's revenue and to indicate the fluctuations in value of peasant property. Gradually, however, Byzantinists have begun to ask questions that were not treated by the Byzantines and have forced the *praktika* to yield information on demographic trends—the size and movements of population—on the relation between property and the tax imposed on it, and on other subjects that were not addressed by the compilers of the documents.

Another type of source that is composed primarily of formulas is the late Byzantine deed of purchase, designed to legalize the transfer of allotments; at first sight deeds of purchase differ from one another only in the descriptions of the property transferred. The direct information in these deeds has given scholars valuable insights into the growth of monastic estates at the expense of smallholders.[21] On this question, the interests of the fourteenth-century notaries who drew up the documents and of the modern scholars who study them coincided, and the scholar asked questions that could be answered by the notary. But new questions gradually arose, such as the important and debated problem, touched on in chapter 2, of the relation between the size of the property that was purchased and its price. In some cases the documents give rise to the even more difficult problem of the interdependence of property, price, and rent. The simple description of acts, one after another, would be insufficient for such a purpose, and only the comparison of various deeds combined in a special table can shed light on a question that would not have occurred to a Byzantine notary.

The standard clauses of deeds of purchase can be investigated from a special point of view. The formulas of late Byzantine charters, both in Greece and in southern Italy,[22] were once regarded as uniform, but a detailed analysis has shown the existence in the thirteenth century and the first half of the fourteenth of at least four local chanceries, at Thessalonica, Serres, Miletus, and Smyrna, and has even shown that the formulas of the chancery at Smyrna changed slightly during the thirteenth century.[23] These local variations to some extent contradict the traditional idea of official Byzantine uniformity.

Various scholars have used Byzantine chrysobulls for different ends. Their content is obviously of first rate importance for both the political and socioeconomic history of Byzantium. The formulas of their preambles were regarded with scorn by generations of Byzantinists, however, until Herbert Hunger found in them a way of reconstructing imperial political ideology.[24] Each preamble, taken separately and treated as a concrete case, reflected the attitude of a single emperor toward a single monastery or town in a particular situation. The scribe of the imperial chancery, while establishing this text, was concerned only with the particular situation. But taken together the preambles create a broad image independent of the consciousness of individual scribes and emperors.

The tax collectors who included peasants' names in Byzantine inventories could not have foreseen the questions raised by Angeliki Laiou-Thomadakis in her demographic study. For the tax collectors the names were simply identifications of dependent holders of monastic lands, but for a modern scholar they serve, taken together, to designate crafts and professions and as a basis for some preliminary conclusions about the ethnic composition of the Macedonian countryside in the fourteenth century.[25]

The family names of Byzantine nobles reveal a perhaps even

more intricate picture. The Byzantine nobility of the eleventh and twelfth centuries can be divided into two groups: the military aristocracy and the families connected primarily with the civil service. The etymology of the patronymics appear to have been different for each group (see table 4).

Although no firm conclusions can be drawn from this evidence, it implies that the civil nobility had more connections than the military aristocracy with crafts and trade and with Constantinople. The military aristocracy, on the other hand, seem to have had closer ties with small provincial sites that either gave their names to or took them from aristocratic patronymics. The social reality was thus reflected in the etymology of patronymics,[26] which were given quite apart from the conscious will of the writers of our sources.[27]

The indirect literary information contained in Byzantine texts is even more thoroughly hidden. Until recently Byzantine literature was studied primarily from the standpoint of its direct content, but beneath this level other levels of imaginative system and language exist. The content of a text is consciously created by the author and is roughly tantamount to direct information. Each single image is likewise produced by the author's will, but the imaginative system is on

Table 4
Etymology of Aristocratic Patronymics of the
Eleventh and Twelfth Centuries

Type or Origin	Percentage of Names	
	Military Aristocracy	Civil Nobility
Biblical or ancient roots	4	4.5
First names	4.5	5
Characteristics		
Scornful	28	24
Neutral	7	6.5
Praiseworthy	1.5	15
Offices	5.5	2
Professions	7.5	13
Toponyms		
Great centers	15	10
Small centers	22	6
Constantinopolitan area	1.5	8.5
Provincial monasteries	3.5	5.5

the whole independent of the author's intent. In other words, if the images of a text are studied not as a simple sum of individual and independent phenomena but as a coherent system, the sphere of psychology, hidden underneath the level of pure content, is entered. It is thus possible to see that most of the imaginative system of Symeon the Theologian is formed of images drawn from the life of the imperial court and the activity of merchants and craftsmen, while the twelfth-century religious mystic Helias Ekdikos made use principally of agrarian and military images. Symeon's predilection reveals his social and political sympathies, which are barely perceptible within the framework of his direct information. It can be observed further that Nicetas Choniates liked frightening and tragic images—wild animals, fire, death, and so on—and, when speaking about storms at sea, as a rule emphasized unavoidable ruin and shipwreck, while in the works of Michael Psellos or Nicephorus Gregoras the image of a ship safely reaching a harbor after a tempest is dominant. The tragic outlook of Choniates, who wrote his history just before and immediately after the capture of Constantinople by the crusaders, is consistently reflected in his imaginative system.

The language of Byzantine authors has hitherto been studied primarily from the viewpoint of its antique heritage, and Byzantine authors have been divided into groups according to the extent of their dependence upon Greek classics. Malalas and Theophanes thus represented a style full of everyday expressions and readily intelligible to the people, whereas Gregoras is esteemed as a writer whose simple classical style is reminiscent of Plato.[28] Whether or not this type of criticism is correct, it has no connection with the question of language as a means of literary effect. Although, for instance, the simplicity of the language of Kantakuzenos has often been stressed,[29] it has not been associated with his clear desire to influence the reader and create an atmosphere of sincerity. Another characteristic of Kantakuzenos's vocabulary is that in spite of the stress, in the content of his works, on the courage, honesty, and self-denial of his hero his text is full of words designating cowardice, profit, and deceit. This apparent contradiction between intent and language on the one hand reveals the real cares and troubles of the historian and on the other hand creates an artistic tension, since the author seems to be in constant inner dispute. He is prepared, unlike Gregoras, to recognize the critics of his hero, but to refute them he needs to prove his point and appear trustworthy to the reader.

Linguistic analysis can contribute in other ways to a better understanding of Byzantine texts.[30] A crucial point in Byzantine history is marked by the reign of Andronicus I, who has been praised by some scholars as a wise ruler trying to carry out necessary reforms and has been criticized by others as a tyrant who ruined the healthiest elements in Byzantine society. In this dispute the evidence of Nicetas Choniates, according to Winfred Hecht, is decisive, for although the rhetoricians of the time of Isaac II, who reproached Andronicus after his deposition, were untrustworthy, the testimony of Choniates is regarded by Hecht as reliable.[31] Hecht tried to defend the foreign policy of Andronicus, saying that Choniates distributed praise and blame evenly in his characterization of the emperor, but he and other scholars failed to see that the actual attitude of Choniates toward Andronicus can best be grasped on the linguistic level, since he almost never referred to Andronicus as *basileus*. He referred to Isaac II by this title 139 times in the history of his reign, and to Alexius III 153 times, but Andronicus was called *basileus* only 14 times. In this way Choniates consistently treated him as an illegal usurper. The terminology by itself reveals Choniates' judgment of Andronicus.

Indirect information can rarely be taken from the available sources before they have been dissected into their constituent elements, out of which secondary or intermediary sources can be built in the form of tables, statistical data, geographical maps, and so on. Such secondary sources are in some cases constructed as a first step in a given scholarly task, as were the tables in the works of Patlagean and Laiou-Thomadakis. In other instances they have been created without a special purpose and can be used in various ways. The simplest and most regularly used secondary sources are dictionaries and indexes, in which words are arranged in alphabetical order, destroying the inner sequence of the developed texts. The prosopographical lexicon of the Palaeologan period, now being prepared by the Austrian Academy of Sciences, is another example of a secondary source.[32] After its completion it will be useful not only for simple references but also for investigations of other kinds, including the social analysis of late Byzantine society.

To develop a secondary source seems at first sight a subjective and therefore dangerous undertaking, since it can lead to a distortion of reality, whereas a traditional commentary on a text is apparently objective. As was seen in the introduction, however, neither the technique of commenting nor the earlier narrative method was free from historical distortion. Both the choice of material and the degree or direction of criticism were determined by definite interests and prejudices and opened the way for discrepancies reflecting political, social, philosophical, and religious viewpoints. An objective picture of the past is not buried in the sources and cannot be mechanically extracted from them. Every generation attempts to create a picture fitted to its own needs and aims, and every generation distorts and restores the past according to its own devices. In any case, is a secondary source that is independent of the author's conscious intention either more or less objective than an original source permeated by varied assumptions and interests?

Subjectivity should be seen not only as a means of distorting the past but also as a way of reconstructing an historical model or image of reality. Beck, in the small book cited earlier more than once, emphasized the apparently unexpected fact of the effect of literature on scholarship.[33] A poetic insight can be deeper and closer to the truth than an erudite description. The great Russian poet Marina Cvetaeva affirmed that Pushkin was closer to the truth in his novel *The Captain's Daughter* than in his history of Pugachev's mutiny.[34]

Byzantine *taktika* of the ninth and tenth centuries are the most important source of information about the Byzantine administrative system, and they have long been the object of special research. Although they have been published more than once and commented upon,[35] however, they have not been used to explain how Byzantine bureaucracy worked. This is in part because the *taktika* are lists of dignitaries designed to describe their behavior during various imperial ceremonies and banquets rather than their administrative activities. More information is needed in order to reconstruct the Byzantine administrative system as it functioned, and since this is scattered and exceedingly scanty, it must be supplemented by modern political experience, ethnological observations, and ancient and medieval parallels. It is possible, for example, to look at the life of modern collegiate institutions in order to get a better understanding of, let us say, medieval monasticism.

The exegetical technique presupposes a smooth flow of events and phenomena, each with a unique place in the stream of history. The construction of coherent historical models, however, requires comparative techniques. The traditional method was not alien to comparison, but the comparisons were primarily of contradictory versions of sources. The essence of modern investigation is the comparison of models, phenomena, and events.

This kind of comparison is present in an inchoate form in any historical work. Even if the comparison remains subliminal, it is reflected in the author's attitude toward the events described and in applied terminology. By naming the Byzantine gold coin "the dollar of the Middle Ages,"[36] for example, Robert Lopez implicitly compared the sway of Byzantine economic activity with the model of modern economic life. George Ostrogorsky had the model of western medieval society in mind when he described the Byzantine military system as based on the feudal device of conditional grants, called the *pronoia* an expression of the inner strength of Byzantine feudalism,[37] and, writing about the Byzantine aristocracy, identified the *exkousseia* with the immunities found in the medieval West,[38] although he never explicitly set the Byzantine and western institutions as models side by side. Every textbook on Byzantine art or literary history is likewise permeated by implicit or explicit comparisons, as with antique prototypes, though there is still no detailed comparison between two cultural models.

Any appreciation of events in Byzantium presupposes a comparison with a scale of established moral and social values. Justinian I can thus be considered either an enlightened ruler who contributed greatly to the development of law, art, and science in his day or a cruel tyrant whose expansionist policy failed, but both views depend upon a comparison with modern political experience and standards for an ideal ruler. While the critical historians of the nineteenth century perfected in their studies on the Fourth Crusade the comparative analysis of the western and Byzantine sources, they did not compare the styles of thought of writers from the East and from the West, who not only distorted and interpreted differently even eyewitness evidence but also presented events in different ways, and this variation reflected different cultural models. Although implicit comparisons of this type are unavoidable in descriptions of the past, modern scholars have tried to introduce comparison not as a silent presupposition but as a method of investigation (see chapter 1).

In studying the theological disputes between the West and Byzantium inaugurated by the conflict between the Patriarch Photius (858–67, 877–86) and Pope Nicholas I (858–67), earlier scholars tended to concentrate either on the initial task of examining the statement of polemical exaggerations on both sides or on the theological task of establishing a list of divergences ranging all the way from the most important to the least important issues. Scholars recently have also tried, however, to understand the theological differences as part of general cultural development and to incorporate them into the models of Byzantine and western medieval civilization.

This method implies not only comparing the Byzantine and non-Byzantine social and cultural models but also grasping the differences within the framework of the Byzantine world. It is common to accept the idea of an unchangeable Byzantine uniformity of opinions, mode of life, and style of manners, but this view has been asserted almost without any serious comparison of different authors. There has recently been a shift in historiography with regard to this point. One of the first steps in this direction was in a study of the polemic between two Byzantine scholars on the threshold of the fourteenth century, Theodore Metochites and Nicephorus Choumnos, by Ihor Ševčenko, who attempted to show that serious political contradictions underlay the surface of slight scholarly differences.[39] This principle was applied by Jakov Ljubarskij to the literary activity of Michael Psellos, who is presented in his various relations with his contemporaries.[40]

The traditional approach to Byzantine literature consisted, as has already been stressed, in emphasizing the filiation of ideas and imitation of forms. The recent comparative method allows a new appreciation of the elements of difference and opposition, which show up less in the general statements of Byzantine writers, which were shaped under the influence of Christianity and Greek classical inheritance, than in minor distinctions in opinions, terminology, and imaginative systems.

Differences signified distortions for the positivistic historians of the nineteenth century, whose principal aim was to choose the correct version from a mass of contradictory evidence or to discover the sources from which an author derived each passage of his narrative. Theophanes' account of the speech by Justin II (565–78) on the occasion of the appointment of Tiberius as Caesar in 574 followed Theophylact Simocatta with one exception, where Theophanes put *stratiotai* in place of *sycophants* in Justin's advice: "Do not be arrogant and do not receive sycophants." The editor Carl de Boor regarded this variant as an error, and corrected it to agree with Theophylact, disregarding the whole manuscript tradition.[41] A modern scholar would never introduce an alteration of this sort. In fact, the change by Theophanes in his *Chronography* reflected his hostility toward the army, and this antimilitarist attitude was developed later by John Zonaras, who attributed to Justin the words: "Do not permit *stratiotai* to claim more than their due."[42]

Nineteenth-century historians often acted like judges condemning false testimony and accepting truthful evidence. In recent years scholars have become more sceptical of a search for truth and more tolerant of alien points of view. Although historical research cannot advance without a discussion of dates, localizations, or names of the participants, the history of such events is being transformed from an end in itself into a means of research. The sources from which Ammianus Marcellinus or Theophanes gathered their (partially distorted) information now matters less than the image of the world they created. The naïve, biased, fantastic, and sometimes openly falsified image of the world in the Life of a saint or chronicle derives its real value from the fact not that it is correct but that it reflects the human vision of the cosmos and microcosm. Whereas positivistic scholars looked for a single truth of event, modern historians try to build various world-models and models of human vision. Nineteenth-century historians often treated Byzantium as a false and evil monarchy in comparison with the medieval world in the West (or vice versa), but scholars have now begun to understand that there were at least two equal systems of European medieval society and culture and two world-models. The method of investigation is a part of the new understanding of the past.

The search for indirect information is, as noted earlier, closely connected with the statistical elaboration of source material. The evidence of coins or seals has been added up in tables, as have the data of late Byzantine *praktika* concerning taxes and peasant property. Even the number of noble families can be calculated on the basis of references to them in narrative, legal, and other texts. This statistical elaboration of evidence has indisputable merit because it makes it possible to compare numbers rather than vague, spontaneous observations and impressions and thus opens the way for quantitative analysis. Günter Weiss argued that the families of the Byzantine civil nobility were of short duration. They entered history suddenly and vanished as quickly as they had come. He cited as examples the five families of the Tzirithons, Hexamilites, Serblias, Romanites, and Chaldos.[43] At least two of these do not support his point, however, since the Chaldos were known from the time of Basil II (976–1025) until that of Alexius I Comnenus (1081–1118) and the Serblias from the middle of the eleventh century to the middle of the twelfth, which cannot be called a short duration. Even if these five families had disappeared rapidly, however, this fact would not have proved Weiss's theory, since there were at least eighty-one families in the civil nobility of the eleventh and twelfth centuries, some of which survived for more than two centuries.

Statistics can be used, however, and the scanty evidence concerning the duration of Byzantine noble families during these two centuries can be summarized in order to establish what can be called an index of noble stability. For the whole period under investigation can be divided into five subperiods, and the duration of each family tentatively estimated with figures ranging from 0 for families known through only one generation or subperiod and 5 for those that existed from before 976, the beginning of Basil II's reign, to about 1204. This calculation shows that the familial index of stability for the military aristocracy was 2.32 and for the civil nobility 1.7, which gives a more precise idea of the duration of Byzantine noble families. The bureaucratic families occupied the stage for approximately two or three generations or subperiods and were of short duration in comparison with the military aristocracy.[44]

Numbers exert a magic spell on human minds, particularly if they are presented with the help of computers. It is therefore necessary to be very careful with Byzantine numerical data and to keep constantly in mind how meager they are and how strongly their evaluation depends upon subjective principles, which underlie all statistical investigations.[45] Neither simple human calculations nor the more intricate and sophisticated work of a computer can provide a completely objective picture or create a secondary source of unshakable significance. But despite its many limitations and restrictions, statistical evidence provides better, clearer, and more reliable conclusions than the accumulation of occasional and separate examples.

Scholars must crosscheck statistical results lest they be deceived by the apparent persuasiveness of statistics. It is necessary to grasp the social or historical sense of the numbers and to ascertain whether this sense coincides with conclusions drawn from other sources of information. The numismatic evidence indicating the decline of Byzantine minting from the mid-seventh century onward, for instance, could not be accepted without support and confirmation from domestic and foreign narrative sources. And any numerical speculation concerning the structure and development of the Byzantine aristocracy must be supported by observations on terminology, by the testimony of contemporary foreigners, and by the direct formulations of legislative texts.

The construction of historical models must consequently be based not only on the comparative investigation of statistically elaborated secondary sources but also, to a great extent, on an appreciation of the self-awareness of the past. Many "eternal" concepts of morality, politics, and economics have been inserted into the past, especially into the Byzantine past, and have been judged by later criteria that make them into a straitjacket of modern conceptions of ideal behavior or property. Western medievalists have recently emphasized the need to understand the world of the Middle Ages within the framework of its own concepts and terminology,[46] and the same purpose has been presented to Byzantinists. We must ask how the Byzantines looked at themselves and their institutions and values. It is dangerous to keep applying to Byzantium general sociological and cultural concepts derived from various epochs or regions.

It is equally dangerous, however, to reject the apparatus of concepts solely because they were not used by the Byzantines themselves. Is it possible, for instance, to deny the existence of classes in Byzantine society simply because no Byzantine source mentions the concept of social class and the Byzantines did not realize that they had classes? Byzantine society was not a classless collective but was divided into clear social strata, each endowed with distinct rights, performing different functions in the production of wealth, and receiving different shares of the national income. These classes were peculiar, flexible, and unstable, with vague and confused borders, but with regard to wealth and power they differed from each other no less than the *ordines* of contemporary society in the West. The proper task of historians is to bring into consonance the two languages, the one of scholarship and the other of the age they are studying.

The development of Byzantine studies in recent decades has been strongly influenced by western medieval research in both methodology and source studies. The quantity and quality of available Byzantine sources are certainly less than those for countries such as England, France, and Germany in the Middle Ages, and the economic and social history of Byzantium cannot be reconstructed in as great detail as that of the West. Nevertheless, the scarcity of Byzantine source material does not present an insuperable obstacle to the future development of Byzantine studies. We have proposed in this book various approaches, methods, and techniques, some of which derive from other fields of scholarly investigation, that can be used to put new questions to old sources. Answers can in this way be found to the questions that are of the greatest interest and concern to people in the modern world, and a window can be opened onto the real life of people in Byzantium, showing how they both resembled and differed from other peoples living in their own time and today.

NOTES

Notes to Introduction

1. W. Ullmann, *The Future of Medieval History* (Inaugural Lecture; Cambridge, 1973), 24–26 called for the integration of Byzantium into the history of medieval Europe, saying that Rome and Constantinople were "the two cornerstones upon which the development of medieval history rested" (p. 25). See also K. Bosl, "Wünsche der Mediävistik an die Byzantinistik," in *Polychordia: Festschrift F. Dölger* (Amsterdam, 1966), 1:30–48, and the thoughtful article of G. von Grunebaum, "Parallelism, Convergence, and Influence in the Relations of Arab and Byzantine Philosophy, Literature, and Piety," *DOP*, 18 (1964), 91–111.

2. *XVe Congrès des études byzantines. Séance de clôture. Athènes, 11e Septembre 1976.*

3. Beck, *Byzantinistik*, 7 f.

4. *Ibid.*, 13.

5. *Ibid.*, 30.

6. *Ibid.*, 31 ff. See also Beck, *Jahrtausend*, 13.

7. S. Markiš, *Gomer i ego poemy* (Moscow, 1962), 104–14.

8. G. Duby, *Hommes et structures du moyen âge* (Paris and The Hague, 1973), 104.

9. E. A. R. Brown, "The Tyranny of a Construct: Feudalism and Historians of Medieval Europe," *American Historical Review*, 79 (1974), 1063–88.

10. The great medievalist G. G. Coulton asked in his *Fourscore Years: An Autobiography* (Cambridge, 1944), 324, "Why should not even the most scientific historian content himself with Goethe's confession of faith: 'I can promise to be sincere, but not to be impartial.'"

11. Even Erwin Panofsky, in his essay "In Defense of the Ivory Tower," *The Centennial Review of Arts and Science*, 1 (1957), 111–22, argued that the tower was a watchtower from which scholars, the watchmen, should sound the alarm when liberty is threatened.

12. It seems to us exaggerated by Herbert Hunger in the last part of his excellent *Reich der neuen Mitte* (Graz, Vienna, and Cologne, 1965), 377–82.

13. It is curious that many English dictionaries, including the *Oxford English Dictionary*, fail to record this use of the term, which is common today. It was also used to mean "sophisticated and subtle," but with an implication of "too subtle."

14. On Le Beau, see Ch. Diehl, "Les études byzantines en France," *BZ*, 9 (1900), 2; A. A. Vasiliev, *History of the Byzantine Empire* (Madison, 1952), 11 f.; A. Kazhdan, "Zagadka Komninov," *VizVrem*, 25 (1964), 56–58; J. Irmscher, "Charles Lebeau und das deutsche Byzanzbild," *Annales du service des antiquités de l'Egypte*, 62 (1977), 175–84.

15. There are many works on the scholarly activity of Gibbon. Among the most recent is M. Baridou, *Edward Gibbon et le mythe de Rome* (Paris, 1977).

16. Ségur, *Histoire du Bas-Empire*, 3 (Paris, 1826), 248 f.

17. On Fallmerayer, see, among many others, H. O. Eberl, *J. Ph. Fallmerayers Schriften in ihrer Bedeutung für die historische Erkenntnis des gräko-slavischen Kulturkreises*

(Berlin, 1930). See also N. M. Petrovskij, "K voprosu o genezise teorii Fall'merajera," *Žurnal Ministerstva Narodnogo Prosveščenija* 48 (1913), no. 11, 104–149.

18. This is equally true of other areas of historical investigation. "If one looks at three of the most passionate and hard-fought historical battles of the 1950s and 1960s—about the rise or decline of the gentry in seventeenth-century England, about the rise or fall of working-class real income in the early stages of industrialization, and about the causes, nature and consequences of American slavery—all were at bottom debates fired by current ideological concerns": Lawrence Stone, "The Revival of Narrative: Reflections on a New Old History," *PastP*, 85 (1979), 9.

19. Sjuzjumov, "Ikonoborčestvo," 66. The ideas of this work, written more than 30 years ago, were developed by the author in a series of later articles, of which the most important are: "O roli zakonomernostej, faktorov, tendencij i slučajnostej pri perechode ot rabovladel'českogo stroja k feodal'nomu v vizantijskom gorode," *ADSV*, 3 (1965), 5–16 and "Istoričeskaja rol' Vizantii i ee mesto vo vsemirnoj istorii," *VizVrem*, 29 (1968), 32–44.

20. Weiss, "Antike," 529–60. On the Byzantine judicial system see his "Hohe Richter in Konstantinopel. Eustathios Rhomaios und seine Kollegen," *JÖB*, 22 (1973), 117–43.

21. G. Weiss, *Oströmische Beamte im Spiegel der Schriften des Michael Psellos* (Munich, 1973). Is it significant that Weiss follows Bury in using "Eastern Roman" rather than "Byzantine"?

22. F. Uspenskij, "Cari Aleksej II i Andronik Komniny," *Žurnal Ministerstva Narodnogo Prosveščenija*, 219 (1880), 100.

23. On the scientific heritage of Ostrogorsky, see A. Kazhdan, "Koncepcija istorii Vizantijskoj imperii v trudach G. A. Ostrogorskogo," *VizVrem*, 39 (1978), 76–85.

24. G. Ostrogorsky, "Byzantine Cities in the Early Middle Ages," *DOP*, 13 (1959), 47–66, reprinted in his *Zur byzantinischen Geschichte* (Darmstadt, 1973), 99–118.

25. See K. Sontheimer, *Antidemokratisches Denken in der Weimarer Republik* (2nd ed., Munich, 1968), 222 ff., who stresses the connection of the historical concept of empire with the Nazi "Third Empire" and some of the central *topoi* of anti-individualistic thought.

26. This idea is clearly expressed in Hunger, *Prooimion*, 15 f.

27. See, for instance, the Preface by J. Le Goff to *La Nouvelle histoire* (Paris, 1978), 16 f.

28. M. Bloch, *Apologie pour l'histoire* (Paris, 1974), 121.

29. G. Ostrogorsky, *Geschichte des byzantinischen Staates*, 3rd ed. (Munich, 1963), trans. J. Hussey, *History of the Byzantine State* (Oxford, 1968; New Brunswick, 1969).

30. Stone, "Revival of Narrative," 3–24.

Notes to Chapter One

1. See Introduction, n. 29.

2. MM, 4, 165 f. On the date, see H. Ahrweiler, "L'histoire et la géographie de la région de Smyrne," *TM*, 1 (1965), 118.

3. NicCh, 523 f.

4. Lemerle, *Cinq études*, 287.

5. The idea of the economic upsurge of Byzantine cities in the eleventh century was proposed in A. P. Kazhdan, *Derevnja i gorod v Vizantii IX–X vv.* (Moscow, 1960),

248 f. It was developed thereafter by M. Hendy, C. Morrisson, and others.

6. E. Th. Tsolakes, *Ioannes Skylitzes Continuatus* (Thessalonike, 1968), 171.6–10.

7. Ch. Diehl, *Choses et gens de Byzance* (Paris, 1926), 177, 181, 211.

8. *Ibid.*, 174 ff. An attempt to reconsider the political role of Justinian II was made recently by Constance Head (*Justinian II of Byzantium* [Madison, Milwaukee, and London, 1972]), who tried to see his activity in a more balanced light. The author emphasizes more than Diehl does that Justinian's rule might be described as typically Byzantine and that he belonged to a particular state and to a particular historical era (p. 152) but even here this quality of belonging to a particular time and space appears as an "acquittal" rather than an explanation of a human character. Head does not tell us what was "typically Byzantine."

9. A. P. Kazhdan and M. A. Zaborov, "Gijom Tirskij o sostave gospodstvujuščego klassa v Vizantii," *VizVrem*, 32 (1971), 48 f.

10. Kinnamos, *Epitome*, ed. A. Meineke (Bonn, 1836), 68.20–69.3. Translation by C. M. Brand in *Deeds of John and Manuel Comnenus by John Kinnamos* (New York, 1976), 59 f.

11. NicCh, 410.61–72.

12. *PG*, 138, col. 176 CD.

13. John Chrysostom, *Sur la vaine gloire et l'éducation des enfants*, ed. A. M. Malingrey (Paris, 1972), 146.648–650, 92.196–202.

14. S. Vryonis, "Byzantine Attitudes toward Islam during the Late Middle Ages," *Greek, Roman and Byzantine Studies*, 12 (1971), 272–74. In Muslim cities the basic units of society were quarters, while guilds remained extremely weak; cf. I. M. Lapidus, "Muslim Cities and Islamic Societies," in *Middle Eastern Cities* (Berkeley and Los Angeles, 1969), 49 f.

15. See the discussion of Kekaumenos's world outlook: A. P. Kazhdan, "K voprosu o social'nych vozzrenijach Kekavmena," *VizVrem*, 36 (1974), 160–67, and Litavrin's answer, *ibid.*, 171–77. On Kekaumenos see also S. Vryonis, "Cultural Conformity in Byzantine Society," in *Individualism and Conformity in Classical Islam* (Wiesbaden, 1977), 128–32. The treatise on kingship, entitled *Logos Nouthetikos*, which according to Vryonis was distinct from the *Strategicon* and was written "by a provincial general" (p. 120), seems in fact to be an integral part of the *Strategicon*.

16. Romanos the Melodist, *Cantica*, ed. P. Maas and C. A. Trypanis (Oxford, 1963), 1:462–71, trans. M. Carpenter, *Kontakia of Romanos, Byzantine Melodist* (Columbia, Mo., 1970–73), 2:239–48.

17. Agathias of Myrina, *Historiarum libri quinque*, 5.5–7, ed. R. Keydell (Berlin and New York, 1967), 171 f., trans. J. D. Frendo (Berlin and New York, 1975), 141 f. On the discussion of the causes of earthquakes, see Averil Cameron, *Agathias* (Oxford, 1970), 113 f.

18. George Pachymeres, *De Michaele et Andronico Palaeologis libri 13*, ed. I. Bekker (Bonn, 1835), 1:304.

19. P. V. Bezobrazov, *Vizantijskij pisatel' i gosudarstvennyj dejatel' Michail Psell* (Moscow, 1890).

20. Ljubarskij, *Psell*, 79–90.

21. F. Tinnefeld, "'Freundschaft' in den Briefen des Michael Psellos. Theorie und Wirklichkeit," *JÖB*, 22 (1973), 151–68.

22. NicCh, 17.41–42, 18.63–64, 97.67–68, 199.51, and others.

23. *Ibid.*, 201.12. See also 131.88–89 and the cliché "kinsman and friends" (41.17, 386.88).

24. *Ibid.*, 267.51.

25. *Ibid.*, 353.22.

26. Nicetas Choniates, *Orationes et epistulae*, ed. I. A. van Dieten (Berlin and New York, 1972), 165.26, 196.7–9.

27. Symeon the Theologian, *Chapitres théologiques, gnostiques et pratiques*, ed. J. Darrouzès (Paris, 1957), pt. 1, 83.

28. On the importance of this concept for earlier history, see P. A. Brunt, "'Amicitia' in the Late Roman Republic," *Proceedings of the Cambridge Philological Society*, 191, N.S. 11 (1965), 1–20.

29. H. Ahrweiler, "Recherches sur la société byzantine au XIe siècle: nouvelles hiérarchies et nouvelles solidarités," *TM*, 6 (1976), 117 f.

30. Lemerle, *Cinq études*, 186 ff.

31. Weiss, *Kantakuzenos*, 23–53.

32. NicCh, 642.81–85.

33. *Ibid.*, 130 f.

34. On Pančenko's theory, see M. Ja. Sjuzjumov, "Naučnoe nasledie B. A. Pančenko," *VizVrem*, 25 (1964), 41–49.

35. On the dualism of the Byzantine village community, see Kazhdan, *Derevnja i gorod*, 21–56.

36. *Vie de Théodore le Sykéon*, ed. A.-J. Festugière, 1 (Brussels, 1970), 113, no. 143.1–2.

37. On the internal weakness of the Byzantine guild, see M. Ja. Sjuzjumov, "Remeslo i torgovlja v Konstantinople v načale X v.," *VizVrem*, 4 (1951), 11–41. Cf. his Introduction to *Vizantijskaja kniga eparcha* (Moscow, 1962), 33–42.

38. E. Frances, "La disparition des corporations byzantines," *Actes du XIIe Congrès international d'études byzantines*, 2 (Belgrade, 1964), 98.

39. See, for example, J. H. Scheltema, "Byzantine Law," *CMH*, 2:72.

40. *Kek*, 120.16–20, 118.7, 200.23–24.

41. Sathas, 5:298.12–16.

42. *EustOp*, 92.3–4, 32–36.

43. MichAk, 183.3–15.

44. H. Hunger, "Christliches und Nichtchristliches im byzantinischen Eherecht," *Österreichisches Archiv für Kirchenrecht*, 18 (1967), 305–25. The importance of familial ties in Byzantium is also stressed by A. Ducellier, *Le drame de Byzance* (Paris, 1976), 16–20.

45. See K. Ritzer, *Formen, Riten, und religiöses Brauchtum der Eheschliessung in den christlichen Kirchen des ersten Jahrtausends* (Münster, 1962), 104.

46. Divorce by mutual consent and by repudiation of the wife by the husband were both known in early medieval Gaul, in spite of ecclesiastical opposition; see Ch. Galy, *La famille à l'époque mérovingienne* (Paris, 1901), 106–7.

47. I. Kajanto, "The Emergence of the Late Single Name System," *L'onomastique latine* (Paris, 1977), 421–28.

48. In addition to the old, but still valuable, work by B. Phillpotts, *Kindred and Clan in the Middle Ages and After* (Cambridge, 1913), see D. Bullough, "Early Medieval Social Groupings: The Terminology of Kinship," *PastP*, 45 (1969), 9–18.

49. D. Jacoby, *La féodalité en Grèce médiévale* (Paris and The Hague, 1971), 35.

50. Laiou, *Peasant*, 80.

51. Sym *Hymnes*, 1:286 (n. 15.127–28).

52. W. H. C. Frend, "The Monks and the Survival of the East Roman Empire in the Fifth Century," *PastP*, 54 (1972), 3–24 stressed the flexibility of Byzantine as contrasted with western monasticism.

53. R. Janin, "Le monachisme byzantin au moyen âge. Commende et typica

(x^e–xive siècle)," *REB*, 22 (1964), 5–44 analyzes the features of Byzantine monastic life reflected in the 32 published *typika* (acts of foundation).

54. Hunger, *Prooimion*, 93 f.

55. Sym *Cat*, 2:284 f. (n. 18.247–260).

56. Nicephorus Gregoras, *Byzantina historia*, ed. L. Schopen, 2 (Bonn, 1830), 796.

57. G. Podskalsky, *Byzantinische Reichseschatologie* (Munich, 1972), 101 f.

58. W. E. Kaegi, *Byzantium and the Decline of Rome* (Princeton, 1968), 135–42.

59. P. Guilhiermoz, *Essai sur l'origine de la noblesse en France au moyen âge* (Paris, 1902), 151–54, 349 ff., etc.

60. See Vryonis, "Cultural Conformity," 138.

61. There is repeated stress on the firmness or security of status, liberty, and payments in the *Liber memorialis* of Remiremont, which contains entries from the ninth to the twelfth centuries: see G. Constable, "The *Liber memorialis* of Remiremont," *Speculum*, 47 (1972), 273.

Notes to Chapter Two

1. Much material relevant to our topic is found in F. Braudel, *The Mediterranean and the Mediterranean World in the Age of Philip II*, trans. S. Reynolds (London, 1972).

2. J. Koder, F. Hild, *Hellas und Thessalia*. in *Tabula Imperii Byzantini*, 1 (Vienna, 1976).

3. Guillou, *Civilisation*, 19–39.

4. F. Hild, *Das byzantinische Strassensystem in Kappadokien* (Vienna, 1977).

5. I. P. Medvedev, "Fenomen transurbanizacii i ego rol' v stanovlenii feodal'nogo vizantijskogo goroda," *ADSV*, 6 (1969), 79–85 with reference to the works of Zakythinos and other scholars. See also C. Foss, *Ephesus after Antiquity* (Cambridge, 1979), 106 f.

6. R. M. Harrison, "Lycia in Late Antiquity," *Yayla*, 1 (1977), 14.

7. E. Honigmann, *Die Ostgrenze des byzantinischen Reiches von 363 bis 1071* (Brussels, 1935).

8. See above all V. von Falkenhausen, *Untersuchungen über die byzantinische Herrschaft in Süditalien vom 9. bis ins 11. Jahrhundert* (Wiesbaden, 1967); new Italian edition: *La dominazione bizantina nell' Italia meridionale dal IX all' XI secolo* (Bari, 1978).

9. G. G. Litavrin, *Bolgarija i Vizantija v XI–XII vv.* (Moscow, 1960), 250–88. Cf. now V. Tŭpkova-Zaimova, *Dolni Dunav—granična zona na vizantijskija Zapad* (Sofia, 1976), 34–70. On the problem of the Byzantine frontier zone in general, see H. Ahrweiler, "La frontière et les frontières de Byzance en Orient," *Actes du XIVe Congrès international des études byzantines*, 1 (Bucharest, 1974), 209–30 and the accompanying reports.

10. The frontier has attracted considerable interest among recent western medievalists, especially in Spain, on which, see in particular the pioneering articles (which apply to the Old World some of the concepts developed by F. J. Turner for the New) of C. J. Bishko, including "The Castilian as Plainsman: the Medieval Ranching Frontier in La Mancha and Extremadura," *The New World Looks at Its History* (Austin, Texas, 1963), 47–69, and the works of R. I. Burns, such as *The Crusader Kingdom of Valencia: Reconstruction on a Thirteenth-Century Frontier* (Cambridge, Mass., 1967).

11. The synoptic edition is by E. Trapp, *Digenes Akrites* (Vienna, 1971). The text of the Grottaferrata version, with English translation, is in *Digenes Akrites*, ed. J. Mavrogordato (Oxford, 1956). On the epic, see N. Oikonomidès, "'L'«épopée» de Digénis et la frontière orientale de Byzance aux Xe et XIe siècles," *TM*, 7 (1979), 375–97.

12. For a productive attempt to use Byzantine miniatures for the reconstruction of "a collective ethnic portrait," see V. Christides, "Pre-Islamic Arabs in Byzantine Illuminations," *Le Muséon*, 83 (1970), 167–81.

13. On the settlement of foreign groups in Byzantium, see S. Vryonis, "Byzantine and Turkish Societies and their Sources of Manpower," in *War, Technology and Society in the Middle East* (London, 1975), 126–40.

14. See the remarks in the Introduction on the propensity of scholars to praise centralization and deplore regionalism.

15. G. von Grunebaum, *Medieval Islam*, 2nd ed. (Chicago, 1953), 9 (citing Rambaud).

16. See, for instance, Kinnamos's description of Dorylaion (Kinnamos, *Epitome*, ed. A. Meineke [Bonn, 1836], 294.12–21) or Attaleiates's description of Hierapolis (Michael Attaleiates *Historia*, ed. I. Bekker [Bonn, 1853], 111.18–23).

17. MichAk, 2:258.12–16.

18. Braudel, *The Mediterranean*, 25–53.

19. The title of the article of H. Evert-Kappesowa, "Morze w kulturze bizantyjskiej," in *La mer et les civilisations mondiales* (Warsaw, 1976), 283–94, is to some extent misleading since it deals primarily with the political and economic aspects of the sea, not with its effect on the culture and social psychology of the Byzantines.

20. *PG*, 126, cols. 501C–504A.

21. S. Doanidu, "Ἡ παραίτησις Νικολάου τοῦ Μουζάλωνος ἀπὸ τῆς ἀρχιεπισκοπῆς Κύπρου," *Hellenica*, 7 (1934), 119.266.

22. H. Ahrweiler, *Byzance et la mer* (Paris, 1966), 414 f.

23. J. Lefort, "Rhétorique et politique. Trois discours de Jean Mauropous en 1047," *TM*, 6 (1976), 285–93.

24. E. Herman, "La 'stabilitas loci' nel monachismo bizantino," *OChP*, 21 (1955), 116–42.

25. Published in A. Vasiliev, *Anecdota graeco-byzantina* (Moscow, 1893), 135–65.

26. I. Troickij, "Ioanna Foki skazanie vkratce o gorodach i stranach ot Antiochii do Ierusalima," *Pravoslavnyj Palestinskij sbornik*, 8 (1899), pt. 2.

27. R. S. Lopez, "The Dollar of the Middle Ages," *Journal of Economic History*, 11 (1951), reprinted in his *Byzantium and the World around it: Economic and Institutional Relations* (London, 1978), pt. 7, 209–34.

28. A. Bellinger and P. Grierson, *Catalogue of the Byzantine Coins in the Dumbarton Oaks Collection*, II, 1 (Washington, D.C., 1968), 7.

29. M. F. Hendy, "On the Administrative Basis of the Byzantine Coinage c.400–c.900 and the Reforms of Heraclius," *University of Birmingham Historical Journal*, 12 (1970), 129–54; A. R. Bellinger, "The Coins and Byzantine Imperial Policy," *Speculum*, 31 (1956), 70 f.

30. Michel Italikos, *Lettres et discours*, ed. P. Gautier (Paris, 1972), 209 f. See V. Laurent, "Numismatique et folklore dans la tradition byzantine," *Cronica numismatica şi arheologica*, 15, no. 119/120 (1940), 250–63; T. Bertelè, "Costantino il Grande e S. Elena su alcune monete bizantine," *Numismatica*, 14 (1948), 91–106.

31. The latest edition, with bibliography, is by P. Gautier, "Le Typikon du Christ Sauveur Pantocrator," *REB*, 32 (1974), 1–145.

32. Ioannes Tzetzes, *Epistulae*, ed. P. A. M. Leone (Leipzig, 1972), 81.16–82.2.

33. P. Lemerle, "Esquisse pour une histoire agraire de Byzance," *Rhist*, 219 (1958), 254–84.

34. Patlagean, *Pauvreté*, 377, 379.

35. Ostrogorsky, *Féodalité*, 317. See also K. Chvostova, *Količestvennyj podchod k srednevekovoj social'no-ekonomičeskoj istorii* (Moscow, 1980), 102–19. On the breakdown of the

old system of municipal tax collection in the fourth century and its replacement by imperial taxation based on land and, eventually, direct taxation of the individual, see W. Goffart, *Caput and Colonate: Towards a History of Late Roman Taxation* (Toronto, 1974).

36. K. V. Chvostova, *Osobennosti agrarnopravovych otnošenij v pozdnej Vizantii* (Moscow, 1968), 126. In spite of these clear-cut numbers, Chvostova surmised no more than a tendency towards the transformation of the *telos* into a hearth tax (p. 158). Cf. J. Lefort, "Fiscalité médiévale et informatique. Recherches sur les barèmes pour l'imposition des paysans byzantins du XIVe siècle," *Rhist*, 252 (1974), 315–52, who emphasizes, on the contrary, the survival of the traditional forms of taxation. On Lefort's technique, see K. V. Chvostova, "Sud'by parikii i osobennosti nalogoobloženija parikov v Vizantii XIV v.," *VizVrem*, 39 (1978), 63–75.

37. See the tables in E. Schilbach, *Byzantinische Metrologie* (Munich, 1970), 63–65.

38. A. P. Kazhdan, *Agrarnye otnošenija v Vizantii XIII–XIV vv.* (Moscow, 1952), 159.

39. *Akty russkogo na sv. Afone monastyrja sv. Panteleimona* (Kiev, 1873), 120.24–27.

40. MM, 4:397.27–398.10.

41. On some of these developments in the West as well as the East, see L. White, Jr., *Medieval Technology and Social Change* (Oxford, 1962). The earliest windmills in England are now dated to the twelfth century.

42. E. Ashtor, *A Social and Economic History of the Near East in the Middle Ages* (London, 1976), 45 f.

43. G. R. Davidson, "A Mediaeval Glass-Factory at Corinth," *American Journal of Archaeology*, 44 (1940), 302.

44. A. P. Rudakov, *Očerki vizantijskoj kul'tury po dannym grečeskoj agiografii* (Moscow, 1917), 142.

45. Ioannes Tzetzes, *Epistulae*, 33.3–16.

46. W. Nissen, *Die Diataxis des Michael Attaliates von 1077* (Jena, 1894), 108.

47. Dietrich Claude, *Die byzantinische Stadt im 6. Jahrhundert* (Munich, 1969), 63, refers very cautiously to the effort of merchants and artisans to bring their shops into the street. Clive Foss, *Byzantine and Turkish Sardis* (Cambridge, Mass., and London, 1976), 42 f., lays greater stress on this phenomenon.

48. G. G. Litavrin, "Otnositel'nye razmery i sostav imuščestva provincial'noj vizantijskoj aristokratii vo vtoroj polovine XI v.," in *Vizantijskie očerki* (Moscow, 1971), 164–68.

49. PL, 201, col. 734 AB. See S. Runciman, *A History of the Crusades*, II (Cambridge, 1952), 350.

50. Weiss, *Kantakuzenos*, 12.

51. Toynbee, *Constantine*, 39 f.

52. A large-scale investigation of late Byzantine and early Ottoman demography is now being conducted under the joint auspices of Dumbarton Oaks and the Center for Byzantine Studies at the University of Birmingham.

53. Laiou, *Peasant*, 271 f.

54. Michael Psellos, *Chronographie*, ed. E. Renauld, 2 (Paris, 1928), 151 (chap. 27.8).

55. Nicholas I, Patriarch of Constantinople, *Letters*, ed. R. J. H. Jenkins and L. G. Westerink (Washington, D.C., 1973), 200 (ep. 29.47–49).

56. S. Lampros, Κερκυραϊκὰ ἀνέκδοτα (Athens, 1882), 48.21–23.

57. See A. Hofmeister, "Puer. Iuvenis. Senex. Zum Verständnis der mittelalterlichen Altersbezeichnungen," in *Papsttum und Kaisertum* (Festschrift P. Kehr), ed. A. Brackmann (Munich, 1926), 316, and J. de Ghellinck, "Juventus. gravitas. senectus," in *Studia medievalia in honorem . . . Raymundi Josephi Martin* (Bruges, 1948), 39–59.

58. *Tusculum Lexikon*, ed. W. Buchwald, A. Hohlweg, and O. Prinz (Munich, 1963).

59. Laiou, *Peasant*, 292–94.

60. Anna Comnena, *Alexiade*, ed. B. Leib (Paris, 1967), 107.25–26.

61. K. Schmid, "Über das Verhältnis von Person und Gemeinschaft im früheren Mittelalter," *Frühmittelalterliche Studien*, 1 (1967), 225–49, and D. Herlihy, "Family Solidarity in Medieval Italian History," in *Economy, Society, and Government in Medieval Italy: Essays in Memory of Robert L. Reynolds* (Kent, Ohio, 1970), 173–84.

62. A. L. Jakobson, "O čislennosti naselenija srednevekovogo Chersonesa," *Viz Vrem*, 19 (1961), 154 f.

63. D. Jacoby, "La population de Constantinople à l'époque byzantine," *Byzantion*, 31 (1961), reprinted in his *Société et démographie à Byzance et en Romanie latine* (London, 1975), pt. 1, 107.

64. B. Berenson, *Studies in Medieval Painting* (New Haven, 1930), 8–9, who stressed (p. 8) that "The economic factor is not to be ignored in judging works of art."

65. Koukoules, 5:9–135.

66. J. L. Teall, "The Grain Supply of the Byzantine Empire," *DOP*, 13 (1959), 98–100.

67. Patlagean, *Pauvreté*, 36–53, 92–101.

68. M. Rouche, "La faim à l'époque carolingienne: essai sur quelques types de rations alimentaires," *Rhist*, 250 (1973), 295–320.

69. A. I. Papadopulos-Kerameus, *Noctes Petropolitanae* (St. Petersburg, 1913), 13.

70. MM, 5:306, 320. The typikon speaks of an annonical modios monthly.

71. Prodrom, 41. *Medimnos* was an archaic word for *modios*. It is not clear what kind of modios is meant, but it does not change the calculation radically.

72. *EustOp*, 155.69–71.

73. E. Schilbach, *Byzantinische Metrologie*, 57, A.6.

74. Ž. Vŭžarova, *Slavjano-bŭlgarskoto selišče kraj sela Popina, Silistrensko* (Sofia, 1956), 89.

75. Ju. P. Glušakova, "O putešestvii igumena Daniila v Palestinu," in *Problemy obščestvenno-političeskoj istorii Rossii* (Moscow, 1963), 86.

76. H. Antoniadis-Bibicou, "Villages désertés en Grèce," in *Villages désertés en histoire économique* (Paris, 1965), 364.

77. Particularly important in this context is C. Foss, "The Persians in Asia Minor and the End of Antiquity," *EHR*, 90 (1975), 721–47. See also his monographs *Byzantine and Turkish Sardis*, 57–76, with additions by A. Kazhdan in *Byzantina*, 9 (1977), 478–84, and "Late Antique and Byzantine Ankara," *DOP*, 31 (1977), 84 f.

78. R. B. K. Stevenson, *The Pottery 1936–1937: The Great Palace of the Byzantine Emperors* (Oxford, 1947), 33–35.

79. P. Charanis, "The Monk as an Element of Byzantine Society," *DOP*, 25 (1971), 65 f.

80. D. M. Metcalf, *Coinage in the Balkans* (Thessalonica, 1965), 25, 36.

81. M. F. Hendy, *Coinage and Money in the Byzantine Empire, 1081–1261* (Washington, D.C., 1969), 320; Angold, *Exile*, 141 f.

82. C. Morrisson, "La dévaluation de la monnaie byzantine au XI⁰ siècle," *TM*, 6 (1976), 24 f.; Lemerle, *Cinq études*, 272–93. This view of the Byzantine eleventh century is close to that of Cyril Mango, "Les monuments de l'architecture du XI⁰ siècle et leur signification historique et sociale," *TM*, 6 (1976), 352 ff., and especially of his *Byzantium: The Empire of New Rome* (London, 1980), where chap. 3 is entitled "The Disappearance and Revival of Cities," 60–87.

Notes to Chapter Three

1. See W. Jaeger, *Paideia: the Ideal of Greek Culture*, trans. G. Highet, I–III (Oxford, 1939–44), especially the Introduction (I:xii–xxix), as well as Averincev, *Poetika*, especially 57–83.

2. Modern scholars tend to accentuate the influence of Greek thought on early Christianity rather than their differences; see, for example, W. Jaeger, *Early Christianity and Greek Paideia* (Cambridge, Mass., 1961).

3. L. Rydén, *Das Leben des heiligen Narren Symeon von Leontios von Neapolis* (Stockholm, Göteborg, and Uppsala, 1963), 145–48.

4. On this scheme, see S. V. Poljakova, "Fol'klornyj sjužet o ščastlivom glupce v nekotorych pamjatnikach agiografii VIII v.," *VizVrem*, 34 (1973), 130–36.

5. On this concept, see H. Ahrweiler, *L'idéologie politique de l'Empire byzantin* (Paris, 1975), 129–47.

6. Constantine Porphyrogenitus, *Le livre de cérémonies*, ed. A. Vogt, 1 (Paris, 1935), 2.19–24.

7. Sathas, 5:68.26–72.17.

8. Michael Psellos, *Scripta minora*, ed. E. Kurtz and F. Drexl, 1 (Milan, 1936), 67.23–68.1.

9. H. Maguire, "Truth and Convention in Byzantine Descriptions of Works of Art," *DOP*, 28 (1974), 114.

10. Ammianus Marcellinus, bk. 16, 10.10; bk. 21, 16.7. trans. J. Rolfe (London and Cambridge, Mass., 1937), 2: 177. See R. MacMullen, "Some Pictures in Ammianus Marcellinus," *Art Bulletin*, 46 (1964), 440 f.; L. W. Bonfante, "Emperor, God and Man in the 4th Century: Julian the Apostate and Ammianus Marcellinus," *La Parola del Passato*, 19 (1964), 427.

11. Ljubarskij, *Psell*, 237.

12. Sym *Cat*, 3:72 (no. 26.28–31).

13. Nicholas Mesarites, "Description of the Church of the Holy Apostles at Constantinople," ed. G. Downey, *Transactions of the Amer. Philos. Soc.*, 47 (1957), 908, § 26.6.

14. J. Lefort, "Rhétorique et politique. Trois discours de Jean Mauropous en 1047," *TM*, 6 (1976), 285–93.

15. Sym *Cat*, 3:182–84 (no. 29.199–200 and 230–34). See also Sym *Hymnes*, 418 (no. 33.80–82).

16. *Vita Euthymii Patriarchae CP*, ed. P. Karlin-Hayter (Brussels, 1970), 75.25–28, 77.23–27.

17. On various aspects of ritualization, see J. Huxley, ed., *A Discussion on Ritualization of Behavior in Animals and Man*, Philosophical Transactions of the Royal Society of London B. 251 (London, 1966), 247–556, especially the essays of E. Gombrich on art and M. Fortes on divination.

18. Koukoules, 4:22 f.

19. E. Kurtz, *Zwei griechische Texte über die hl. Theophano, die Gemahlin Kaisers Leo VI* (St. Petersburg, 1898), 2.28–34.

20. For instance W. Kroll, "Astrologisches," *Philologus*, 57 (1898), 131.

21. John Tzetzes, *Scholia in Lycophronis Alexandriam*, ed. E. Scheer (Berlin, 1908), 1.88.

22. Photius, *Lexicon*, ed. S. A. Naber, 2 (Leiden, 1865), 128.6–9, s.v. ῥάμνος.

23. Michael Psellos, *De operatione daemonum*, ed. J. F. Boissonade (Nuremberg, 1838), 25 f.

24. Sathas, 5:11.17–21.

25. See David Herlihy, "The Generation in Medieval History," *Viator*, 5 (1974), 347–64, esp. 359–61.

26. Koukoules, 4:103–5 and 154–87.

27. J. W. Baldwin, "The Intellectual Preparation for the Canon of 1215 against Ordeals," *Speculum*, 36 (1961), 613–36.

28. Angold, *Exile*, 172 f.

29. G. Karlsson, *Idéologie et cérémonial dans l'épistolographie byzantine*, 2nd ed. (Uppsala, 1962); H. Hunger, *Die hochsprachliche profane Literatur der Byzantiner*, 1 (Munich, 1978), 214–33.

30. NicCh, 10.52–56.

31. *Ibid.*, 148.86–90.

32. Cf. the forthcoming article by G. Constable, "Miracles and History in the Twelfth Century."

33. Theodoret, *Kirchengeschichte*, bk. 5, chap. 26, ed. L. Parmentier (Berlin, 1954), 328.2–6.

34. R. Guilland, "Etudes sur l'Hippodrome de Constantinople. L'arène," *JÖB*, 6 (1957), reprinted in his *Etudes de topographie de Constantinople byzantine*, 1 (Berlin, 1969), 442–61. See also A. Cameron, *Circus Factions* (Oxford, 1976), 230 f.

35. A. Cameron, *Porphyrius the Charioteer* (Oxford, 1973), 256 f.

36. R. Guilland, "Etudes sur l'Hippodrome de Byzance," *BS*, 23 (1962), 205 f.

37. *PG*, 87:3, col. 3020 A. See Cameron, *Circus Factions*, 247.

38. R. Guilland, "La disparition des Courses," in *Mélanges offerts à O. et M. Merlier* (Athens, 1955), reprinted in his *Etudes de topographie*, 542–45.

39. W. Hörandner, *Theodoros Prodromos. Historische Gedichte* (Vienna, 1974), 95. On hunting in Byzantium in the twelfth century, see Ph. Koukoules, Κυνηγετικὰ ἐκ τῆς ἐποχῆς τῶν Κομνηνῶν καὶ τῶν Παλαιολόγων, *Epeteris Hetaireias Byzantinon Spoudon*, 9 (1932).

40. R. Guilland, "Etude sur l'Hippodrome de Byzance," *BS*, 27 (1966), 289–307.

41. Christopher of Mitylene, *Die Gedichte*, ed. E. Kurtz (Leipzig, 1903), no. 136.

42. *PG*, 137, col. 727 D.

43. *Ibid.*, col. 741 B–D.

44. S. G. Vilinskij, "Žitie sv. Vasilija Novogo v russkoj literature," *Zapiski Novorossijskogo universiteta, Ist.-filol. fak.*, 6–7 (1911–13). See G. da Costa-Louillet, "Saints de Constantinople aux VIIIe, IXe, Xe siècles," *Byzantion*, 24 (1954), 492–510.

45. See D. Abrahamse, "The Transformation of the Saint in Early Medieval Byzantium," *Byzantine Studies/Etudes byzantines*, 2.2 (1975), 122–31.

46. *PL*, 170, col. 524 D.

47. The earliest reference to trousers in Byzantine literature is by Eustathius of Thessalonica in the twelfth century: see Koukoules, 6: 286.

48. Sym *Hymnes*, 1:288 and 294 (no. 15.149–53 and 207–8).

49. Nicholas I, *Letters*, 220 (ep. 32.101–3).

50. Sym *Hymnes*, 1:190 (no. 4.11–14).

51. Prodrom, 52.80–81.

52. Kek, 174.28–29.

53. MichAk, 2:235.13–19.

54. *EustOp*, 311.42–54, 311.81–312.27.

55. NicCh, 594.1–5.

56. Liutprand of Cremona, *De legatione Constantinopolitana*, 11, 13, 20, 32, ed. J. Becker, 3rd ed. (Hanover and Leipzig, 1915), 181–82, 183, 186, 192. See J. Koder and Th. Weber, *Liutprand von Kremona in Konstantinopel* (Vienna, 1980), 71–99.

57. Th. Khoury, *Manuel II Paléologue. Entretiens avec un musulman* (Paris, 1966), 82–88.

58. Theoph, 2:5 f.

59. E. Sargologos, *La vie de Saint Cyrille le Philéote, moine byzantin* (Brussels, 1964), 48, chap. 3.1.

60. S. V. Poljakova, *Iz istorii vizantijskogo romana* (Moscow, 1979), 37–41.

61. Sym *Hymnes*, 2:476 (no. 39.14).

62. Sym *Hymnes*, 1:292–96 (no. 15.174–75, particularly verses 220–30).

63. *AASS Novembris* IV:692–705.

64. Sathas, 5:7.11.

65. George et Demetrios Tornikes, *Lettres et discours*, ed. J. Darrouzès (Paris, 1970), 243.10–245.1, 245.25–26.

66. See the observations of William Ramsay, *Pauline and other Studies in Early Christian History*, 2nd ed. (London, 1908), 184–88.

67. H. G. Beck, *Kirche und theologische Literatur im byzantinischen Reich* (Munich, 1959), 105 f.

68. Attaleiates, *Historia*, 88.13–15.

69. Laiou, *Peasant*, 78. They headed between 17 and 22 percent of all households she investigated (p. 89).

70. According to Laiou, *Peasant*, 295, a Byzantine girl was ready to marry at fifteen.

71. Prodrom, no. 1.

72. Laiou, *Peasant*, 295.

73. Michael Psellos, *Scripta minora*, 2 (Milan, 1941), 307.2–4. On the place of the infant in the Byzantine family see E. Patlagean, "L'enfant et son avenir dans la famille byzantine (IVe–XIIe siècles)," *Annales de démographie historique* (Paris, La Hague, 1973), 85–93.

Notes to Chapter Four

1. H. A. Wolfson, *The Philosophy of the Church Fathers*, 2nd ed. (Cambridge, Mass., 1964), 362 f.

2. *The Cambridge History of Later Greek and Early Medieval Philosophy*, ed. A. H. Armstrong (Cambridge, 1970), is typical of this isolationist approach, by which philosophical development is studied in a social, political, and cultural vacuum and where there is no reference to the Trinitarian controversy. H. G. Beck regards Byzantine theology as a specific scholarly discipline but emphasizes the necessity of confronting theology with other disciplines and connecting it with "the whole scholarly world," since it "of necessity falls into decay if it is isolated," and the need to study the relation between theology and the religious needs of an average Byzantine in everyday lay life; see Beck, *Jahrtausend*, 166 f., 204 f.

3. H. Grégoire, "The Byzantine Church," in *Byzantium*, ed. N. H. Baynes and H. St. L. B. Moss (Oxford, 1948), 89.

4. H. Jedin, ed., *Handbuch der Kirchengeschichte* (Freiburg, Basel, and Vienna, 1963), 1: 474 f.

5. R. Browning, *The Emperor Julian* (Berkeley and Los Angeles, 1976), 167.

6. On these developments, which affected both pagan and Christian thought and attitudes, see E. R. Dodds, *Pagan and Christian in an Age of Anxiety: Some Aspects of Religious Experience from Marcus Aurelius to Constantine* (Cambridge, 1965).

7. H. Jonas, *The Gnostic Religion* (Boston, 1958), 42–47. See *Gnosis und Gnostizismus*, ed. K. Rudolf (Darmstadt, 1975), with bibliography.

8. H. Ch. Puech, *Le Manichéisme* (Paris, 1949), 74–85; O. Klíma, *Manis Zeit und Leben* (Prague, 1962), 203–10. See also the collection of articles *Der Manichäismus*, ed. G. Widengren (Darmstadt, 1977).

9. A. H. Armstrong, *The Architecture of the Intelligible Universe in the Philosophy of Plotinus* (Amsterdam, 1967).

10. Ch. Elsas, *Neuplatonische und gnostische Weltablehnung in der Schule Plotins* (Berlin and New York, 1975), 172 f.

11. J. Meyendorff, *Byzantine Theology* (New York, 1974), 180.

12. On the contradictions in the Christology of Athanasius of Alexandria, see J. Roldanus, *Le Christ et l'homme dans la théologie d'Athanase d'Alexandrie* (Leiden, 1977), 363 f.

13. The modern tendency to prove that Nestorius was orthodox, as in L. I. Scipioni, *Nestorio e il concilio di Efeso* (Milan, 1974), is not supported by any serious evidence.

14. R. C. Chesnut, *Three Monophysite Christologies* (Oxford, 1976), esp. 142 f.

15. For opposing views on this point, see J. Jarry, *Hérésies et factions dans l'Empire byzantin du IVe au VIe siècle* (Cairo, 1968), 552 f., and A. Cameron, "Heresies and Factions," *Byzantion*, 44 (1974), 92–120.

16. See the study by T. E. Gregory, *Vox populi: Popular Opinion and Violence in the Religious Controversies of the Fifth Century A.D.* (Columbus, Ohio, 1979), who stresses the various ways in which public opinion, especially in the towns, was shaped and the involvement of the urban crowd in religious controversies.

17. P. Charanis, *Church and State in the Later Roman Empire* (Madison, 1939; 2nd ed., Thessalonica, 1974), 60; I. Engelhardt, *Mission and Politik in Byzanz* (Munich, 1974), 174.

18. Philostorgius, *Hist. eccl.* 2:2.

19. Manlio Simonetti, *La crisi ariana nel IV secolo* (Rome, 1975), 554–59 acknowledges in general the effect of social conflicts on the "Arian crisis" but stresses the primarily religious character of the movement.

20. E. E. Lipšic, *Očerki istorii vizantijskogo obščestva i kul'tury. VIII–pervaja polovina IX veka* (Moscow and Leningrad, 1961), 421 f.

21. K. N. Uspenskij, *Očerki po istorii Vizantii* (Moscow, 1917), 258 f.

22. Sjuzjumov, "Ikonoborčestvo," 104 f.

23. M. V. Anastos, "Iconoclasm and Imperial Rule, 717–842," *CMH*, 1:67 f. S. Gero, *Byzantine Iconoclasm during the Reign of Leo III* (Louvain, 1973), 131, also says that Byzantine Iconoclasm was not Muslim, Jewish, or Anatolian in its origin, but appeared as "an imperial heresy," born in the royal palace.

24. O. Grabar, "Islam and Iconoclasm," in *Iconoclasm* (Birmingham, 1977), 49 f.

25. L. Barnard, "The Ideology of Images," in *Iconoclasm* (Birmingham, 1977), 13. S. Gero, "The Eucharistic Doctrine of the Byzantine Iconoclasts and its Sources," *BZ*, 68 (1975), 21. See also his evaluation of Iconoclasm following the idea of Paparrhegopoulos as an "unsuccessful attempt at a reformation" in his "Byzantine Iconoclasm and the Failure of a Medieval Reformation," in *The Image of the Word* (Missoula, Montana, 1977), 56 f. Peter Brown, "A Dark-Age Crisis: Aspects of the Iconoclastic Controversy," *EHR*, 88 (1973), 1–34, is one of the few who sees Iconoclasm as a controversy in connection with contemporary sociocultural problems. He considers these to be concentrated on the role of the holy man in society and ideology and thus on the struggle of centripetal and centrifugal forces. His article immediately evoked a traditionalist answer: P. Henry, "What was the Iconoclastic Controversy About?" *Church His-*

tory, 45 (1976), 16–31, which emphasized, in contrast, that "the Iconoclastic controversy was a grappling with ancient and fundamental issues" (p. 30)—"the things that only the historian of Christianity notices" (p. 21). A recent article by Kathryn M. Ringrose, "Monks and Society in Iconoclastic Byzantium," *Byzantine Studies/Études byzantines*, 6 (1979), 130–51, reveals an attempt at a social approach to the problem. The author stresses the divergence of monastic groups, whose attitudes toward Iconoclasm depended upon their social origins and connections. According to her (p. 146), Iconoclastic emperors supported, and were supported by, itinerant hermit monks rather than monastic communities.

26. A. Guillou, "Transformations des structures socio-économiques dans le monde byzantin du VIᵉ au VIIIᵉ siècle," *ZRVI*, 19 (1980), 76 f.; J. F. Haldon, *Recruitment and Conscription in the Byzantine Army c.550–950* (Vienna, 1979), 46 f.

27. The public character of early liturgy in Constantinople is emphasized by Thomas Mathews, *The Early Churches of Constantinople: Architecture and Liturgy* (University Park, Pa., and London, 1971). N. K. Moran, "The Musical 'Gestaltung' of the Great Entrance Ceremony in the 12th Century in Accordance with the Rite of Hagia Sophia," *JOB*, 28 (1979), 167–71, places the origin of the Great Entrance procession, as presented in sources from the tenth to twelfth centuries, not at the outside skeuophylakion but at the side altar.

28. G. Lange, *Bild und Wort* (Würzburg, 1968), 219.

29. P. Alexander, "The Iconoclastic Council of St. Sophia (815) and its Definition (*Horos*)," *DOP*, 7 (1953), reprinted in his *Religious and Political History and Thought in the Byzantine Empire* (London, 1978), pt. 8, 44.

30. P. Scazzoso, "La teologia antinomica dello Pseudo-Dionigi," *Aevum*, 50 (1976), 195–234. In this connection it is also important to stress that the antinomian imaginative system of Pseudo-Dionysius resembled the enigmatic structure of phrases in his contemporary Nonnus of Panopolis; see chapter 5.

31. H. Goltz, *Hiera mesiteia. Zur Theorie der hierarchischen Sozietät im Corpus areopagiticum* (Erlangen, 1974), 23–29.

32. H. G. Beck, *Kirche und theologische Literatur im byzantinischen Reich* (Munich, 1959), 348 f.

33. On this subject, see A. P. Kazhdan, "Predvaritel'nye zamečanija o mirovozzrenii vizantijskogo mistika X–XI vv. Simeona," *BS*, 28 (1967), 1–38. Walther Völker, *Praxis und Theoria bei Symeon dem Neuen Theologen* (Wiesbaden, 1974), began with an important statement that Symeon acted not "in an empty vacuum" and was to be understood only "in a concrete ecclesiastical situation" (p. 8), but came to a conventional conclusion concerning Symeon's dependence upon tradition and particularly Maximos the Confessor (p. 454).

34. Symeon the Theologian, *Traités théologiques et éthiques*, ed. J. Darrouzès (Paris, 1966–67), 2: 150.429–31; 1: 306.477–485. See especially the case cited by Symeon in his 18th catechesis (see above, chap. 1, note 55).

35. See E. Herman, "Die Regelung der Armut in den byzantinischen Klöstern," *OChP*, 7 (1941), 406–60.

36. On Palamas, see, above all, J. Meyendorff, *A Study of Gregory Palamas* (London, 1964), previously published in French as *Introduction à l'étude de Grégoire Palamas* (Paris, 1959). See also G. C. Papademetriou, *Introduction to St. Gregory Palamas* (New York, 1973), and especially G. Podskalsky, "Gottesschau und Inkarnation. Zur Bedeutung der Heilsgeschichte bei Gregorios Palamas," *OChP*, 35 (1969), 5–44.

37. It does not matter for our point of view whether the border line was between the East and the West or between the South (the Mediterranean) and the North, as

suggested by P. Brown, "Eastern and Western Christendom in Late Antiquity," in *The Orthodox Churches and the West* (Oxford, 1976), 3 f. The first traces of this "parting of the ways," whether they were social or purely religious, must be sought in the cultural development of the late antique empire.

38. J. Gauss, *Ost und West in der Kirchen- und Papstgeschichte des 11. Jahrhunderts* (Zurich, 1967), 21 f.

39. J. A. W. Hellmann, *Ordo. Untersuchung eines Grundgedankens in der Theologie Bonaventuras* (Munich, Paderborn, and Vienna, 1974), especially 68–92.

40. N. Festa, "Nicetas di Maronea e i suoi dialoghi sulla processione dello Spirito Santo," *Bessarione*, 3a ser., 9 (1912), 99.21–27.

41. *Ibid.*, 103.8–15, 105.7.

42. See, for example, the works by John Phurnes in A. Demetracopulos, *Bibliotheca ecclesiastica*, 1 (Leipzig, 1866), 40.7–9.

43. W. de Vries, *Orient et Occident* (Paris, 1974), 245, marks the following distinctions in the structure of both churches: the role of the councils, the unity of the church, the hierarchical structure of the church, the part played by the emperor in ecclesiastical matters, and above all the primacy of the pope.

Notes to Chapter Five

1. H. Hunger, *Die hochsprachliche profane Literatur der Byzantiner*, 1–2 (Munich, 1978). Cf. A. Kazhdan, "Der Mensch in der byzantinischen Literaturgeschichte," *JÖB*, 28 (1979), 1–21; J.-L. van Dieten, "Die byzantinische Literatur—eine Literatur ohne Geschichte," *HistZ*, 231 (1980), 101–9.

2. F. H. Marshall, "Byzantine Literature," in *Byzantium*, ed. N. H. Baynes and H. St. L. B. Moss (Oxford, 1948), 221. See also S. Runciman, *Byzantine Civilization* (London, 1961), 240.

3. F. Dölger, "Byzantine Literature," *CMH*, 2:207.

4. Guillou, *Civilisation*, 334, 339.

5. P. Lemerle, *Prolégomènes à une édition critique et commentée des "Conseils et Récits" de Kékauménos* (Brussels, 1960), 95.

6. Beck, *Byzantinistik*, 19. Elsewhere Beck admits the *Aktualität* of Byzantine literature, while emphasizing that this actuality was superficial and insignificant; cf. Beck, *Jahrtausend*, 132, 142.

7. S. V. Poljakova, *Iz istorii vizantijskogo romana* (Moscow, 1979), 43–53.

8. J. Leclercq, *Monks and Love in the Twelfth Century* (Oxford, 1979), 62–85.

9. Cf. Hans Belting, *Das illuminierte Buch in der spätbyzantinischen Gesellschaft* (Heidelberg, 1970), 96, who said that there was no distinction between lay and monastic patrons in the selection and ornament of illuminated manuscripts.

10. Dölger, "Byzantine Literature," 210.

11. Symeon Seth, *Syntagma de alimentorum facultatibus*, ed. B. Langkavel (Leipzig, 1868), 35.22–36.26; *Kek*, 210.15–16.

12. For one of many examples, see Franz Grabler, "Niketas Choniates als Redner," *JÖB*, 11–12 (1962–63), 57–58, whose main conclusion is that Nicetas was an educated master of eloquence.

13. Averincev, *Poetika*, 129–49. As noted in chapter 4, in Pseudo-Dionysius this approach coincides with a consistently antinomian world view.

14. Averincev, *Poetika*, 214 f. This principle is not consistently observed by Ro-

manos. In several stanzas the idea of the destruction of Herod's power is expressed in a direct form. So, in the first stanza Herod weeps that his power will quickly be destroyed: Romanos the Melodist, *Hymnes*, ed. J. Grosdidier de Matons, 2 (Paris, 1965), 206.11–12. See also the second and third stanzas, p. 208. For an English translation, see *Kontakia of Romanos, Byzantine Melodist*, trans. M. Carpenter (Columbia, Mo., 1970–73), 1:26–34.

15. I.S. Čičurov, *Mesto "Chronografii" Feofana (načalo IX v.) v rannevizantijskoj istoriografičeskoj tradicii (IV–nač. IX v.)* (Moscow, 1975), 5 f.

16. C. Mango, "Who Wrote the Chronicle of Theophanes?", *ZRVI*, 18 (1978), 9–17.

17. Ch. Loparev, "Vizantijskie žitija svjatych VIII–IX vekov," *VizVrem*, 17 (1910), 18.

18. *Vie de Théodore de Sykéon*, ed. A.-J. Festugière (Brussels, 1970), 19.1–2, 17 (ch. 22); see also trans. in E. Dawes and N. Baynes, *Three Byzantine Saints* (Oxford, 1948).

19. A. Heisenberg, *Nikolaos Mesarites. Die Palastrevolution des Johannes Komnenos* (Würzburg, 1907), 19.24–20.10.

20. H. G. Beck, *Das literarische Schaffen der Byzantiner* (Vienna, 1974), 11 f. Beck, *Jahrtausend*, 123, calculated that there were about 15 emperors among literati; high-ranking officials formed 20 percent and upper clergy—from the bishops upward—more than 30 percent.

21. A. P. Kazhdan, "Chronika Simeona Logofeta," *VizVrem*, 15 (1959), 128, note 24.

22. Kazhdan, *Sostav*, 205 f.

23. H. Hunger, "Klassizistische Tendenzen in der byzantinischen Literatur des 14. Jh.," *Actes du xive Congrès international des études byzantines*, 1 (Bucharest, 1974), 148.

24. I. Ševčenko, "Society and Intellectual Life in the Fourteenth Century," *ibid.*, 1:69–76.

25. I. P. Medvedev, *Vizantijskij gumanism XIV–XV vv.* (Leningrad, 1976), 18.

26. This fact was recently emphasized by C. Mango, "The Availability of Books in the Byzantine Empire, A.D. 750–850," in *Byzantine Books and Bookmen* (Washington, D.C., 1975), 43 f. According to G. Cavallo, "La circolazione libraria nell'età di Giustiniano," in *L'imperatore Giustiniano: storia e mito* (Milan, 1978), 201–36, the crisis was less severe in the eastern provinces of the empire than in the western.

27. J. Vogt, "Etudes sur le théâtre byzantin," *Byzantion*, 6 (1931), 623–40.

28. Augustine, *Confessions*, bk. 6, chap. 3, trans. W. Watts (London and New York, 1931), 272 f.

29. J. Balogh, "Voces paginarum," *Philologus*, 82 (1926–27), 84–109 and 202–40.

30. Averincev, *Poetika*, 184–87.

31. In the *Lexikon zu Dionysika des Nonnos*, ed. W. Peek, 1 (Berlin, 1968), 21 and 336, the verb ἀείδω is registered 41 times, including such traditional expressions as Διόνυσον ἀείσω, while γράφω is mentioned only 13 times, in most instances without any connection with poetical labor.

32. He could exclaim: "Let us sing a hymn": George of Pisidia, *Poemi*, ed. A. Pertusi, 1 (Ettal, 1960), 199.502. On 258.154 he "described" the levying of soldiers.

33. A. Lord, *The Singer of Tales* (Cambridge, Mass., 1960).

34. S. S. Averincev, "Vizantijskie eksperimenty s žanrovoj formoj klassičeskoj grečeskoj tragedii," *Problemy poetiki i istorii literatury* (Saransk, 1973), 255–70.

35. O. Demus, *Byzantine Mosaic Decoration* (London, 1947; repr. New Rochelle, N.Y., 1976), 6 f.

36. E. Kitzinger, *The Art of Byzantium and the Medieval West* (Bloomington, Ind., and London, 1976), 200 f.

37. K. Weitzmann, "The Study of Byzantine Book Illumination," in *The Place of Book Illumination in Byzantine Art* (Princeton, 1975), 3.

38. Erich Auerbach commented on this characteristic of western medieval literary style in *Mimesis*, trans. Willard Trask (New York, 1957), in the chapter on Gregory of Tours, when language "lives in the concrete side of events, it speaks with and in the people who figure in them" (p. 78).

39. A. P. Kazhdan, "Robert de Klari i Nikita Choniat (Nekotorye osobennosti pisatel'skoj manery)," in *Evropa v srednie veka: ekonomika, politika, kul'tura* (Moscow, 1972), 294–99.

40. See for instance N. el-Khoury, "Willensfreiheit bei Ephraem dem Syrer," *Ostkirchliche Studien*, 25 (1976), 60–66.

41. For instance, K. Krumbacher, *Geschichte der byzantinischen Literatur*, 2nd ed. (Munich, 1897), 730. See the new edition, by H. Criscuolo, of Theodosius the Deacon, *De Creta capta* (Leipzig, 1979).

42. The same tendency can be seen in Muslim accounts and depictions of battles with Christians, only there the characteristics are reversed and the Muslims appear as bright and their foes as dark.

43. K. N. Uspenskij, "Feofan i ego chonografija," *VizVrem*, 3 (1950), 427–34. Paul Speck, *Kaiser Konstantin VI* (Munich, 1978), tried to establish various sources used by Theophanes.

44. P. Brown, "The Rise and Function of the Holy Man in Late Antiquity," *Journal of Roman Studies*, 61 (1971), 91 f., argued that the East Roman holy man wielded his idealized power through a type of social inversion.

45. F. H. Tinnefeld, *Kategorien der Kaiserkritik in der byzantinischen Historiographie* (Munich, 1971), 174–77.

46. Ljubarskij, *Psell*, 230–42.

47. *PG*, 133, cols. 1251B–1252B.

48. L. Petit, "Monodie de Théodore Prodrome sur Etienne Skylitzès métropolitain de Trébizonde," *Izvestija Russkogo Archeologičeskogo Instituta v Konstantinopole*, 8.1–2 (1902), 13.211–34.

49. H. Heisenberg, *Nikolaos Mesarites*, 27.5–10, 28.11–13, 45.11–18.

50. A. Grabar, *La sculpture byzantine au moyen âge*, 2 (Paris, 1976).

51. E. Kitzinger, *The Art of Byzantium*, 257 f.

52. This function of the Byzantine image was especially emphasized by V. V. Byčkov, *Vizantijskaja estetika* (Moscow, 1977).

53. On the role of the Virgin in art as the protectress of Constantinople, see A. Cutler, *Transfigurations: Studies in the Dynamics of Byzantine Iconography* (University Park, Pa., 1975), 111–41.

54. NicCh, 332.37–40.

55. This trait is emphasized by I. Spatharakis, *The Portrait in Byzantine Illuminated Manuscripts* (Leiden, 1976), 255 f.

56. H. Belting, *Das illuminierte Buch*, 72 f. Among the few exceptions to this kind of representation of the social role, Belting (p. 88 f.) cites the portrait of John VIII Palaeologus (1425–48), which he attributes to an Italian master, perhaps Pisanello.

57. T. Whittemore, *The Mosaics of Hagia Sophia at Istanbul* (Boston, 1942), pl. xiv, xxx.

58. H. Maguire, "The Depiction of Sorrow in Middle Byzantine Art," *DOP*, 31 (1977), 173 f.

59. On this monastery see P. Miljković-Pepek, *Nerezi* (Belgrade, 1966).

60. I. Ševčenko, "Storia letteraria," in *La civiltà bizantina dal IX all'XI secolo* (Bari, 1978), 99–101, insists that it was Constantine himself who wrote the book, about 950.

61. *Kek*, 284.8–10.

62. A. P. Kazhdan, "Social'nye vozzrenija Michaila Attaliata," *ZRVI*, 17 (1976), 5–14.

63. A. Carile, "La Ὕλη ἱστορίας del cesare Niceforo Briennio," *Aevum*, 43 (1969), 254–64.

64. M. Vickers, "Sirmium or Thessaloniki? A Critical Examination of the St. Demetrius Legend," *BZ*, 67 (1974), 341.

65. M. Hendy, *Coinage and Money in the Byzantine Empire, 1081–1261* (Washington, D.C., 1969), 437 f.

66. A. V. Bank, "Gemmy-steatity-molivdovuly," *Palestinskij sbornik*, 23 (1971), 47.

67. See the survey of the monuments in E. Voordeckers, "A Byzantine Bronze Relief in the Mayer van den Bergh Museum in Antwerp," *Orientalia Lovanensia Periodica*, 1 (1970), 189 f.

68. M. V. Alpatov, "Obraz Georgija voina v iskusstve Vizantii i Drevnej Rusi," *Trudy Otdela Drevnerusskoj literatury*, 12 (1956), 295–98. See also V. N. Lazarev, "Novyj pamjatnik stankovoj živopisi XII v. i obraz Georgija-voina v vizantijskom i drevnerusskom iskusstve," *VizVrem*, 6 (1958), 186–222.

69. C. Erdmann, *The Origin of the Idea of Crusade*, trans. M. Baldwin and W. Goffart (Princeton, 1977), 14, 45–52, on the appearance of saints' banners about the year 1000 and, 273–81, on the patronage of war by saints, especially in the East. See also E. Kantorowicz, "Gods in Uniform," in his *Selected Studies* (Princeton, 1965), 7–24, who associated the appearance of saints in late Antiquity in military garb with the parallel pagan practice.

70. Orderic Vitalis, *The Ecclesiastical History*, 6:2, ed. and trans. M. Chibnall, 3 (Oxford, 1972), 216–17; see also note 3. Cf. Erdmann, *Origin*, 277, and P. Brown, "Eastern and Western Christendom in Late Antiquity," in *The Orthodox Churches and the West* (Oxford, 1976), 16, in whose account Gerold is called Hugh.

71. A. E. Laiou, "The Role of Women in Byzantine Society," *XVI. Internationaler Byzantinistenkongress, Akten* I/1 (Vienna, 1981), 233–60, is the most recent work on this subject.

72. *PG*, 87:3, col. 3705 AB; *AASS Novembris*, IV:228 D.

73. J. Anson, "The Female Transvestite in Early Monasticism: The Origin and Development of a Motif," *Viator*, 5 (1974), 1–32.

74. S. Papadimitriu, "'Ο Πρόδρομος τοῦ Μαρκιανοῦ κώδικος XI, 22," *VizVrem*, 10 (1903), 155–63.

75. See for instance V. Lazarev, *Storia della pittura bizantina* (Turin, 1967), 124 f. Cf. K. Weitzmann, "The Character and Intellectual Origins of the Macedonian Renaissance," in his *Studies in Classical and Byzantine Manuscript Illumination* (Chicago, 1971), 176 f.

76. Photius, *Bibliothèque*, ed. R. Henry, 1 (Paris, 1959), 57 f.

77. Theodosius the Deacon, 2. 255–59.

78. R. Browning, "Homer in Byzantium," *Viator*, 6 (1975), 25 f.

79. Cited by H. G. Beck, *Das literarische Schaffen der Byzantiner* (Vienna, 1974), 7.

80. NicCh, 253.93–95.

81. A. P. Kazhdan, *Kniga i pisatel' v Vizantii* (Moscow, 1973), 107–11.

82. Trans. C. Mango, *The Art of the Byzantine Empire, 312–1453* (Englewood Cliffs, N.J., 1972), 232.

83. V. Nabokov, *Ada; or, Ardor: A Family Chronicle* (New York, 1970), 166–68; cf. also p. 54 and 85 ff.

Notes to Chapter Six

1. Toynbee, *Constantine*, 524. See p. 10 above on other modern uses of the term.

2. Weiss, "Antike," 529–60.

3. Averincev, *Poetika*, 88–104.

4. Z. V. Udal'cova, "K voprosu o genezise feodalizma v Vizantii," *Vizantijskie očerki* (Moscow, 1971), 9f., although on p. 25 she wrote, "Admitting the considerable number of antique elements preserved in all spheres of the life of Byzantine society, we cannot however neglect the fact that they were essentially altered by the synthesis with the tribal organization of the barbarians." This seems to refer to the second model and the predominance of barbarian elements rather than to the third one. Udal'cova's idea met with severe criticism from M. Ja. Sjuzumov, "Zakonomernyj perechod k feodalizmu i sintez," *ADSV*, 12 (1975), 33f., who emphasized that this approach led to the concept of a "mechanical mixture of Roman and Germanic [principles]."

5. An attempt to reconstruct the effect of barbarian style on Byzantine art has been made by Vadim Polevoj, *Iskusstvo Grecii*, 2 (Moscow, 1973), 94f. He stresses, however, that the barbarian style neither became dominant nor was preserved as an independent force in Greek culture.

6. See for instance E. E. Lipšic, "O putjach formirovanija feodal'noj sobstvennosti i feodal'noj zavisimosti v balkanskich i maloazijskich provincijach Vizantii," *VizVrem*, 13 (1958), 42–53; M. Ja. Sjuzumov, "K voprosu o processach feodalizacii v Rimskoj imperii," *Vestnik drevnej istorii* (1955), no. 1, 66 f.

7. On this point, see E. A. R. Brown, "The Tyranny of a Construct: Feudalism and Historians of Medieval Europe," *American Historical Review*, 79 (1974), 1063–88.

8. G. Ostrogorsky, *History of the Byzantine State* (New Brunswick, N.J., 1969), 304.

9. See for instance, H. Hunger, *Aspekte der griechischen Rhetorik von Gorgias bis zum Untergang von Byzanz* (Vienna, 1972). On the other hand, he stressed that it was rather an imitation than a reproduction of classical contents: H. Hunger, "On the Imitation (Mimesis) of Antiquity in Byzantine Literature," *DOP*, 23–24 (1969–70), reprinted in his *Byzantinische Grundlagenforschung* (London, 1973), pt. 15, 21.

10. H. Ahrweiler, *L'idéologie politique de l'Empire byzantin* (Paris, 1975).

11. Lemerle, *Cinq études*, 251.

12. A. Guillou, *Les actes grecs de S. Maria di Messina* (Palermo, 1963), 46 and 107, nos. 1.10 and 11.6. See the editor's comment on the latter act, *ibid.*, 29 f.

13. P. Lemerle, A. Guillou, N. Svoronos, and D. Papachryssanthou, *Actes de Lavra*, 1 (Paris, 1970), 233f., no. 42, especially lines 4–6 and 11–12.

14. To cite the German original: "Es liegt vor, wenn sich wesentliche Erscheinungsformen und Wirkungsweisen sozialen Verhaltens umformen," Weiss, "Antike," 530.

15. The shortage of the *summa honoraria* paid by the citizens of the African *municipia* can be stated only after 235: A. Burgarel-Musso, "Recherches économiques sur l'Afrique romaine," *Revue africaine*, 75 (1934), 114.

16. M. T. W. Arnheim, *The Senatorial Aristocracy in the Later Roman Empire* (Oxford, 1972), 170 f. See the statistical tables on pp. 216–19.

17. The decline of ancient social values in the third century in the East, and especially of the mechanisms that channeled the ambition of rival urban aristocracies into constructive activities, is discussed in P. Brown, *The Making of Late Antiquity* (Cambridge, Mass., 1978).

18. For a comparison of the Muslim *iqtā'* with the Byzantine *pronoia*, for example, see A. K. S. Lambton, "Reflections on the iqtā'," in *Arabic and Islamic Studies in Honor of H. A. R. Gibb* (Cambridge, Mass., 1965), 373.

19. R. Browning, *Byzantium and Bulgaria* (London, 1975).

20. Dimitri Obolensky has repeatedly emphasized the significance of Byzantine cultural diffusion in eastern Europe and the influence of Byzantium on religion, law, art, and literature. But even he pointed out in *The Byzantine Commonwealth* (London, 1971), 308 f., that the veneration of the national dynasty in Russia had no model in Byzantium. It is not simply "a cult of national rulers." It is a different organization of power.

21. P. Lemerle, "Esquisse pour une histoire agraire de Byzance," *Rhist*, 219 (1958), 33–49. In his *Le premier humanisme byzantin* (Paris, 1971), Lemerle prefers to apply a periphrastic title: *Les trois premiers siècles de l'Empire* (pp. 43–73).

22. Georgij Kurbatov, *Osnovnye problemy vnutrennego razvitija vizantijskogo goroda v IV–VIII vv.* (Leningrad, 1971), 207, admitted that the decay of urban life was particularly significant in the small centers. On the slow transformation of the city in this period see also G. Dagron, "Le christianisme dans la ville byzantine," *DOP*, 31 (1977), esp. 25.

23. Patlagean, *Pauvreté*, 170–81.

24. G. Tchalenko, *Villages antiques de la Syrie du Nord. Le massif du Bélus à l'époque romaine*, 1 (Paris, 1953); Brown, *Making of Late Antiquity*, 84.

25. A. H. M. Jones, "Census Records of the Later Roman Empire," *Journal of Roman Studies*, 43 (1953), 49–64. On the other hand, the article by I. F. Fikhman, "U istokov krupnogo zemlevladenija v Oksirinche," *VizVrem*, 38 (1977), 12–18, indicates, in spite of the author's tendency, how weak and doubtful are the data concerning great estates in the Egypt of the fourth and fifth centuries.

26. See J. Percival, "Seigneurial Aspects of Late Roman Estate Management," *EHR*, 84 (1969), 449–73, who concluded that "At the end of the Roman period the villa estate was showing signs of turning into a manor."

27. Weiss, "Antike," 552 f.

28. F. Dvornik, *Early Christian and Byzantine Political Philosophy* (Washington, D.C., 1966), 2:720.

29. J. B. Bury, "The Constitution of the Later Roman Empire," in his *Selected Essays* (Cambridge, 1930; rev. ed., Amsterdam, 1964), 103 f., 109.

30. I. Shahid, "The Iranian Factor in Byzantium during the Reign of Heraclius," *DOP*, 26 (1972), 295–320.

31. For the last survey of the factions' activity in the sixth century, see A. A. Čekalova, "Vosstanie Nika i social'no-političeskaja bor'ba v Konstantinopole v konce V—pervoj polovine VI v.," in *Vizantijskie očerki* (Moscow, 1977), 158–81.

32. For criticism of the so-called "district theory" of the circus parties' movement, see G. Prinzing, "Zu den Wohnvierteln der Grünen und Blauen in Konstantinopel," *Studien zu Frühgeschichte Konstantinopels* (Munich, 1973), 27–48. Prinzing quotes the pioneering work by M. Ja. Sjuzjumov (41, n. 11), which is practically unknown to western scholars.

33. A. Cameron, *Circus Factions: Blues and Greens at Rome and Byzantium* (Oxford, 1976), 271–96, 309 f. Cf. G. L. Kurbatov, "Ešče raz o vizantijskich dimach," *Srednevekovyj gorod*, 3 (Saratov, 1975), 3–21; A. S. Fotiou, "Byzantine Circus Factions and their Riots," *JÖB*, 27 (1978), 1–10; J. Gascou, "Les institutions de l'Hippodrome en Egypt byzantine," *Bulletin de l'institut français d'archéologie orientale*, 76 (1976), 185–212.

34. Victor of Tunnuna, *Chronica*, ed. T. Mommsen, in *Monumenta Germaniae historica: Auctores antiquissimi*, 11 (Berlin, 1894), 195.18–19.

35. The old tradition of Byzantine circus games was emphasized recently by Gilbert Dagron, *Naissance d'une capital* (Paris, 1974), 320–64.

36. Weiss, "Antike," 555 f.

37. *Historia monachorum in Aegypto*, ed. and trans. A.-J. Festugière (Brussels, 1971), 35 f.

38. Daniel the Stylite, a holy man who lived on top of a pillar, was in touch with emperors and the highest clergy. When he heard of the usurpation of Basiliscus (475–76), he came down and proceeded to the palace of Hebdomon, at times carried by the crowd, while the "impious Basiliscus" implored him to return: H. Delehaye, "Vita S. Danielis Stylitae," *Analecta Bollandiana*, 32 (1913), 191–94, trans. in E. Dawes and N. Baynes, *Three Byzantine Saints* (Oxford, 1948), 52–54. In the seventh century another holy man, Theodore of Sykeon, actively intervened in the administration of properties that belonged to the church: *Vie de Théodore de Sykéon*, ed. A.-J. Festugière (Brussels, 1970), 63, no. 76.1–5, trans. in Dawes and Baynes, *Three Byzantine Saints*, 139. On the role of monks as the conscience of society, see W. H. C. Frend, "The Monks and the Survival of the East Roman Empire in the Fifth Century," *PastP*, 54 (1972), 3–24.

39. K. Baus, in *Handbuch der Kirchengeschichte*, 2:1 (Freiburg, Basel, and Vienna, 1973), 383f.

40. K. N. Uspenskij, *Očerki po istorii Vizantii*, 1 (Moscow, 1917), 183–97.

41. Sjuzjumov, "Ikonoborčestvo," 81–89.

42. C. Mango, "Storia dell'arte," in *La civiltà bizantina dal IV al IX secolo* (Bari, 1977), esp. 321.

43. W. E. Kaegi, *Byzantium and the Decline of Rome* (Princeton, 1968), 136–39.

44. G. Dagron, "L'Empire romain d'Orient au IVe siècle et les traditions politiques de l'hellénisme," *TM*, 3 (1968), 180–83.

45. S. S. Averincev, "Imperator Julian i stanovlenie "vizantinizma," *Tradicija v istorii kul'tury* (Moscow, 1978), 79–83.

46. I. Ševčenko, "Hagiography of the Iconoclast Period," in *Iconoclasm* (Birmingham, 1977), 113–29.

47. A. P. Kazhdan and I. S. Čičurov, "O strukture vizantijskogo obščestva VII–IX vv.," in *Vizantijskie očerki* (Moscow, 1977), 119–37.

48. That is emphasized by P. A. Yannopoulos, *La société profane dans l'Empire byzantin des VIIe, VIIIe et IXe siècles* (Louvain, 1975), 125.

49. P. Brown, "A Dark-Age Crisis: Aspects of the Iconoclastic Controversy," *EHR*, 88 (1973), 30–34.

50. Lemerle, *Le premier humanisme*, 267.

51. *Scriptores originum Constantinopolitanarum*, ed. Th. Praeger, 1 (Leipzig, 1901), 78 f.

52. Ioannes Skylitzes, *Synopsis historiarum*, ed. H. Thurn (Berlin, 1973), 340.88–95.

53. See, for example, S. Vryonis, "Byzantine Δημοκρατία and the Guilds in the Eleventh Century," *DOP*, 17 (1963), 287–314. An analysis of the social structure of Byzantium in the eleventh and twelfth centuries is found in Kazhdan, *Sostav*, of which there is a summary in French by I. Sorlin in *TM*, 6 (1976), 367–80.

54. P. Joannou, "Der Nominalismus und die menschliche Psychologie Christi. Das Semeioma gegen Eustratios von Nikaia (1117)," *BZ*, 47 (1954), 373.

55. Angold, *Exile*, 3 f.

56. The economic decline of the late Byzantine urban population must not be exaggerated. The existence of a Greek bourgeoisie in the fourteenth and fifteenth centuries, in spite of the poverty of the imperial court, has recently been emphasized by N. Oikonomidès, *Hommes d'affaires Grecs et Latins à Constantinople (XIIIe–XVe siècles)* (Paris, 1979).

Notes to Chapter Seven

1. Beck, *Byzantinistik*, 22 f. See the Introduction on this lecture.

2. R. Jenkins, *Byzantium: The Imperial Centuries, A.D. 610–1071* (London, 1966), 319, 331.

3. G. G. Litavrin, in *Istorija Vizantii*, 2 (Moscow, 1967), 219 f.

4. Kazhdan, *Sostav*, 255–57. For a defense of the traditional appreciation of Basil's reign, see Litavrin, *Obščestvo*, 266 f.

5. P. V. Bezobrazov, *Očerki vizantijskoj kul'tury* (Petrograd, 1919), 12.

6. R. Guilland, "La noblesse de race à Byzance," *BS*, 9 (1948), reprinted in his *Recherches sur les institutions byzantines*, 1 (Berlin and Amsterdam, 1967), 15.

7. D. Bullough, "*Europae Pater*: Charlemagne and His Achievement in the Light of Recent Scholarship," *EHR*, 85 (1970), 76–78; see also J. Fleckenstein, "Die Entstehung des niederen Adels und das Rittertum," in *Herrschaft und Stand*, ed. J. Fleckenstein (Göttingen, 1977), 21 f.

8. Cf. R. Anderson, *Traditional Europe* (Belmont, Cal., 1971), 29–32.

9. G. Ostrogorsky, "Observations on the Aristocracy in Byzantium," *DOP*, 25 (1971), 3.

10. M. T. W. Arnheim, *The Senatorial Aristocracy in the Later Roman Empire* (Oxford, 1972), 170.

11. A. P. Kazhdan, "Ob aristokratizacii vizantijskogo obščestva VIII–XII vv.," *ZRVI*, 11 (1968), 52; Kazhdan, *Sostav*, 223–25.

12. Leo, *Tactica*, chap. 2, pars. 19–21, ed. R. Vári, 1 (Budapest, 1917), 27–29. On the rise to prominence in Byzantium of many families of foreign origin, see S. Vryonis, "Byzantine and Turkish Societies and their Sources of Manpower," in *War, Technology and Society in the Middle East* (London, 1975), 136.

13. *Jus*, 1:264.16–18.

14. According to R. W. Bulliet, *The Patricians of Nishapur* (Cambridge, Mass., 1972), 20, the power and prestige of the Muslim "patriciate" was based on one or more of three sources: landholding, trade, or religion. The main traits of the Byzantine and medieval Muslim trading classes deserve special comparative study.

15. George Pachymeres, *De Michaele et Andronico Palaeologis libri 13*, ed. I. Bekker (Bonn, 1835), 1:64.10–65.11: the Tzamanturi, Strategopuli, Philae, Apreni, Labadarii, and Philanthropeni are known only from the thirteenth century, while the Tornikii, Raul, Palaeologi, Vatatzae, Kavallarii, Nestongi, Kamytzae, Angeli, Tarchaneiotae, and Kantakuzeni originated in the eleventh and twelfth centuries.

16. See, for example, M. Ja. Sjuzjumov, "Ekonomičeskie vozzrenija L'va VI," *VizVrem*, 15 (1959), 35 f., and particularly G. G. Litavrin, "Problema gosudarstvennoj sobstvennosti v Vizantii X–XI vv.," *VizVrem*, 35 (1973), 51–74, and M. Ja. Sjuzjumov, "Suverenitet, nalog i zemel'naja renta v Vizantii," *ADSV*, 9 (1973), 57–65.

17. J. Danstrup, "The State and Landed Property in Byzantium to c.1250," *Classica et mediaevalia*, 8 (1947), 241. See also Guillou, *Civilisation*, 243 f.

18. The pioneering work of V. Makušev appeared in 1874. The best survey of Byzantine *pronoia* from this standpoint is Ostrogorsky, *Féodalité*, 1–257, first published in Serbian in 1951.

19. A. Hohlweg, "Zur Frage der Pronoia in Byzanz," *BZ*, 60 (1967), 288–308, and the reply of G. Ostrogorsky, "Die Pronoia unter den Komnenen," *ZRVI*, 12 (1970), 41–54.

20. Litavrin, *Obščestvo*, 107–9. See also V. A. Arutjunova-Fidanjan, *Tipik Grigorija Pakuriana* (Erevan, 1978), 28–30.

21. "The monarchical art of Byzantium," according to A. Grabar, *L'empereur dans l'art byzantin* (Paris, 1936; repr. London, 1979), 263, "was to establish by the means of the image the traditional features of the superhuman possessor of the supreme power."

22. Ju. Trifonov, "Svedenija iz starobŭlgarskija život v Šestodneva na Joana Ekzarcha," *Spisanie na Bŭlgarskata Akad. na naukite*, 35. *Klon istor.-filol.* (1926), 14 f.

23. P. A. Lavrov, "Materialy po istorii vozniknovenija drevnejšej slavjanskoj pis'mennosti," *Trudy slavjanskoj komissii*, 1 (Leningrad, 1930), 13.

24. V. Minorsky, "Marvazi on the Byzantines," in *Mélanges H. Grégoire*, 2 (Brussels, 1950), 460.

25. H. G. Beck, "Konstantinopel. Zur Sozialgeschichte einer frühmittelalterlichen Hauptstadt," *BZ*, 58 (1965), reprinted in his *Ideen und Realitäten in Byzanz* (London, 1972), pt. 10, p. 14.

26. Michael Psellos, *Chronographie*, ed. E. Renauld, 2 (Paris, 1928), 115, 121.

27. On Byzantine monarchy, see H. Hunger in *Das byzantinische Herrscherbild* (Darmstadt, 1975), 1–12, with an abundant bibliography by O. Kresten (p. 415–48). See also A. P. Kazhdan, "O social'noj prirode vizantijskogo samoderžavija," *Narody Azii i Afriki* (1966), no. 6, 52–64.

28. H. G. Beck, "Storia della chiesa," in *La civiltà bizantina dal IV al IX secolo* (Bari, 1977), 246, substitutes for *caesaropapism* the term "political orthodoxy," which implies, he says, "bilateral usurpation" and the inseparability of the emperor and religion and of politics and belief.

29. Guillou, *Civilisation*, 175–95.

30. D. J. Geanakoplos, "Church and State in the Byzantine Empire: A Reconsideration of the Problem of Caesaropapism," *Church History*, 34 (1965), 398.

31. Cf. K. Sontheimer, *Antidemokratisches Denken in der Weimarer Republik*, 2nd ed. (Munich, 1968), 250–59, on the importance of the concepts of community, nation, and organism in German historiography.

32. *Cronaca dei Tocco di Cefalonia di Anonimo*, ed. G. Schirò (Rome, 1975), *passim*.

33. A century earlier, between 1248 and 1258, the heir to the Latin Empire, Philip of Courtenay, was mortgaged to two Venetian merchants: R. L. Wolff, "Mortgage and Redemption of an Emperor's Son: Castile and the Latin Empire of Constantinople," *Speculum*, 29 (1954), 47–84.

34. A. P. Kazhdan, "Vizantijskaja armija v IX–X vekach," *Učenye zapiski Velikoluksogo ped. instituta* [1] (1954), 23–25.

35. The problem of the centrifugal and centripetal forces in Byzantium of 1071–1261 was discussed at the XVth International Congress of Byzantine studies, in the papers by Hélène Arhweiler, Vera Hrochova, I. Karayannopulos, A.P. Kazhdan, N. Oikonomidès, and Zinaida Udal'cova.

36. NicCh, 152–54.

37. S. G. Vilinskij, "Žitie sv. Vasilija Novogo v russkoj literature," *Zapiski Novorossijskogo universiteta, Ist.-filol. fak.*, 6–7 (1911–13).

38. Theophanes Continuatus, ed. I. Bekker (Bonn, 1838), 53.7, 54.3–5. For money seized from tax collectors and divided among the people, see Genesius, *Regum libri quattuor*, ed. A. Lesmüller-Werner and H. Thurn (Berlin and New York, 1978), 23: 90–92.

39. Theophanes Continuatus, 388.8–10.

40. Theophanes Continuatus, 443.13–18; *Jus*, 1:226.5–7.

41. Pseudo-Lucian, "Philopatris," in Lucian, ed. M. D. Macleod, 8 (London, 1967), 450, cap. 20.

42. Litavrin, *Obščestvo*, 262. He suggests further that the aim of riots in provincial towns also was the abolishment of taxes (p. 273).

43. M. M. Frejdenberg, "K istorii klassovoj bor'by v Vizantii v XII veke," *Učenye zapiski Velikolukskogo pedinstituta* [1] (1954), 32f.

44. E. Herman, in *Dictionnaire de droit canonique*, 2, cols. 706–35.

45. Constantine Porphyrogenitus, *De cerimoniis aulae byzantinae*, ed. J. J. Reiske, 1 (Bonn, 1829), 657.12–20.

46. W. E. Kaegi, "The Byzantine Armies and Iconoclasm," *BS*, 27 (1966), 50, 68 f.; "Some Reconsiderations on the Themes (seventh–ninth centuries)," *JÖB*, 16 (1967), 41 f. On the contrary, H. Ahrweiler, "L'organisation des campagnes militaires à Byzance," in *War, Technology, and Society in the Middle East* (London, 1975), 89–96, evaluates the army of the "theme regime" as a specimen of courage and discipline.

47. Theoph, 1:376.19–24, 377.4–5, 490.5–7.

48. A. Sharf, *Byzantine Jewry from Justinian to the Fourth Crusade* (London, 1971).

49. The Patriarch Joseph Galesiotes (1266–75) called them "ill and rebellious people": V. Laurent, *Les regestes des actes du Patriarcat de Constantinople*, 1, pt. 4 (Paris, 1971), 195, no. 1400.

50. Metropolitan Cyril of Tyre was elected patriarch of Antioch in 1287 but was not confirmed because he was accused of communicating with Armenians, *ibid.*, 356, no. 1568.

51. The most recent, though not full, survey is E. Bauer, *Die Armenier im byzantinischen Reich und ihr Einfluss auf Politik, Wirtschaft und Kultur* (Yerevan, 1978).

52. The secondary literature is huge: see M. Graebner, "The Slavs in Byzantine Population: Transfers of the seventh and eighth Centuries," *Etudes balkaniques*, 11 (1975), no. 1, 40–52; also P. Lemerle, "Les anciens recueils des miracles de saint Démétrius et l'histoire de la péninsule balkanique," *Bulletin de la classe des lettres de l'Académie de Belgique*, 5th Ser., 65 (1979), 395–415.

53. W. Hecht, *Die byzantinische Aussenpolitik zur Zeit der letzten Komnenenkaiser* (Neustadt [an der Aisch], 1967), 35.

54. E. Th. Tsolakis, "Das Geschichtswerk des Michael Attaleiates und die Zeit seiner Abfassung," *Byzantina*, 2 (1970), 263.

55. Ja. N. Ljubarskij, in Anna Komnina, *Aleksiada* (Moscow, 1965), 35 f.

56. F. Chalandon, *Les Comnène*, 2 (Paris, 1912), 204, n. 1.

57. S. Papadimitriu, "'Ο Πρόδρομος τοῦ Μαρκιανοῦ κώδικος, XI, 22," *VizVrem*, 10 (1903), 155–63.

58. A. P. Kazhdan, "Vizantijskij publicist XII v. Evstafij Solunskij," *VizVrem*, 28 (1968), 71 f.

59. J. Darrouzès, "Les documents byzantins du XIIᵉ siècle sur la primauté romaine," *REB*, 23 (1965), 79–82.

60. On the concept of *mimesis* in medieval and Renaissance literature, see the work of E. Auerbach cited in n. 38 to chap. Five.

61. Sym *Cat*, 1:454 (no. 5, 916–22); 3:76 (no. 26, 73–75) and 114 (no. 28, 222–27).

62. NicCh, 176.55–56.

63. MichAk, 1:109.28–30.

64. A. P. Kazhdan, "Vizantijskij publicist XII v. Evstafij Solunskij," *VizVrem*, 28 (1968), 74 f.

65. See, in particular, K. Bosl, "Potens und Pauper," in *Alteuropa und die moderne Gesellschaft. Festschrift für Otto Brunner* (Göttingen, 1963), 60–87, who distinguishes the concepts of social and economic poverty in the West.

66. Patlagean, *Pauvreté*, 25–35.

67. M. A. Poljakovskaja, "K voprosu o social'nych protivorečijach v pozdnevizantijskom gorode (po Alekseju Makremvolitu)," *ADSV*, 8 (1972), 95–107.

68. See Toynbee, *Constantine*, 39 f.

69. D. J. Constantelos, *Byzantine Philanthropy and Social Welfare* (New Brunswick, N.J., 1968), 3–61; Hunger, *Prooimion*, 143–53.

70. Sym *Cat*, 2:110 and 126 (no. 9, 75–77 and 268–79).

71. F.-E. Morard, "Monachus. Moine. Histoire du terme grec jusqu'au 4ᵉ siècle," *Freiburger Zeitschrift für Philosophie und Theologie*, 20 (1973), 333–411.

72. On the concept of *oikonomia*, H. Thurn, Οἰκονομία *von der frühbyzantinischen Zeit bis zum Bilderstreit* (Munich, 1960), 143–47. See also P. Rai, "L'économie dans le droit canonique byzantin des origines jusqu'au XIᵉ siècle," *Istina*, 18 (1973), esp. 281 f.

Notes to Chapter Eight

1. See *La Nouvelle histoire*, ed. J. Le Goff (Paris, 1978).

2. Beck, *Byzantinistik*, 28.

3. The high point of this type of approach is the *Typologie des sources du moyen âge occidental*, ed. L. Genicot (Turnhout, 1972 ff.), of which the object is to establish both the nature of every type of source and rules for the use of each.

4. See M. A. Zaborov, *Istoriografija krestovych pochodov* (Moscow, 1971), 212–61.

5. F. Hirsch, *Byzantinische Studien* (Leipzig, 1876).

6. F. Dölger and P. Wirth, *Regesten der Kaiserurkunden des oströmischen Reiches* (Munich and Berlin, 1924–65; rev. ed. of vol. 3, Munich, 1977); V. Grumel, V. Laurent, and J. Darrouzès, *Les regestes des actes du Patriarcat de Constantinople* (Paris, 1936–79).

7. The pioneer work is P. A. Jakovenko, *Issledovanija v oblasti vizantijskich gramot* (Juriev, 1917), but see now F. Dölger and J. Karayannopulos, *Byzantinische Urkundenlehre* (Munich, 1968).

8. P. Lemerle, *L'émirat d'Aydin* (Paris, 1957).

9. Lemerle, *Cinq études*.

10. H. Grégoire, "Etudes sur le neuvième siècle," *Byzantion*, 8 (1933), 515, 534. According to Grégoire, "The Amorians and Macedonians, 842–1025," *CMH*, 1:105, the traditional neglect of Michael III was "one of the more serious failures of modern Byzantine historians." It is, of course, "a kind of paradoxical exaggeration" (Ch. Diehl and G. Marçais, *Le monde oriental de 395 à 1081* [Paris, 1936], 319).

11. W. Hahn, *Moneta Imperii Byzantini*, 1–2 (Vienna, 1973–75).

12. *Digesta*, 48.2, 10. See K. E. Zachariä von Lingenthal, *Geschichte des griechischrömischen Rechts*, 3rd ed. (Berlin, 1892; repr., Aalen in Würtemberg, 1955), 276, n. 926.

13. Constantine Harmenopulus, *Manuale legum sive Hexabiblos*, bk. 1, chap. 6:33, ed. W. E. Heimbach (Leipzig, 1851), 106.

14. Patlagean, *Pauvreté*, 11–35. On the notion of wealth from the seventh century to the ninth, see P. A. Yannopoulos, *La société profane dans l'Empire byzantin des VIIᵉ, VIIIᵉ et IXᵉ siècles* (Louvain, 1975), 22 f.

15. See Weiss, *Kantakuzenos*, 7 f.

16. Synopsis minor E 22 in *Jus*, 6:388. See also Balsamon in *PG*, 137, col. 929D. On the Byzantine *emphyteusis* see G. Weiss, "Die Entscheidung des Kosmas Magistros über das Paroikenrecht," *Byzantion*, 48 (1978), 488–90.

17. MM, 3:50.7, 53.25, 55.6. See also κομμέρκιον ἢ ἐμφύτευμα in an act of 1423 (*ibid.*, 165.19).

18. MM, 4:320 f.

19. L. Petit and B. Korablev, "Actes de Chilandar," *VizVrem*, 17 (1911), Appendix, no. 21. 49–53.

20. The best survey is in Ostrogorsky, *Féodalité*, 259–368.

21. See, for example, J. Lefort, *Actes d'Esphigménou* (Paris, 1973), 21–27, where deeds of purchase are used along with the other documents.

22. G. Ferrari, "I documenti greci medioevali di diritto privato dell' Italia meridionale e loro attinenze con quelli bizantini d'Oriente e coi papiri greco-egizii," *Byzantinisches Archiv*, 1 (1910), 100.

23. A. P. Kazhdan, *Agrarnye otnošenija v Vizantii XIII–XIV vv.* (Moscow, 1952), 28–36. I. Medvedev, "Diplomatika častnogo vizantijskogo akta," *Problemy istočnikovedenija zapadnoevropejskogo srednevekov'ja* (Leningrad, 1979), 139, still emphasized "the standardized and uniform shape and language" of Byzantine documents, but even he did not deny "natural modifications of the same formulary."

24. Hunger, *Prooimion*, 15–18. See the comparable work on western documents, also by a scholar from Vienna, Heinrich Fichtenau, *Arenga. Spätantike und Mittelalter im Spiegel von Urkundenformeln* (Graz and Cologne, 1957).

25. Laiou, *Peasant*, 108–41.

26. Kazhdan, *Sostav*, 185–96, table 6.

27. No proper study of Byzantine first names has yet been made. Recent research in the West suggests that standard Christian and noble names increasingly replaced individualized pre-Christian names after about 1100: cf. K. W. Littger, *Studien zum Auftreten der Heiligennamen im Rheinland* (Munich, 1975).

28. See for instance F. Dölger, "Byzantine Literature," *CMH*, 2:232–35.

29. Beginning with V. Parisot, *Cantacuzène, homme d'état et historien* (Paris, 1845), 4 f.

30. On the relation of language to culture and social actions, see the various works of Leo Spitzer, esp. *Essays in Historical Semantics* (New York, 1948), and *Linguistics and Literary History* (Princeton, 1948).

31. W. Hecht, *Die byzantinische Aussenpolitik zur Zeit der letzten Komnenenkaiser* (Neustadt [an der Aisch], 1967), 88 f.

32. *Prosopographisches Lexicon der Palaiologenzeit*, 1–4 (Vienna, 1976–80).

33. Beck, *Byzantinistik*, 26 f.

34. M. Cvetaeva, *Moj Pushkin* (Moscow, 1967), 105–60.

35. The best edition and commentary is N. Oikonomidès, *Les listes de préséance byzantines des IXe et Xe siècles* (Paris, 1972). More data are available for the early period, but even in this branch the traditional method of investigation is dominant: see, for example, A. Giardina, *Aspetti della burocrazia nel basso impero* (Rome, 1977), dedicated to the *agentes in rebus*. More important is the work of T. F. Carney, *Bureaucracy in Traditional Society* (Lawrence, Kan., 1971), whose "impressionistic generalizations" (to use his own words, p. 7) concerning the bureaucratic structure of the empire were strongly influenced by an interdisciplinary approach to the problem.

36. R. S. Lopez, "The Dollar of the Middle Ages," *Journal of Economic History*, 11 (1951), reprinted in his *Byzantium and the World around it: Economic and Institutional Relations* (London, 1978), pt. 7, 209–234.

37. Ostrogorsky, *Féodalité*, 53.

38. G. Ostrogorsky, "K istorii immuniteta v Vizantii," *VizVrem*, 13 (1958), 55–106;

the French translation: "Pour l'histoire de l'immunité à Byzance," *Byzantion*, 28 (1958, published in 1960), 165–254.

39. I. Ševčenko, *Etudes sur la polémique entre Théodore Métochite et Nicéphore Choumnos* (Brussels, 1962).

40. Ljubarskij, *Psell*. See also the comparative studies of Byzantine writers of the twelfth century by A. Kazhdan, especially "Vizantijskij publicist XII veka Evstafij Solunskij," *VizVrem*, 27–29 (1967–68), and "Nikifor Chrisoverg i Nikolaj Mesarit," *Viz Vrem*, 30 (1969), 94–112.

41. Theoph, 1:249.1 and note.

42. John Zonaras, *Epitome historiarum*, ed. Th. Büttner-Wobst, 3 (Bonn, 1897), 178.13.

43. G. Weiss, *Oströmische Beamte im Spiegel der Schriften des Michael Psellos* (Munich, 1973), 11.

44. Kazhdan, *Sostav*, 182 f.

45. A work dedicated to the problem of the verification of Byzantine statistics is Jurij Bessmertnyj's critical review of Kazhdan's *Sostav* in *Istoriko-filologičeskij žurnal* (1976), no. 2, 236–42. See also the review of Laiou-Thomadakis's study by P. Karlin-Hayter, *Byzantion*, 48 (1978), 580–85.

46. Stimulating in this respect is the research on the medieval notion of freedom, including H. Grundmann, "Freiheit als religiöses, politisches, und persönliches Postulat im Mittelalter," *HistZ*, 183 (1957), 23–53, and A. Ja. Gurevič, *Problemy genezisa feodalisma v Zapadnoj Evrope* (Moscow, 1970), 195–213.

INDEX

abasement before power, 125–26
Abasges, 154
Abelard, 138
Abu al-Faraj, 154
acceptilatio, 121
acclamations, 67
Achilles, 3, 114
Achilleus Tatios, 71
Acre, 51
actors, 67, 103. *See also* mimos; theater
administrative system: Byzantine, 13, 35, 119, 146–47, 151, 173; Roman, 12. *See also* government
Adonis, 85
Adriatic Sea, 56
adultery, 71–72
Aegean basin, 128, 134
Aeschylus, 3, 103
Aetios, 85
age groups, 63
Agnes (widow of Alexius II), 72
agrarian conditions, 15. *See also* holdings; landlords; rent
agricultural produce, 56, 131
Ahrweiler, Hélène, 30, 120
Alans, 154
Alexander (Byzantine emperor), 20
Alexandria, 76, 77, 129, 134; Alexandrian school of theology, 118. *See also* Cyril
Alexius (brother of Nicephorus *drungarius*), 74
Alexius I Comnenus, 10, 48, 72, 87, 111, 113, 138, 176
Alexius II Comnenus, 72
Alexius III Angelus, 21, 172
alienation, estrangement, 36, 125
allotment. *See* holdings
Alypiou monastery, 47
Ambrose (saint), 103
Ammianus Marcellinus, 61, 175

Amphion, 50
Anastasius I, 129
Anastasius II, 134
Anastos, Milton, 86
Anatolikon, 134
Andronicus I Comnenus, 11, 14, 42, 62, 65, 72, 108, 110, 115, 136, 138, 155, 172
Angeli, 136, 146
angels, 79, 93, 107
Angold, Michael, 57, 138
Anna (Theophano's mother), 63
Anthemius of Tralles, 27
antihero, 106, 108, 114
Antioch, 134; Antiochene school of theology, 118
Antoniadis-Bibicou, Hélène, 56
Apokaukos, Alexius, 13, 92
apostles, 12, 66
apprentice, 31–32, 49
Arab authors, 149
Arabs, 39, 86, 107, 133, 152, 153, 154
archaeology, excavations, 54, 56, 57, 127
archons, in Gnostic thought, 80
Archontitzes, Michael, 47
Argyros (Byzantine general), 92
aristocracy, 15, 51, 86, 92, 102, 136, 143; military and civil, 112; aristocratic families, 40, 54, 176. *See also* landlords; military magnates; nobility
Aristophanes, 103
Aristotle, 78, 138
Arius, Arians, 83, 85
Armeniakon, 134, 151
Armenians, 40, 63, 72, 153
army, 51, 150, 151–52, 153. *See also* mercenaries; military
Arnheim, M. T. W., 123
Artabasdes, 134
asceticism, 28, 70, 89. *See also* values, ascetic